THEOLOGY IN A
POST-TRAUMATIC CHURCH

Theology in a
Post-Traumatic Church

John N. Sheveland
Editor

ORBIS BOOKS
Maryknoll, New York 10545

Founded in 1970, Orbis Books endeavors to publish works that enlighten the mind, nourish the spirit, and challenge the conscience. The publishing arm of the Maryknoll Fathers and Brothers, Orbis seeks to explore the global dimensions of the Christian faith and mission, to invite dialogue with diverse cultures and religious traditions, and to serve the cause of reconciliation and peace. The books published reflect the views of their authors and do not represent the official position of the Maryknoll Society. To learn more about Maryknoll and Orbis Books, please visit our website at www.orbisbooks.com

Portions of Chapter 7, "Malignant Narcissism and Clericalism: Psychological Perspectives on a Culture of Abuse," originally appeared in "Seminary Human Formation: Lessons from the Causes and Context of Sexual Abuse Study," *Seminary Journal* 19, no. 2 (2013): 10–19.

Portions of Chapter 3, "What Is Redemption?" originally appeared in "Clergy Sexual Abuse and the Work of Redemption: Gestures toward a Theology of Accompaniment," *Buddhist-Christian Studies* 41 (2021): 71–86. doi:10.1353/bcs.2021.0011.

"Rewriting Psalm 55 Reflecting on Sexual Abuse" by Rev. Dr. Brad Hambrick is used with permission from the author.

Manufactured in the United States of America.
Manuscript editing and typesetting by Joan Weber Laflamme.

Library of Congress Cataloging-in-Publication Data

Names: Sheveland, John N., 1973– editor.
Title: Theology in a post-traumatic church / John N. Sheveland, editor.
Identifiers: LCCN 2022059670 (print) | LCCN 2022059671 (ebook) | ISBN 9781626985209 (trade paperback) | ISBN 9781608339822 (epub)
Subjects: LCSH: Child sexual abuse—Religious aspects—Catholic Church. | Child sexual abuse by clergy.
Classification: LCC BX1912.9 .T444 2023 (print) | LCC BX1912.9 (ebook) | DDC 261.8/3272088282—dc23/eng/20230309
LC record available at https://lccn.loc.gov/2022059670
LC ebook record available at https://lccn.loc.gov/2022059671

Contents

Foreword　　　　　　　　　　　　　　　　　　　　　ix
　　HANS ZOLLNER, SJ

Introduction　　　　　　　　　　　　　　　　　　　　1
　　JOHN N. SHEVELAND

1. **Resiliency, Hope, Healing**
   Victims Assistance Ministry in a Trauma-Sensitive
   　　Theological Context　　　　　　　　　　　　　17
   　　HEATHER T. BANIS, PhD
   　　Principle 1: Be Victim-Centric　　20
   　　Principle 2: Honor the Sacred Story　　21
   　　Principle 3: Betrayal Trauma　　31
   　　Conclusion　　37

2. **Critical Reflections on the Discourse on a**
   "Traumatized Church"　　　　　　　　　　　　39
   　　JENNIFER E. BESTE
   　　Trauma and Its Effects　　39
   　　The Discourse of Traumatization in the
   　　　　Catholic Clergy Sexual Abuse Crisis　　43
   　　Ethical and Theological Implications of the
   　　　　"Traumatized Church" Discourse　　47
   　　The Need to Reject Sweeping Claims of a
   　　　　"Traumatized Church"　　49

Theological Implications of Rejecting the
"Traumatized Church" Discourse   61
Conclusion   63

3. **What Is Redemption?**   64
    JOHN N. SHEVELAND

4. **What Can Make Churches Unsafe?**
    The Catholic Church as Total Institution   87
    CRISTINA LLEDO GOMEZ
    Church Abuse of Vulnerable and Non-Vulnerable
        Persons   92
    Organizational Culture and Abuse Vulnerability
        in Churches   101
        *The Catholic Church as Alternative Moral
            Universe*   103
        *Catholic Churches and Human Nature and
            Transformation*   105
        *The Catholic Church and Total Institutions'
            Extinguishing of Member Identities*   106
        *The Catholic Church and Promoting
            Secrecy*   108
        *The Catholic Church and Unique Power
            Structures*   110
        *Unique Informal Group Dynamics in the
            Catholic Church*   113
    Conclusion: From Abuse-Vulnerable to Trauma-
        Informed Churches   115

5. **Visions of Survivor Healing and Empowerment in
    Response to Trauma**   117
    SCOTT R. A. STARBUCK
    Pastoral Context   118

Prophetic Critique   119
Isaiah 40—66   123
Isaiah 55:1–13   124
Isaiah 61:1–11   130
A Healing and Restorative Path   134

6. **Psycho-theological Functions of Laments**
    Giving Voice to Anger and Grief   138
    LINDA S. SCHEARING
    Laments and Trauma   139
    Psalm 55 and Sexual Abuse   142
    Psalm 88 and Sexual Abuse   150
    Conclusion   154

7. **Malignant Narcissism and Clericalism**
    Psychological Perspectives on a Culture of Abuse   155
    FERNANDO A. ORTIZ
    Evaluation of Personality Risk Factors   161
    Evaluating Protective Factors   164
    Conclusion   170

8. **Understanding and Resisting Clericalism and
    Social Sin**   173
    B. KEVIN BROWN
    Clericalism and the Clergy Sexual Abuse
        Crisis   174
        Clericalism and Bias   174
        *Clericalism and the Clergy Sexual Abuse
            Crisis*   177
    Understanding Clericalism within the Church
        as Social Sin   181
        Social Sin and Bias   182
        Addressing the Social Sin of Clericalism   186

Resisting Clericalism through Theological
      Renewal   189
   The Theological Roots of Clericalism   189
   Toward Theological Renewal   197

9. **Worship among the Ruins**
   *Foundations for a Theology of Liturgy and
      Sacraments "after Abuse"*   201
      Joseph C. Mudd
   Clerical Culture and the Dialectic of
         Authority   202
      Clericalism and Dramatic Bias   206
      Ecclesial Illness and Psychic Conversion   208
      Redeeming Sacrifice after Abuse   211
      Idolatry and Deviated Transcendence   213
      Sacrifice as Self-Offering in Christ   215
   Sacraments and Healing after Abuse   217
      *Reconciliation: Transformation of Histories of
         Suffering*   218
      Healing and Worship   221
   Conclusion   223

Contributors   225

Index   227

Foreword

Hans Zollner, SJ

In February 2019, just before the start of the Child Protection Summit in the Vatican, representatives of victims associations and survivors from different countries met with the summit organizers. Some of the survivors vented their anger. Others expressed their hopes for change. All of them recounted horrible experiences of abuse by clergy and other church employees. One of them directly addressed the organizers—two cardinals, an archbishop, two priests, and myself among them. Speaking in a calm, composed, and compelling voice, the survivor made this affirmation: "I do not believe in God because he did not help me in my suffering." Then, looking us right in the eye, this person added: "And I think neither do you believe in God. Because if you did, you and your church would stand by victims and do everything possible to make sure no more abuse happens." These words and the deadly serious tone with which they were spoken shook me deeply at the time and have accompanied me ever since. These were the words that rang in my ears while I read this book, in which elements of a theology in a post-traumatic church are developed.

Wouldn't it be better for the church and its theologians to just keep quiet? Wouldn't it be better to avoid all theological talk about abuse and its cover-up and about the trauma it triggers? Theological, spiritual, liturgical, or pastoral displays and practices often leave victims of abuse feeling uncomfortable. For many of them, talking about God in the face of deep wounds inflicted by God's ministers is nothing more than a red herring.

To them, it seems as though the church is trying to evade their present pain, fierce anger, and abysmal despair by seeking refuge in pious platitudes.

This book shows that this does not always have to be the case. There really can be some form of theological reflection in the face of the unspeakable suffering caused by sexual violence. In every chapter the language used, the topics covered, and the overall tone indicate that this is not abstract, "pie in the sky" theology or an attempt at self-immunization against the traumas explored. Explicitly and implicitly, the victims of sexualized violence and their experiences form the starting point of the theological reflection. Over the millennia Christian theology has always taken up the language, symbols, and concepts of respective cultural and scientific contexts, discussed them critically, and used them as the starting point for answering the question of how God and God's work can be conceived in a changing world and in society. This theology believes in a God who is actively involved in this world, and in his Son, who has taken on human form to be like us in everything but sin. Such a theology cannot help but speak, in a time-bound and thus always provisional way, of the eternal and otherworldly God who takes care of his people. That is why it is so important that in recent years there has been an increased interest in theological debate in the face of abuse and its cover-up, at least in Anglo-Saxon and Central European countries.

When dealing with the various aspects of abuse in theological research and teaching, it quickly becomes clear that all theological disciplines have to deal with it. They can all contribute something from their respective perspectives and speak about God in a broken world that's desperately in need of healing: *biblical studies* and the search for biblical images for healing and redemption in calamitous situations; *systematic theology* that poses questions such as "Where is God in the face of suffering? What does redemption mean?" But also, "What does the church stand for? What does it have to do in order to credibly fulfil its mission?"; *moral theology*, which among other things poses the question of how justice and mercy relate to each other in the case of such serious crimes and sins as sexual violence; *liturgy* and the search for a sacrificial language in personal and communal prayer; *pastoral theology* and the primacy of those who cannot defend themselves and claim what is rightfully theirs. *Canon law* and *church history* have much homework of their own to do here.

Appropriately defining key terms like *trauma, vulnerable adult,* and *spiritual abuse,* remains an urgent task. There are various difficulties of understanding, or conceptual ambiguities, regarding each of these terms. The present volume attempts to address some of these issues, but it is particularly striking to compare how these and other central concepts are treated in the individual articles. There are two reasons why such variations cannot easily be avoided: first, this is a relatively new field in theology in which a common language has yet to be found; and second, these concepts come from other scholarly disciplines, so their respective hermeneutics and the corresponding discussion of content are also involved. Understanding and interpreting them require strong interdisciplinary knowledge.

Which is why a greater and more precise ability to speak about abuse and its cover-up is necessary—in terms of vocabulary, and in terms of the will and ability actually to utter these words, or to bring them into scientific and ecclesiastical discourse. Greater willingness and increased competence in seeking to strike the right tone and to use expressions correctly are the best ways to avoid misunderstandings and prevent divisions. Among these divisions is the mutual alienation of academic theology and church leadership. Only by wrestling with each other—as arduous as that may be—can we reach mutual understanding and arrive at a common approach. Anything else will result in repeated clashes and failing to utilize existing resources instead of developing creative ideas on core theological concepts and ensuring regular feedback to the everyday life of the church.

Personally, I hope this anthology will stimulate further theological reflection and influence church leaders in their actions—especially with regard to listening to victims, even the most angry and disillusioned ones. In this way it will both inform and help shape how we report on the abuse and denial of the past and present—and how we promote commitment to safeguarding in the future.

—HANS ZOLLNER, SJ

Introduction

John N. Sheveland

In October 2021, Pope Francis called the church into a synodal process that will continue through 2024. For Christians, to be synodal means to walk a path together, to journey together, as a community collectively shaped and animated by experiences of dialogue and reciprocity in which the Holy Spirit is discerned to be present, calling all in the church to a deeper conversion to the mission of the church. It enjoins participative and inclusive ecclesial processes so that everyone—especially those on the margins or peripheries—can speak, be heard, and contribute to the body of the church. Synodality recognizes and promotes the irreducible human diversity of God-given gifts and charisms bestowed upon humanity for the benefit of all, and it seeks to render these more audible, visible, and participatory. Importantly, as the Preparatory Document describes:

> Synodality represents the main road for the Church, called to renew herself under the action of the Spirit and by listening to the Word. The ability to imagine a different future for the Church and her institutions, in keeping with the mission she has received, depends largely on the decision to initiate processes of listening, dialogue, and community discernment, in which each and every person can participate and contribute. (no. 9)[1]

---

[1] Preparatory Document for the 16th Ordinary General Assembly of the Synod of Bishops, "For a Synodal Church: Communion, Participation, and Mission" (July 9, 2021). Official church documents referenced herein are available on the Vatican website.

1

This book began as a collaborative project in 2019, motivated by a desire among us as theologians to offer constructive theological engagements with the Catholic Church's self-inflicted abuse crisis in the wake of the Theodore McCarrick situation and the Pennsylvania grand jury report, both of which rocked the US Catholic Church in the summer of 2018 and revealed more dimensions to the ongoing story of abuse and cover-up. For us as authors, constructive theological engagement with the dynamics of abuse and traumatic wounding has not been a dispassionate academic study. As theologians and other professionals, we have endeavored to draw close to the wounds of victims, to their experiences of vulnerability, manipulation, abuse, and cover-up, as a mode of being church together and, from that context, to offer theological expression to the phenomena of abuse and healing. We have endeavored to contribute to a theology that is "victim-centric." We have endeavored to listen carefully, to feel deeply, and to bring to bear upon these crimes and sins a wide range of biblical, theological, ecclesiological, liturgical, ethnographic, and psychological resources. Just as the church becomes incoherent if its people do not journey together, we feel that a theological program unaffiliated with, unallied with, or indifferent to the crimes and sins of abuse inflicted upon other members of the body of Christ is a theology in crisis, a theology that offers no functional meaning for the church of which it is a part.

The Preparatory Document connects the synodal process to victim-survivors of abuse while drawing heavily upon Pope Francis's August 2018 "Letter to the People of God." The Preparatory Document states:

> In particular, we cannot forget the suffering experienced by minors and vulnerable people "due to sexual abuse, the abuse of power and the abuse of conscience perpetrated by a significant number of clerics and consecrated persons." We are continually challenged "as the People of God to take on the pain of our brothers and sisters wounded in their flesh

and in their spirit." For too long the cry of the victims has been a cry that the Church has not been able to hear sufficiently. These are deep wounds that are difficult to heal, for which forgiveness can never be asked for enough and which constitute obstacles, sometimes imposing ones, to advancing in the direction of "journeying together." The whole Church is called to deal with the weight of a culture imbued with clericalism that she inherits from her history, and with those forms of exercising authority on which the different types of abuse (power, economic, conscience, sexual) are grafted. It is impossible to think of "a conversion of our activity as a Church that does not include the active participation of all the members of God's People:" together let us ask the Lord for "the grace of conversion and the interior anointing needed to express before these crimes of abuse our compunction and our resolve courageously to combat them." (no. 6)

Here the Preparatory Document conjoins the opportunity for synodal renewal of the church with the stark and overwhelming challenge of listening carefully to the pained voices of survivors, to accompany them, to deconstruct the culture of clericalism onto which different types of abuse are grafted, to tell the truth about the ecclesial conditions that gave rise to abuse, and to recognize our shared need for the "grace of conversion" and "interior anointing" to meet these challenges as a community.

The authors of this volume are aware that much has been researched and written analyzing the causes and conditions of abuse, of clericalism, and of the pathological narcissism associated with abuse. Significantly less constructive theological work interfacing with victim experience has been undertaken by theologians. Hans Zollner, SJ, director of the IADC Safeguarding Institute at the Pontifical Gregorian University in Rome, was correct in 2017 when he wrote that theologians have not quite shown up with their skillset to contribute to the church's reform of the causes and conditions of abuse:

During the last two years, at international colloquia, we were
able to see that on the issue of sexual abuse one could find
many publications in the fields of spiritual, psychological
and pastoral studies, but that, up to now, almost nothing
has been written in the field of systematic theology. Bishops
usually delegate the problem to psychologists and Canon
lawyers.[2]

That judgment has remained largely accurate even as, since
2018, theologians have begun to show up and offer explicitly
theological engagement with the issue, both in our principal
academic university contexts and in service on local diocesan
review boards and on the USCCB National Review Board, both
boards being mandated by the 2002 "Charter for the Protection
of Children and Young People" (The Dallas Charter).[3] The authors of this volume intend to do so in a victim-centric modality.
That is, when we listen to victim-survivors of abuse, what do
we hear? What are the theological implications of their witness,
and will their witness be recognized as making a claim or even a
demand upon our attention so as to be viewed as authoritative?
How do we retain our victim-centric orientation in an ecclesial
environment that, to date, has struggled to do so? So too, what
do the church and theologians learn when they approach matters of abuse not simply with a view to how to help survivors or
others affected by the abuse of loved ones, but with a view to
what survivors can teach us about trauma, whether and how to
come back from betrayal, the conditions for the possibility of
healing, and the effective ministry that can facilitate it? Synodality
primes the church not merely to be present and to accompany,
important as these are, but, through accompaniment, synodality

---

[2] Hans Zollner, SJ, "Sexual Abuse in the Church: A Call to Change
Our Way of Seeing Things," *Vidyajyoti Journal of Theological Reflection*
81 (2017): 255.

[3] See United States Conference of Catholic Bishops, "Charter for the
Protection of Children and Young People" (2002; rev. June 2018) articles
2, 10.

also readies the church to ask—and to learn—what survivors of abuse can teach about how God actively relates to brokenness, what theological insights emerge from survivors' lived experience and the processing of wounds and healing, and what is revealed as lost to persons and to the church when these wounds remain unprocessed, unhealed, over a lifespan.

The synodal process requires significant patience on the part of the church as a listening body. Because all are invited to speak out with courage, including specifically the marginalized and excluded who have been subjected to prejudice or stereotyping, the community of the church is tasked with making space for authentic, transparent forms of communication that identify, interrogate, and interrupt those same prejudices and stereotypes. The spirit of freedom and courage to speak forthrightly finds its corollary in a humbled, listening church made ready by the Spirit to receive what is new, authentic, and corrective from among us. This suggests that the church's ongoing work of processing its wounds of abuse will find opportune chances for doing so in local environments where there is serious commitment to and conversion toward the synodal process.[4] Where a lack of conversion to the synodal process is evident, or where the results of the synodal process are neglected or not taken seriously by leadership or laity, we are less likely to find an environment conducive to survivors, to their witness, and to the shared responsibility to accompany them on the journey of healing, which is the church's own journey.

It is nearly impossible to take a static picture of the church's response to the crisis. Any such picture would fail to capture what in reality is a continually evolving dynamic environment. One sees variation at the local level of dioceses, parishes, and schools where people live out their faith lives and encounter the structural realities of the institutional church and personnel responsible for safe environment and protection. At the institutional levels of the USCCB and the Holy See, one observes ongoing evolution in policies and procedures that have been designed, implemented, and revised since 2002 to protect the

---

[4] Preparatory Document, nos. 30.II, 30.III.

vulnerable from abuse, to be accountable to the church's own codes of conduct, and to heal the very real and deep wounds of both primary and secondary victims of abuse. The environment of the Catholic Church is in constant flux for these reasons. The reality of the church is in fact pluriform, because the conditions of the church pertaining not only to matters of abuse and healing but to all matters are distinct from diocese to diocese under the impact of different leaders and local cultural dynamics. The abuse crisis brings into sharp focus the hierarchical governance of the church with regard to the dynamics of power, but equally the decentralization of the church with regard to local experiences of life-affecting inconsistencies across dioceses, parishes, schools, and other institutions. Indeed, in the judgment of Karen Terry, the principal investigator of the John Jay College's "Causes and Context Study,"[5] the Catholic Church's decentralized organizational structure functions as a risk factor for abuse. It is not enough to rest content with the USCCB's "Charter for the Protection of Children and Young People," or upon the latest revision of the same, or the latest Motu Proprio issued by a pope. All such achievements, important as they are, must be implemented in numerous local dioceses, parishes, and schools to be effective. Where there is indifference or only a minimalist response—checking boxes—among local actors responsible for implementing safe-environment standards, vulnerability persists. As important as mandatory policies and procedures are, focus must fall upon the culture of the church itself, on whether the church in its manifold local iterations has embraced an ethos of protection and healing, or, in the words of the former chair of the USCCB National Review Board, Francesco Cesareo, in many of the last USCCB *Annual Reports: Findings and*

---

[5] Karen J. Terry, "The Causes and Context of Sexual Abuse of Minors by Catholic Priests in the United States, 1950–2010" (Washington, DC: USCCB Communications, 2011). Frequently referred to as the "Causes and Context Study."

Recommendations, there are "signs of complacency" and "a lack of diligence" on the part of some dioceses.[6]

The annual reports provide a yearly assessment of whether and how dioceses have been in compliance with the "Charter for the Protection of Children and Young People." The USCCB commissions Stonebridge Business Partners to conduct onsite audits of diocesan compliance with the charter, and the results provide the USCCB and the National Review Board with data on both successful implementation of the charter and the specific reasons some dioceses may fall out of compliance with it. This data provides a somewhat useful window through which to observe the culture of the church around matters of safe environment as it plays out in varied ways in local stakeholders and contexts.

The *2018 Annual Report* is of particular interest. Francesco Cesareo begins his comments in that report by noting the depth of frustration and disappointment among many in the church stemming from the situation with (former Archbishop) Theodore McCarrick and the Pennsylvania grand jury report. Many wondered, Cesareo writes, whether the implementation of the charter "has been more concerned with 'checking-off the box' as opposed to creating a culture of safety within dioceses." Not merely an abstract speculation, this sentiment was supported, Cesareo indicated, in the results of the 2018 audit, which reinforced the findings of audits in years past. They would also be shown to be consistent with audits in the years to come (2019–21).[7] He goes on to explain in greater detail:

> During the last several years the Annual Report has pointed out recurring concerns that speak to the issue of complacency. This year is no exception. We continue to see failure

---

[6] USCCB, *2017 Annual Report: Findings and Recommendations*, vii; *2018 Annual Report: Findings and Recommendations*, vi–vii; *2019 Annual Report: Findings and Recommendations*, viii; *2021 Annual Report: Findings and Recommendations*, vi.

[7] Cesareo, *2018 Annual Report*, vi.

to publish reporting procedures in the various languages in which the liturgy is celebrated; poor record keeping of background checks; failure to train children not trained, especially in religious education programs; lack of cooperation by parishes and implementation of safe environment requirements or responding to requests from safe environment personnel; lack of a formal monitoring plan for priests who have been removed from ministry; failure to update policies and procedures in light of the 2011 *Charter* revisions. These are just some of the concerns highlighted in this year's Annual Report that need attention. While not widespread, the fact that in some dioceses these recurring problems are still evident points to lack of diligence that puts children's safety at risk.

In the contexts of a society and of youth-serving organizations in which child vulnerability is ubiquitous, the fact that Cesareo notes these problems are not widespread is an indication of just how successful the implementation of safe environment has been in Catholic dioceses. Always balanced in his assessment of the data, Cesareo confirmed in the same Annual Report that the majority of current bishops have seriously confronted clerical sexual abuse. The unevenness, the variability in buy-in among local stakeholders, nonetheless, remains a concern. Each year, despite stakeholders knowing that a diocesan review board that fails to meet at least once during that year causes the entire diocese to fall out of compliance with the charter, a number of diocesan review boards continue to be inactive or dysfunctional; this fact is an example of this concerning variability.[8] It reflects upon the quality of the culture around protection of vulnerable children and persons in that diocese. Dioceses in which parishes

---

[8] According to the *2021 Annual Report: Findings and Recommendations*, three dioceses and one eparchy were non-compliant with Article 2 of the charter, which requires diocesan review boards to meet during the audit period. Each year, a small number of dioceses and eparchies have been non-compliant with the charter for this reason.

resist training children in the safe environment practices in which they are entitled—and required—to be trained, also reflect on the quality of that particular diocese's commitment and vigilance for protection of vulnerable children and persons.

Into this ground-level assessment of problems and concerns that continue to occur in an environment that is generally compliant with the charter, one may ask what difference theology can make to the culture of a church. Are the efforts of theologians to build up constructive theological responses to abuse and ecclesial conditions that make abuse more likely able to offer any meaningful contribution to people harmed directly and indirectly by abuse? With an eye fixed upon the horizon of an unfolding future, can theology make a difference to people who may be, or someday may become, vulnerable to abuse? We think so.

Constructive theological and ethical engagements with clergy-perpetrated abuse tend to come in articles of chapter length. Few current volume-length treatments focus upon theological engagement with victim-survivors of abuse. By collecting a variety of authors and theological sub-disciplines into one volume, we intend not to say the best or final word on the subjects addressed, but rather to demonstrate first that a wide range of theological sub-disciplines do have much to offer a victim-centric ecclesial culture and, second, that the gifts and efforts of other theologians from these and additional theological sub-disciplines stand to make important contributions going forward. Such focus upon a victim-centric orientation combined with a breadth of theological perspectives—systematic theology, ethics, ecclesiology, biblical studies, liturgical studies—along with clinical psychological expertise has not yet occurred within one volume.

Chapter 1, "Resiliency, Hope, Healing: Victims Assistance Ministry in a Trauma-Sensitive Theological Context," is written by Heather T. Banis, PhD, a clinical psychologist with theological training who specializes in trauma-informed counseling. Banis has served on the faculty at Occidental College and is currently the Victims Assistance Coordinator for the Archdiocese of Los Angeles. She serves also as a consultant to the USCCB Committee for the Protection of Children and Young People. This chapter situates the church's victim assistance ministry in terms of an ongoing relationship of learning from those harmed how best to respond to victim-survivors of abuse in order to nurture authentic healing. With his permission, she describes the call "Joe" placed to her office as the beginning of a long relationship that was therapeutic for him but also instructive to her in terms of how to develop attunement to survivors. This chapter combines research on trauma and theology with victim assistance ministry experienced in real time and with real people. It develops a variety of best principles to govern such ministry, including how to be victim-centric, how to honor the sacred story of survivors, and how to understand clergy-perpetrated sexual abuse as a betrayal trauma. Her work with Joe provides some suggestive possibilities of the difference victim assistance ministry can make in the cultivation of resilience and renewal.

Chapter 2, "Critical Reflections on the Discourse of a Traumatized Church," written by Jennifer E. Beste, the Koch Chair of Catholic Thought and Culture at the College of Saint Benedict and a leading researcher in this field in the United States, provides a helpful corrective to a misunderstanding of the meaning of the title of this book. Is the church traumatized? Is it the case that people of God are traumatized by the phenomenon of clergy sexual abuse and its cover-up? Emphatically, this is not the case. This chapter embodies a victim-centric perspective in its clarification, based on Beste's three decades of research on trauma, that trauma and post-traumatic stress are clinical terms that do not apply to the entire church as synonyms for people's grief, anxiety, disorientation, and even crises of faith that can attend confrontation with abuse and cover-up. Such responses are distinct from trauma, and to conflate the two harms our capacity to accompany victim-survivors of abuse and to redress the causes and conditions that led to it. The title of this book, *Theology in a Post-Traumatic Church*, does not mean to convert the clinical application of trauma into a synonym for all who have come to grief over the phenomenon of abuse in their church, whether laity, priests, or bishops. Rather, it underscores the responsibility of theologians to do theology from the perspective of abuse and healing (that is, redemption), to draw constructively upon the resources of the Christian tradition for the entire people of God, which in this focus includes victim-survivors and others harmed indirectly by abuse. Beste enjoins the reader to retain focus upon victims and their children, on the one hand, while calling upon Catholics to accept for themselves the onus for resolving the crisis as collaborators who are co-responsible for the church.

Chapter 3, "What Is Redemption?" by John N. Sheveland, a theologian at Gonzaga University who serves on the Spokane Diocesan Review Board and National Review Board, turns to survivors themselves to learn theologically about what survivors undergo and why when they experience their wounds to be encountered by a God who heals and redeems them over a long developmental process throughout their lifespan. The chapter acknowledges that policies surrounding prevention, while necessary, are not enough, and that one part of the needed change in the culture of the church will include the community's capacity to accompany survivors of any form of abuse. This move beyond a narrow focus on prevention policies implemented by only a few toward a more earnest culture of attunement to global and ecclesial child vulnerability and the flourishing of survivors as a commitment made by many will require sober redress of patterns of clericalism and narcissism among clergy and laity alike. This chapter expands on the compelling ethnographic research of Susan Shooter, proposes an alignment between the principles of high reliability organizations and some features of Catholic ecclesiology, and probes the power of communal liturgical prayer to effect change in the culture of the church.

Chapter 4, "What Can Make the Churches Unsafe: The Catholic Church as Total Institution," by Cristina Lledo-Gomez, an ecclesiologist and research fellow at Charles Sturt University and lecturer at BBI—The Australian Institute of Theological Education, explores the organizational structures of churches that enhance conditions for the abuse of power. Such abuse of power can persist even in ecclesial environments that have committed to zero tolerance for abuse. In this chapter Lledo-Gomez draws upon her concrete experience and roles in position of service to her local church—ranging from youth minister, reader, senior server, and extraordinary minister of holy communion to chair of the Australian Catholic Bishops Commission for Social Justice, pastoral associate for staff, and theology lecturer at a Catholic university, to wife of a permanent deacon—to arrive at the finding that the same churches that support people can also use and abuse them, not only sexually but spiritually. She argues that the safeguarding of children must be widened toward people's generalized vulnerability to the abuse of power, toward specific ways a religious institution can be set up and maintained that cater to spiritual abuse such as manipulation, coercion, and controlling behavior, censorship, isolation as punishment, and compelled obedience to an abuser. These are risk factors for clergy-perpetrated abuse, and they remain risk factors for other kinds of abuse even when clergy-perpetrated abuse is absent. The chapter employs the powerful framework of a "total institution" and investigates whether and how some of its features apply to Catholic experience. Total institutions constitute alternative moral universes, embrace assumptions about human nature, extinguish members' previous identities, promote secrecy, and exhibit unique power structures and unique informal group dynamics. A trauma-informed approach to these risk factors will prioritize safety, trust, choice, collaboration, and empowerment, these being protective factors associated with synodality and a means to measure the integrity of those claiming commitment to safeguarding in the church.

Chapter 5, "Visions of Survivor Healing and Empowerment in Response to Trauma," by Scott R. A. Starbuck, a biblical theologian at Gonzaga University and senior pastor at Manito Presbyterian Church, is the first of two chapters that contemplate the prophetic power of the Hebrew Bible to empower survivors' processing and recovering from traumatic wounding. It is a powerful witness to the ways in which the biblical text itself, in this case the Book of Isaiah, offers anticlerical opportunities for the empowerment of the laity, those wounded by trauma in particular.

Starbuck provides a trauma-informed theological exegesis of Isaiah 55:1–13 and 61:1–11 precisely for those in pastoral contexts who have been failed by the religious institution and who are in need of an anchor in the biblical text itself, which discloses a God who is theologically available to the violated in an unmediated manner. Exegesis of these verses provides a biblical opportunity to foster in victim-survivors a sense of healing and the empowerment of their own personal agency without dependence upon clerical mediation.

Chapter 6 also probes the Hebrew Bible's capacity for victim-centric resources for healing and finds the psalms to have already become a crucial aid in the processing of grief among many survivors. Linda Schearing, professor emerita of Hebrew Bible at Gonzaga University, notes that an analogy can be drawn between the theological and ecclesial tendency to neutralize the themes of anger and lament—despite their ubiquity in the Psalter—and the experiences of many survivors of sexual abuse when their voices are silenced or viewed as unsettling to others. The chapter studies the meaningfulness of the genre of lament for trauma recovery, gives voice to a number of survivors who have written of the importance of Psalm 55 and Psalm 88. It provides a biblical justification for the pastoral reality that survivors need and are entitled to lament, with its depth of feeling, bold truthfulness, inherent messiness, vivid and desperate intonation of divine absence in the midst of interpersonal betrayal, yet with a sense that healing may be possible even if distant and remote. This chapter has significant implications for a community's capacity to accompany and hold space in the midst of survivor witness or testimony, and it challenges the contemporary moment of synodality in the church with another way to appreciate how hard the church must work to incorporate the voices and contributions of all, even and especially those who call out with disruptive testimony from the "pit" (Ps 88:4, 6) in which they have found themselves. It provides a biblical key as well for the trauma-informed pastoral practice of listening in ways that necessarily elongate the processing of trauma, permitting gradual testimony in a space of receptivity without rushing to provide well-intended words of consolation.

Such words are not always to be found in the psalms, and this tells us something vital.

Chapter 7, "Malignant Narcissism and Clericalism: Psychological Perspectives on a Culture of Abuse," is the first of three chapters that conduct "deep dives" into clericalism. It is written by Fernando A. Ortiz, PhD, a clinical psychologist at Gonzaga University and former member of the USCCB National Review Board; he also regularly psychologically evaluates candidates to various US seminaries. This chapter explores clericalism as a danger to the church and gives particular psychological attention to narcissistic personality traits that frequently combine with the culture of clericalism. This chapter is a "must read" for any stakeholders involved in seminary and religious formation desiring the ability to predict risk factors that predispose candidates to an abusive clerical culture. Ortiz stresses the importance of a comprehensive human formation program for priests and seminarians to reduce risk factors and promote resilience, emotional intelligence, problem-solving skills, and healthy support systems.

The author of Chapter 8, "Understanding and Resisting Clericalism and Social Sin," is B. Kevin Brown, a theologian at Gonzaga University and a principal investigator in Fordham University's initiative *Taking Responsibility: Jesuit Educational Institutions Confront the Causes and Legacy of Clergy Sexual Abuse*. This chapter joins another recent study on clericalism by Julie Hanlon Rubio and Paul J. Schutz to provide sophisticated and complementary analyses of various patterns of clericalism as a bias.[9] For Brown, clericalism is a structure of domination rooted in bias that affects and distorts all relationships in the church. It conditions the community's set of meanings and values in ways that enable the dominant group to maintain power and privilege at the expense of others. It appeared repeatedly in four historical patterns of abuse and cover-up: (1) with few exceptions, bishops and priests did not report offending priests to law enforcement; (2) bishops

---

[9] Julie Hanlon Rubio and Paul J. Schutz, "Beyond 'Bad Apples': Understanding Clergy Perpetrated Sexual Abuse as a Structural Problem and Cultivating Strategies for Change" (New York: Fordham University, August 2022).

frequently allowed perpetrators to continue serving in positions of ministry with children; (3) bishops did not inform parishioners that a priest assigned to their community had been accused previously or that children might be in danger as a result; and (4) there was a lack of collaboration between ordained and non-ordained in responding to cases of abuse. Brown proposes creative ways in which clericalism can be resisted for the well-being of all and gestures toward a renewed theology of ministry predicated upon the Spirit's invitation to participate in non-dominating love.

Chapter 9, "Worship among the Ruins: Foundations for a Theology of Liturgy and Sacraments 'after Abuse,'" by Joseph C. Mudd, a theologian and director of Catholic Studies at Gonzaga University, explores the psychic structure of clericalism with the help of the works of Canadian Jesuit theologian Bernard Lonergan. Clericalism is a human phenomenon observable across cultures that locates authority in office, not with authenticity. Authenticity legitimizes authority, whereas unauthenticity destroys it. Mudd explores Lonergan's analysis of dramatic bias and the repressive function of the psyche and applies them to the clericalism in our setting, expressing itself as dishonesty with reality and the choice not to attend to the testimony of victim-survivors due to the attending dread, horror, revulsion, and distaste for abuse and its conditions. For all, psychic conversion is needed to transform the repressive role of the psyche to a constructive one. One liturgical task is to become clear on the role of sacrifice in the liturgy 'after' clergy sexual abuse. Mudd then moves to consider how the sacramental economy of the church presents the opportunity to participate in what Lonergan referred to as the "law of the cross," namely, the experience of evil turned into good by the power of God in Jesus Christ. This can feature clergy and laity working together from their indelible baptismal priesthood to undo patterns of coercion and abuse lodged deeply and unconsciously in a community's way of proceeding and replace them with the sacrificial attitude of Christ, a mutual divine-human interpersonal situation of mutual self-offering in solidarity with victims of abuse. For this reason Mudd suggests every mass should remember victims of clergy-perpetrated abuse, and he speculates that the failure to do so may undermine the meaning of the liturgy. Mudd concludes by reimagining how the sacraments of reconciliation and anointing of the sick might be reimagined for a community 'after' abuse as a way for the community to process what has happened through public penance and collective absolution through, for example, liturgies of lament and masses offered for reconciliation. These may become one way for individuals and communities to reconfigure how authority is expressed in the church, and in so doing, recover authenticity.

This book is indebted to a number of people, and it is a privilege to acknowledge them here. Each author took this task to heart in the midst of difficult pandemic living conditions. I am grateful for their willingness to take on the project and for their resilience in the midst of it. Thomas Hermans-Webster, acquisitions editor for Orbis Books, and before him, Jill O'Brien, offered tremendous insight and energy toward this project at every turn, for which we as authors are deeply grateful. Maria Angelini, managing editor at Orbis, contributed a sharp eye for detail and enhanced the manuscript throughout. I am grateful to members of the Secretariat for Child and Youth Protection at the United States Conference of Catholic Bishops, its director Deacon Bernie Nojadera, Molly Fara, Laura Garner, and former members Lauren Sarmir and Melanie Takinen. These professionals have tirelessly performed the church's front-line work of making the promise to protect and the pledge to heal, and they are true subject-matter experts. I am grateful to past and present members of the National Review Board from whom I have learned deeply, especially Francesco Cesareo and Suzanne Healy, and to members of the Spokane Diocese Review Board. All of us as authors are indebted to our spouses and families who have graciously tolerated our distraction during long and irregular work hours. We dedicate this volume to our children—to all children—and especially to the people of Saint Michael, Alaska—past, present, and future. May we learn from our past and together create a future in which the landscape of child vulnerability and flourishing exceeds even what hope empowers us to imagine.

1.

Resiliency, Hope, Healing

Victims Assistance Ministry
in a Trauma-Sensitive Theological Context

Heather T. Banis, PhD

Joe[1] waited anxiously for an opening to ask his physician the question foremost in his mind—would he ever be able to stop taking the antidepressant medication he had taken for years? The question, once asked, elicited the answer Joe thought he feared the most. "No, Joe" his doctor said. "Never—you are damaged goods—you're going to need those meds for the rest of your life if you want to be able to function." Driving home, devastated, Joe's anger overwhelmed the decades of silence to which he had long ago committed himself. Once home, he raced to the phone, called the Archdiocese of Los Angeles's Office of Victims Assistance Ministry and unleashed his pain through the fiber optics connecting us, demanding that we, meaning me, the coordinator of that office, and the church he had loved as a boy and as a man, listen to his sacred story. In doing

---

[1] It is an honor to relate Joe's story, and I do so with his permission based on what he has shared with me of his past and what we have experienced together. For background information on Joe and his story, see Tom Hoffarth, "Abuse Survivor Finds Healing at Liturgy of Lament in Glendora," *Angelus News* (April 8, 2019).

so, Joe was giving us a chance to acknowledge the unimaginable harm perpetrated against him and to accompany him as he stepped angrily into this next phase of his healing journey.

Although victims assistance ministry is now twenty years old, in the history of the US Catholic Church the best practices of that ministry are continuously evolving as those ministering learn from those harmed how best to respond to victim-survivors in order to nurture authentic healing. This chapter situates the work of victims assistance ministry not on best practices per se but on best principles—principles that are essential and timeless, and therefore able to sustain the continuing evolution of best practices to support healing of clergy-abuse victim-survivors, their loved ones, and the church. Because these principles are grounded in the lived experience of those harmed and those ministering, they prioritize "attunement"—a journey of accompaniment that honors victim-survivors through attentive listening, transparency, and accountability. This discussion of attunement benefits from the trauma-informed work of Jennifer Baldwin, Shelly Rambo, Serene Jones, and Ron Rolheiser. The three principles of attunement are:

1. a commitment to *victim-centric* response protocols that rely upon input from the individual victim-survivor as well as the collective wisdom of other victim-survivors to inform the ministry,

2. an essential understanding of each victim-survivor's experience as a *sacred story* of trauma, perseverance, and resilience, deserving of individualized attention and response,

3. an acknowledgment that clergy sexual abuse is, at its core, a *betrayal trauma* requiring a sincere and ongoing demonstration of trustworthiness, transparency, and accountability by the church as a foundation of reconciliation.

Joe is one of hundreds of victim-survivors to contact the Office of Victims Assistance Ministry in Los Angeles. This chapter tells Joe's story as it unfolded in relationship to victims assistance ministry as the point upon which a trauma-sensitive theological lens is focused. On the day Joe called, his despair doing battle with his courage—hope, vulnerability, and distrust juxtaposed with the need to proclaim truth and seek accompaniment—the healing journey Joe was already on turned a corner, inviting companionship from a stranger representing the very institution in which he was harmed, starting down a path with an unknown landscape and only the vaguest notion of destination.

Jennifer Baldwin describes trauma-sensitive theology as a "theoretical lens, ethical commitment [and] guide for praxis." Trauma-sensitive theology provides a relevant foundation for the church's accompaniment because it illuminates the sacred space the survivor and companion now share.[2] Focused particularly on relational trauma, Baldwin's work is holistic in scope and encompasses spiritual beliefs, practices, and rituals into healing work in both the psychological and spiritual realms. Hers is an affirmative model that acknowledges the victim-survivor's resilience and capacity for attunement as strengths.

Shelly Rambo's focus is contextual and accepts the reality that the victim-survivor has to live with both the trauma and its aftermath. She challenges redemption-based resurrection theology by expanding attention and capacity for the "Holy Saturday" experience of divine love persisting in the face of suffering.[3]

Serene Jones expands the trauma-informed theological focus around those harmed by asking the important question, "What should be the work of the church in the wake of such trauma?" She challenges the church to embrace responsibility for the "reordering [of] the collective imagination of its people" in its response to the collective trauma impacting society and asserts that "healing lies as much, if not more, in the stories we tell and the gestures we offer as in the doctrines we preach."[4]

Ron Rolheiser speaks of responding to what is lost with an affirmation of the new life one already has in Christ. He, too, calls people of faith to cultivate an imagination grounded in the regenerative cycle exemplified in the paschal mystery of Jesus's passion, death, and resurrection. This paschal imagination creates

---

[2] Jennifer Baldwin, *Trauma-Sensitive Theology: Thinking Theologically in the Era of Trauma* (Eugene, OR: Cascade Books, 2018), 6.

[3] Shelly Rambo, *Spirit and Trauma: A Theology of Remaining* (Louisville, KY: Westminster John Knox Press, 2010), 12.

[4] Serene Jones, *Trauma and Grace: Theology in a Ruptured World* (Louisville, KY: Westminster John Knox Press, 2009), 1.

"a vision which inspires one to constantly re-set one's life in the context of union with Christ in a kind of regenerative cycle."[5]

Even as he was able to envision himself healed, the healing process, as Joe anticipated and subsequently experienced, would necessitate encounters with memories, truths, and failings any survivor of abuse would fear. For, as Jones writes, "to be saved is not to be taken elsewhere. It is to be awakened—to mourn and to wonder. And to stand courageously on the promise that grace is sturdy enough to hold it all—you, and me, and every broken, trauma-ridden soul that wanders through our history. To us all, love comes."[6] These life-giving, restorative, and foundational ideas offer a framework for a discussion of the best principles for victims assistance ministry. Collectively, they foster attunement between those harmed, those affected, and those embedded in the structure and hierarchy of the church.

PRINCIPLE 1: BE VICTIM-CENTRIC

Today, the vast majority of clergy-abuse victim-survivors coming to Victim Assistance Ministry in Los Angeles are adults, many sixty years old or older. For decades they have borne the wounds of their trauma, many with self- or other-imposed silence intended to protect others in the face of a deafening silence from their church. In both circumstances silence has exacerbated the losses created in the wake of what was stolen in childhood. Once children and too soon made victims, those harmed present a myriad of manifestations of what it means to be survivors: dignified if often lost; seeking even as they push back against what is offered; wanting to be believed; expecting to be rebuked; overcome by sadness; fueled by anger; despairing, hopeful, scattered, and messy; or with a laser focus and incisive bearing. The harm done decades ago expands and takes shape uniquely throughout each

---

[5] Ron Rolheiser, "Paschal Imagination," February 18, 1991, ronrolheiser.com.

[6] Jones, *Trauma and Grace*, 165.

survivor's life, malforming and deforming typical structures of affect, expectation, and response.

An attuned response from both clergy and laity must be grounded in respect, exhibit breadth and flexibility, and, to truly foster healing, must be steadfast in their willingness to bear the brunt of anger, the burden of blame, and accountability for the depth of the wounds created. Each victim-survivor will bear uniquely configured strengths, needs, and fears warranting a response that is contingent in corresponding and specific ways. Because healing will manifest in equally unique ways, to commit to a victim-centric model is to accept what Jones identifies as "the challenge . . . to think of grace in ways that do not require pure outcomes or an impossible, radical newness."[7]

PRINCIPLE 2: HONOR THE SACRED STORY

Joe's anger was an offering. Even as he gave witness to the prolonged and pervasive impact of clergy sexual abuse, he gave evidence of a capacity to imagine himself and his relationship with God anew, exemplifying the very essence of the renewal of which Rolheiser speaks: "A healthy imagination is the opposite of resignation, abdication, naive optimism or despair. It is the foundation of hope. Through it we turn fate to destiny."[8] Able to separate the priest who perpetrated against him from God and his love for his church, Joe's capacity for healing was embodied in his capacity for relationship. The significance of this ability is profound.

The story of Joe's childhood revolved to a large degree around the family's faith and strong connection to the church. His parents were steadfast volunteers in ministry and significant donors to the parish. Joe and his brothers were altar servers; an older cousin became a priest and then a bishop. Statistics testify to the fact that most children are abused by a known and trusted adult. Such was the case for Joe. The challenge for Joe was how to make any sense

---

[7] Jones, 156.

[8] Rolheiser, "Paschal Imagination."

of what was happening to him in the context of his faith. Thus, it is crucial to explore the concept of sin and its place in the narrative of clergy sexual abuse from the perspective of the victim-survivor.

Baldwin and others define sin as an abuse of relational power.[9] The relationship between a young boy and a beloved priest exemplifies one such imbalanced structure in which an expectation of trustworthiness may be exploited. Joe's relationship with his perpetrator began as one of love and admiration. His trusting and devout parents encouraged the relationship, which Joe believed constituted a shared commitment to serve God and the church. Ordained in the image of Christ, who never abused relational power, Fr. Pat transformed Joe's faith into a vulnerability he could exploit. Terrified, confused, betrayed, and isolated by the abuse, Joe's childhood became a living hell for the duration of the abuse. Even when it ended, as Rambo points out, "the experiences were haunting . . . and present life became organized under the threat of their return."[10]

This organizing effect of trauma can be so pervasive that it redirects neurodevelopmental trajectories, positioning threat detection as the primary cognitive function of the brain even as some or all of the physical experiences of continuing abuse escape awareness.[11] Rambo explains that the "body experiences trauma in ways that escape cognitive functioning and awareness. Traumatic impact is shown to limit the function of the limbic system, therefore stopping the system from passing along the experience to the prefrontal cortex, the part of the brain that assigns to an experience language and meaning."[12] According to Baldwin, "we then begin living through parts enlisted in protecting us from experiencing that form of harm again."[13] Drawing back protective curtains closed these many years, Joe

---

[9] Baldwin, *Trauma-Sensitive Theology,* 115.

[10] Rambo, *Spirit and Trauma,* 20.

[11] Dianna T. Kenny, *Children, Sexuality, and Child Sexual Abuse* (London: Routledge, 2018), 46–51.

[12] Rambo, *Spirit and Trauma,* 20.

[13] Baldwin, *Trauma-Sensitive Theology,* 116.

began the intentional process of healing wounds his physician had deemed irreparable.

Psychologically and spiritually Joe sought to reframe the narrative of his life, which was replete with self-recrimination for allowing the beloved priest to sin against God by sexually abusing him. The self-blame and need for secrecy Joe had carried in his heart since he was a young boy affected his entire life story. While part of what makes the individual stories of victim-survivors sacred is their uniqueness, feelings of self-blame are quite common in the narratives of child sexual abuse survivors. Tragically, in a desperate effort to make sense of the abuse, to retain some sliver of a sense of agency, and sometimes fueled by the despicable and distorted messages of the abuser to the child, many victim-survivors live with the shame that they were somehow to blame for what was perpetrated against them. Baldwin, building on the work of Rita Nakashima Brock, offers an important theological entry point that contradicts the all too frequent assumption that somehow victim-survivors are irreparably damaged by "what they've done," or even that they deserved their abuse.[14] Brock's concept of original grace offers the possibility of reimagining a future of restored grace, in contradiction to commonly internalized messages of original sin that can foster the idea, in the absence of an alternative context, that the child somehow contributed to the sin or was somehow deserving of the abuse: "Instead, the original grace present in self reassures us and roots us in hope of resiliency and faith that we are, in fact, fundamentally 'enough.'"[15]

Contextually, when the idea of original grace is connected with the conceptualization of sin as an abuse of relational power, Jesus exemplifies "optimal relationality" with God and, by lived example, with humanity. Healing is the right relationship with God by which the victim-survivor can reclaim a sense of worthiness as original grace. The concept of original grace is important from a linguistic standpoint, as well. Jones points out the "ways in which language, in its patterns and disruptions, both holds power and

---

[14] Baldwin, 111.
[15] Baldwin, 111.

constructs identities."[16] Original grace offers the imagination a glimpse of what one can reclaim and nurture in order to potentiate healing and, beyond healing, thriving. Baldwin states that by shifting "away from original sin to original offense as the source of our beliefs . . . space for compassion and empathy" develops.[17] Such a shift also relocates the source of the sin from within the victim-survivor to the relational context; it locates the trauma in relationship, envisions healing as a reclaiming of original grace, and invites preventive efforts targeting the structure of the relationship between the victim-survivor and the perpetrator, whether the abuser is an individual or an institution. The significance of this shift is magnified by the reality that clergy sexual abuse is often first disclosed in confession, as a sin in which the victim-survivor participated and, tragically, accepts some measure of responsibility.

Thankfully, Joe never lost his faith in God—he managed to separate the actions of the perpetrating priest from God's will in his heart and mind. Nevertheless, Joe blamed himself for being vulnerable, for not trying harder to stop what was being perpetrated against him, and for not preventing further abuses of other children, ultimately claiming the sin of that abuse, at least in part, as his own. The reclaiming of his original grace has been an important theme in Joe's healing journey, a journey still marked by dark passages and haunting memories even as he walks more and more in the light. Such is the nature of living with trauma.

Those who work with trauma victim-survivors know all too well that the healing process is a complex and challenging one that unfolds in unique ways related to the trauma itself and both the past and current life circumstances of the victim-survivor. Embedded in layers of narrative, the trauma infiltrates the survivor's thoughts, feelings, actions, spirituality, and hopes. Trauma often isolates the individual from sources of support and understanding because such isolation seems to offer safeguards that relationships no longer do. To embark intentionally on a healing journey risks much.

---

[16] Jones, *Trauma and Grace*, 225.
[17] Baldwin, *Trauma-Sensitive Theology*, 117.

Healing truly begins when a sense of safety can develop, even if only in fleeting ways. This sense of safety exists, or does not exist, in the context of relationship with another. To experience such safety can awaken the possibility of feeling safe again, in a larger sense. In this way healing from trauma involves reclaiming more than restoration. Symptoms of post-traumatic stress disorder, depression, or anxiety are persistent physical and psychological reminders of what trauma has disrupted or devastated. The "other" is in a pivotal position to offer the victim-survivor a relational context capable of holding the trauma and its aftermath, as discussed in the chapter by John Sheveland. Experiences of the other that offer both capacity and commitment to hold the trauma(s) can foster feelings of safety and agency, however limited or imperfect. Linguistic, scriptural, and theological references are critical determinants of the character of this relational context and are of particular significance given how frequently victim-survivors turn to the church seeking to disclose, to be received, and to be accompanied in healing, frequently by someone in the church. Thus, it is essential that clergy, victim assistance coordinators, and all the church become attuned to the needs of trauma survivors, intentionally constructing the church and its myriad relational contexts as safe, welcoming havens for those harmed.

Transformation of the pain of the trauma so that self-love, trust, and agency can be reintegrated into the victim-survivor's narrative is critical. Innocence cannot be restored, but the loss of innocence can be transformed. These characteristics of trauma and healing lend themselves to analysis within the Easter narratives, as the trauma of Good Friday offers a similarly dislocating and overwhelming reference experience and the journey of Holy Saturday echoes in the life of the trauma survivor, even years after the actual traumatic event(s). Care must be taken with the triumphant tone of the Easter story, as many victim-survivors do not experience a moment that releases them once and for all from the grip of the trauma, thus completing their healing process. Nonetheless, they can find images of transformation throughout the Easter narratives that resonate as recurring experiences of resurrection offering hope, affirming presence, and bringing something from their pain. In doing so, some victim-survivors can then engage in what Susan Shooter calls "knowing ministry," through which their lived experience of God's transforming presence to traumatic experience becomes service to others.[18]

As a church centered on resurrection, those engaged in pastoral ministry with trauma survivors may unintentionally disconfirm the lived experience of the survivor, by rushing through the trauma of Good Friday and the significance of Jesus's descent into hell of Holy Saturday in a well-intentioned but ill-advised effort to arrive at the resurrection. Rambo's emphasis on the Holy Saturday quality of the survivor's lived experience, and the experience of those who bear witness, provides insight into the nature of the trauma's impact on those directly harmed and on those who, knowingly or unknowingly, are witnessing that impact. Citing Mary Magdalene's experience at the empty tomb, Rambo draws parallels between "her inability to see, locate and identify the body of Jesus . . . as constitutive of what it means to witness . . . much of what she is witnessing is inaccessible to her. Her witness reflects the complexities of seeing in the aftermath of death."[19] The survivor experiences a death of sorts. Both the survivor and those who love that person experience dislocation because of what they observe but do not understand. They lack the words or context to describe what they experienced, and thus, cannot reconcile the experience with their meaning-making system. Citing Mary's tears as the means by which the angels recognize her at the tomb, Rambo asserts that "Mary's inability to directly access the events taking place does not reveal something about her credibility as a witness but instead the nature of what she is witnessing."[20] With hindsight, those who love Joe can now "see" the tears he shed as a child even though they could not then fathom the source of his

---

[18] Susan Shooter, "How Survivors of Abuse Relate to God: A Qualitative Study," in *The Faith Lives of Women and Girls: Qualitative Research Perspectives*, ed. Nicola Slee, Fran Porter, and Anne Phillips (London: Routledge, 2013), 228–31. See also Chapter 3 herein.

[19] Rambo, *Spirit and Trauma*, 83.

[20] Rambo, 91.

distress. This dynamic, so common in the interactions between the victim-survivor and his or her unknowing or disbelieving family and friends, is what gives rise to the profound and elemental need for acknowledgment of the abuse at present. Citing the work of renowned trauma psychologist Judith Herman, Rambo writes, "Having a witnessing is an essential first step to traumatic recovery, she says. A survivor must reconnect to the world; this reconnection is only possible through some form of witness."[21] Joe's despair and anger brought him into connection with the Office of Victims Assistance Ministry and launched a series of disclosures and confrontations that have both created more distress and, at the same time, obliterated barriers in relationships with his family, leading ultimately to his own public presentations and advocacy efforts. Joe actively sought the witnessing he had long needed, and in doing so he is rediscovering his true self—his whole self—reclaiming what was stolen from him in childhood.

To give witness, however, is no easy task for either victim-survivors or their loved ones. Rambo delves into the complexities of what Mary Magdalene gives witness to upon seeing the empty tomb: "She points to a different kind of presence, whose form cannot be readily identified or can only be received through multiple experiences of misrecognitions. She encounters not simply the absence of Jesus, but a mixed terrain of his absence and presence. He is there but not there; he is present in a way that she has not known before."[22] Mary's credibility as a witness to an inexplicable event is diminished by the inaccessibility of what she is witnessing and is compounded by her status as a woman in a culture, time, and place distrustful of her gender. Such challenges align with those experienced by the many children who disclosed abuse by clergy only to be dismissed or disbelieved by the essential unbelievability of the claim, their diminished status as children, and the power of their abusers' role as unquestioningly trusted men of God. Rambo asserts that "Mary's witness is bound up in her inability to see, locate and identify the body of

---

[21] Rambo, 24.
[22] Rambo, 91.

Jesus. The problems she confronts in the process of witnessing in the aftermath of the crucifixion are constitutive of what it means to witness."[23] Mary struggled to understand what she had seen, its implications, and the disbelief it generated in others. So, too, victim-survivors struggle to give voice to what they experienced behind closed doors, choked by shame, and hardly believable by themselves, let alone others. For Rambo, "the beloved disciple's witness points to this double aspect of belief—the fact that a preliminary experience of 'missed' understanding is constitutive of what it means to be a believer."[24]

This analysis suggests that, in witness to the sacred story of the clergy abuse crisis, an acknowledgment of what was "missed" is central to understand both what happened, and how it could happen. Sexual abuse in general is rarely observed by witnesses; typically the only two who know what happened are the victim-survivor and the perpetrator, one of whom has significantly more power and credibility than the other. Thus, much is required of the victim-survivor, loved one, or advocate, giving witness to the sexual abuse perpetrated by clergy to speak the truth of what was not, and cannot be, observed directly or acknowledged, particularly in the face of institutional denial and deflection. Healing and reconciliation demand a shared witness to the abuse—acknowledgments by the offender and by the offending institution are necessary elements of witnessing in the same way that Mary's witnessing to the resurrected Christ demanded recognition by his followers for the significance and impact of the resurrection to be made manifest. As Rambo states, Mary's witness "reflects the complexities of seeing in the aftermath of death."[25] Mary's tears, like the pain of victim-survivors today, give voice to sacred stories that elude words but live nonetheless.

To honor such sacred stories is to recognize and acknowledge complexities of lived experience as beacons to which attention must be redirected. Rambo describes it thus: "Witness is neither

---

[23] Rambo, 83.
[24] Rambo, 93.
[25] Rambo, 83.

a straightforward proclamation of something that has taken place nor a straightforward imitation of what has taken place. It is a tenuous orientation to suffering that presses central theological claims about death and life in and against themselves."[26] This attention enables one to see what remains—"the suffering that does not go away."[27] Rambo suggests that the suffering of a sexual abuse victim-survivor is reflected in the image of Holy Saturday—the middle day. She frames it as "the site of witness to a more complex relationship between death and life . . . not a finality to the cross but rather a confrontation with something of death remaining and extending into the territory of life. Both resist a picture of triumphant life arising out of death."[28] It is the resistance to a triumphal outcome that resonates with the clergy abuse survivor—if the capacity to imagine healing exists within the victim-survivor, his or her persistent lived experience is more similar to a recurrence of Holy Saturday than to the triumphal finality of Easter Sunday. To live as a trauma survivor is to suffer recurring memories, fears, and uncertainties that continuously threaten any earned sense of triumph. Jones writes of the impact of trauma as "wounds [that] are not magically healed but are borne."[29] In part, healing consists of learning how to carry the burden of the trauma, and its aftermath, differently.

To understand sacred stories of recurrent suffering, to respond to them, and to prevent further suffering requires humility. It requires a willingness to hear the essential truth of the experience in the absence of judgment or filter, with an openness to acknowledging one's role in that suffering and a genuine belief that the wisdom engendered by that lived experience must inform response and reparation to it. To do so is to accept victim-survivor witness in its unconventionality as an opportunity for deeper attunement in the midst of disconnection and disbelief. Rambo states that "witnessing is not about attaining a correct and true

---

[26] Rambo, 42.
[27] Rambo, 26.
[28] Rambo, 46.
[29] Jones, *Trauma and Grace*, 160.

story but, in fact, about a capacity to meet these stories, to hear them for all the ways in which they do not cohere."[30] Baldwin explains that "holding both the weight of the wound, the burden of traumatic processing and recovery, and the hope and potential for resiliency (or even flourishing) in appropriate tension is a dynamic challenge—and a requirement for those of us who seek to provide support through the journey."[31] Thus, victims assistance ministry is about both receiving witness and giving witness to clergy sexual abuse and its impact.

In this journey of companionship, the victim-survivor and companion share responsibility for guidance and direction, each informed by the experience, resilience, and wisdom of the other. The church similarly must invite and respect the expressed needs of victim-survivors and their loved ones as central to efforts to foster healing and reconciliation. Rambo suggests that Holy Saturday lends itself to this effort in its embodiment of the concept of "the remaining":

> The language of remaining within theology speaks back to trauma theory, offering a distinctive vocabulary to think about the challenges of traumatic survival. The language of remaining also provides a way, within a theological context, to reframe and reengage questions about divine presence in suffering. The classic question, "Where is God in the midst of suffering?" comes to new expression if read through a traumatic lens.[32]

Reading through a trauma lens also provokes a new encounter with the Easter narratives in the context of Jesus's experience. Jesus's whole life portrays living in full connection with the Divine, particularly in the midst and aftermath of trauma, and illustrates how, even on Holy Saturday, God is what Rambo calls the *remaining*. Thus Baldwin offers Jesus as the exemplar of

---

[30] Rambo, *Spirit and Trauma*, 151.
[31] Baldwin, *Trauma-Sensitive Theology*, 27–28.
[32] Rambo, *Spirit and Trauma*, 17.

"optimal relationality as it negotiates challenges of an embodied life in the world . . . unconstrained by beliefs generated through life's wounds and fears."[33] The church—the people of God—are called to presence there, too.

PRINCIPLE 3: BETRAYAL TRAUMA

At its core, clergy sexual abuse is a betrayal trauma—a violation of trust made manifest in a violation of a child's body and soul. Tragically, such abuses have historically been compounded by pervasive disbelief, denial, and intentional obfuscation of truths that the eyes of those in power perceived as threats to the institution of the church. The Vatican's report on former cardinal Theodore McCarrick offers one such example.[34] Healing and reconciliation for those harmed directly, and the renewal of the church as a whole, require transformative actions that demonstrate understanding, acknowledgment, accountability, and trustworthiness. Rambo's assertion that "divine love is revealed at the point at which it is most threatened"[35] speaks to these issues in important ways. She argues that Jesus's descent into hell manifests his identification with those who believe themselves forsaken and assures by his presence that no place is without God. The significance of this example for the individual victim-survivor is vital because the experience of clergy abuse can include feeling forsaken by God. Such a betrayal can engender self-loathing, isolation, and a loss of personal agency. Rambo's theology of remaining challenges these forms of self-loss by contradicting the victim-survivor's perceived sense of unworthiness and the persistent fear of abandonment that characterizes abuse and its aftermath, while offering hope as an antidote to the sense of powerlessness. With hope comes the

---

[33] Baldwin, *Trauma-Sensitive Theology*, 119.

[34] "Report on the Holy See's Institutional Knowledge and Decision-Making Related to Former Cardinal Theodore Edgar McCarrick (1930–2017)," prepared by the Secretariat of State of the Holy See, November 10, 2020.

[35] Rambo, *Spirit and Trauma*, 68.

capacity for reimagining, and with imagination comes possibility. Jones and Rolheiser suggest that healing from trauma is a healing of imagination. Mindful that "human beings . . . constantly engage the world through organizing stories or habits of mind, which structure our thoughts,"[36] Jones envisions healing as a process in which the survivor brings trauma and grace into new relationship with one another in such a way that God's presence in relationship affirms worth, restores agency, and allows for the envisioning of new possibilities.

Healing, as envisioned by these theologians, requires a willingness on the part of the community to share with the individual harmed the burden of bearing the wounds inflicted as well as the scars of those wounds, as Christ did and does. Baldwin notes: "The scars of traumatic wounding remain. . . . They function as a means of identification as well as a symbol of the capacity for recovery and healing."[37] She cautions that healing work with trauma survivors must be mindful of the ways in which "unhealthy faith and theology can increase injury sustained by trauma."[38] As previously discussed, concepts of original sin can be distorted inadvertently by the victim-survivor or intentionally by the perpetrator so that blame and responsibility are heaped upon the child who was betrayed. Conversely, as Rambo suggests, "theologies of the cross narrate the story of God taking the pain of the world into Godself"[39] and can be understood through the lens of trauma, such that God is recognized in Godforsaken places. In some instances, for the victim-survivor actively engaged in the ongoing struggle to survive and heal, the church's misnaming of persistent symptomatology (for example, hopelessness, suicidal ideation) as indicative of a lack of faith is another traumatic wound. Baldwin asserts that forgiving and forgetting do not constitute healing. Rather, healing is made manifest in both the individual and the church by "the courage to face the darkness

---

[36] Jones, *Trauma and Grace*, 20.
[37] Baldwin, *Trauma-Sensitive Theology*, 137.
[38] Baldwin, 53.
[39] Rambo, *Spirit and Trauma*, 66.

of traumatic injury, process and care for the wounds, and come to new ways of living authentically."[40]

One can argue that this call also holds true for the healing of the church in the wake of clergy sexual abuse—restoration of a pure version of "what was" is not the goal to pursue. Rather, the church, experiencing its own descent, is called to an authenticity made manifest in trustworthiness, transparency, and accountability.

Theological responses to the clergy sexual abuse crisis in particular, and to traumatic events in general, must be trauma-informed if they are to be authentic, relevant, and meaningful. By definition, a traumatic experience is one that overwhelms one's coping resources. Psychologists recognize that faith in God, or in more general terms, one's meaning-making system, is central to the psychological processing of a traumatic event at both the cognitive and emotional levels. Baldwin asserts, "The realization that the core presuppositions of faith are inadequate in providing clarity of meaning or support in the face of traumatizing crisis events is for many people part of what makes trauma so destabilizing."[41] She suggests seeking out narratives in our sacred texts that "honor the harm of traumatic wounding and facilitate healing resiliency."[42] Rambo's interpretation of the passion, the descent, and Easter offers one such narrative. Rambo suggests: "Read through the lens of trauma, the witness of Mary Magdalene and the beloved points to the impossibility of envisioning life ahead. They depict the messy and inconclusive experience of living beyond a death. In the aftermath of Jesus' death, their survival is haunted by Jesus' words of farewell and his instructions about remaining. Survival is given shape through the curious imperative to remain and to love."[43] Victim-survivors live in this space of remaining, but often do so in isolation and without recognition of its significance.

This theology of remaining is not optional. Rambo insists that it is commanded. She describes it as "a presence that takes

---

[40] Baldwin, *Trauma-Sensitive Theology*, 30.
[41] Baldwin, 53.
[42] Baldwin, 88.
[43] Rambo, *Spirit and Trauma*, 109.

the form of bearing with, of enduring, and of persisting. It is an accompanying and attending presence that always carries with it the marks of suffering and death."[44] To remain is to witness, acknowledge, and be compelled to act or speak—breaking the stunned or complicit silence with truth made transparent. The acknowledgment of such a shame-shrouded secret as sexual abuse can initiate a vital reconnection to the world for the victim; it shines the light of day upon an act so heinous that it has been described as soul murder.

Rolheiser invokes the power of the imagination in a critical moment in the journey of healing: "Imagination is the power to create the images we need to understand and respond to what we are experiencing . . . when we stand before our own experience petrified, frozen and unable to accept or cope with what is there; or when we stand before it stunned, benignly unaware that forces are about to destroy us."[45] Joe's vision of healing manifests Rolheiser's esteem for the power of imagination. Joe imagines healing in specific terms that are both unique to his lived experience and universal among clergy abuse survivors. Joe seeks acknowledgment of the abuse by the perpetrator and the church. He seeks an apology from the perpetrator to him and to all his other victims. He seeks increased and expanded outreach by the church to those who have left the church because of abuse experienced directly or dismay at the handling of abuse by the church. Emboldened by his vision of the church as the safe and holy place he once believed it was, Joe's pain and loss are transforming into advocacy and action, even as he continues to wrestle with the recurring symptoms of post-traumatic stress disorder. Joe's journey of healing, full of anger, sorrow, and forgiveness and enlivened by purpose and a sense of calling, exemplifies Rolheiser's faith in what he calls paschal imagination. He explains: "We can respond with a paschal imagination. . . . We can look at the pattern of death and resurrection in Christ and then move on to positively and critically shape our destiny by naming our deaths, claiming our

---

[44] Rambo, 104.
[45] Rolheiser, "Paschal Imagination."

resurrections, letting the old ascend, and living with the spirit that God is actually giving to us."[46]

If Rolheiser's words offer direction in a healing process, Baldwin's definition of healing provides the landmarks by which it will be recognized. She defines healing as "the outflow of establishing reconnection with Self and Spirit, offering healing unburdening of our own internal parts, allowing parts to assume their authentic gifts of flourishing, and enhancing our attuned connections with God and self, and extending that grace to others."[47] The question that remains beyond the healing of the individual is how the healing of the church will be recognizable. Insightfully, Jones reminds that it is the resurrected Jesus who comes to the disciples, not the other way around. She writes that "the disciples, in their pain and fear, do not have to figure out how to reach him. He simply appears, full-bodied and present. Here, then, is God coming to us, even in this moment."[48] Jones posits that it is for the church to proclaim God's presence in the midst of the fear, confusion, and disconnection and to assert that God is already and always with us. Yet, to do so with authenticity requires the acknowledgment of the church's role in the genesis of the clergy sexual abuse crisis. To do so genuinely demands that significant and contingent changes be made in church culture and practice to demonstrate trustworthiness. In Jones's vision, "the shadow cast by the cross becomes a dark womb that holds their brokenness and envelopes their pain. In this space there is no divine justification for suffering, but there is the outstretched gesture of understanding, of solidarity, and of welcoming embrace."[49]

The church has been forever changed by the clergy abuse crisis. While it is too soon to know just how the church will continue to reorder itself, the reordering process requires imagination, just as the healing process does. Rolheiser notes: "So much of the frustration and stagnation in Christian circles today stems from

---

[46] Rolheiser, "Paschal Imagination."

[47] Baldwin, *Trauma-Sensitive Theology*, 156–157.

[48] Jones, *Trauma and Grace*, 39.

[49] Jones, 97.

a failure of imagination. To let ourselves be led by God through ever-changing times requires, on our part, great imagination."[50] To move beyond the Holy Saturday of this crisis into the resurrection, the church might be better served by the image of remembering and reclaiming relationship with God such that the church is what Rambo describes as a "persistent witness to love's survival."[51] Note, however, that Rambo and Rolheiser were speaking to individual or collective traumas not perpetrated by, or within, the church.

The challenge facing the Catholic Church today is that the scourge of abuse comes from within. For Jones, the church's role is to reorder "the collective imagination of its people and to be wise and passionate in this task . . . to bring order to this disorder . . . in a manner that seeks the flourishing of all people."[52] What might this reordering look like, or is it even possible, from within the church itself? Jones writes, "We are called to be those who testify, who try to tell the story of what happened in its fullness; those who witness, who receive the story of the violence and create a safe space for its healing; those who reimage the future by telling yet again—without denying the event of violence now woven into it—the story of our faith."[53] Weaving the clergy sexual abuse crisis into the narrative of our faith is no easy task, and it is one that has met with, and likely will continue to meet with, resistance. Misperceptions about the impact of such trauma, for the individual and for the church, coupled with fear regarding the diminishment or even destruction of the church, have fostered ecclesiastically sanctioned acts that not only fail to protect the church, as was perhaps intended, but damage the church's integrity even further. Perhaps the desire to seek a triumphal outcome has overshadowed the value and integrity of giving witness to the love remaining amid the terror of clergy sexual abuse. Rambo's use of the term *eliding* seems to capture the essence of the church's historical response to allegations of clergy abuse—"instances in

---

[50] Rolheiser, "Paschal Imagination."

[51] Rambo, *Spirit and Trauma*, 110.

[52] Jones, *Trauma and Grace*, 31.

[53] Jones, 33.

which certain truths are suppressed, omitted, ignored or passed over captures the intentionality that is often at play [in response to a crisis and] takes into account the fact that, in many cases, certain parties are invested in suppressing the truth of certain events."[54]

The imperative to change church culture, to acknowledge the systemic support that enabled such abuses to be perpetrated, to eliminate the eliding responses that have been commonplace, and to inculcate a resolve to prevent future abuse, is no easy task. Rolheiser's invitation to envision a new future by letting go of what has died and no longer serves may offer the church what it needs today. He asserts that "we must be able to . . . name where we've died, claim where we've been born, know what old bodies we need to let ascend, and recognize the new spirit that is being given us" as a recurring reliving of the paschal cycle and promise.[55] As highlighted by Rolheiser, just as Christ sparked the apostles' individual and collective imaginations on the road to Emmaus, so too can we be invigorated by what we do not yet understand.

CONCLUSION

"To be saved is not to be taken elsewhere. It is to be awakened— to mourn and to wonder. And to stand courageously on the promise that grace is sturdy enough to hold it all."[56] The clergy sexual abuse crisis has been devastating for the individual lives of victim-survivors, for their loved ones, and for the life of the church. Victims assistance ministry is in a position of privileged responsibility as the designated, dedicated center of response to clergy-abuse victim-survivors. Grounding in the three principles discussed herein—victim-centric response, honoring the sacredness of the abuse story, and understanding how betrayal trauma can be healed—creates the possibility of healing in collective moments of being heard, acknowledged, affirmed, and respected. The theologians whose works inform this chapter and trauma-trained

---

[54] Rambo, *Spirit and Trauma*, 41.
[55] Rolheiser, "Paschal Imagination."
[56] Jones, *Trauma and Grace*, 165.

psychologists agree—"trauma is not something you really ever 'get over,' but rather one develops the capacity to 'bear it.'"[57] And "the story of trauma is a story about the storm that does not go away. It is a story of remaining."[58] Victims assistance ministry is also in the privileged position of witnessing to the impact of clergy sexual abuse within the church and providing through its efforts a model whereby all the church can muster a healing response and renewal efforts. As Baldwin states, "To participate in the binding and soothing of the wounds of traumatic violation and injury, theology must resist its history of valorizing suffering and death and renew its commitment as a resource of healing and inspiration of healthy behavior and relational attachments."[59] The painful memories carried by those harmed can, with support and imagination, transform such that trust and meaning are restored and disruptions in relationships, human and divine, are healed. To accompany a victim-survivor on such a journey is both an honor and a responsibility that demands much and reveals even more of the church. Jones implores the church to "be boldly theological in [its] admission of the importance of the poetic and practical."[60] To do so is to recognize the place for inspiration, ritual, policy, and procedures that are contingent in their responsiveness to expressed needs. Within such a responsive context, the child who was made a victim and then a survivor can imagine thriving in right relationship with God, with loved ones, and with self. With such an understanding as this put into action, demonstrative indicators of accountability, transparency, and trustworthiness take recognizable shape and invite collective renewal, relationship by relationship. Joe's faith, determination, resilience, and right relationship with Victims Assistance Ministry exemplify this ideal. He offers the gift of his pain and his imagination with growing confidence that his church, too, seeks transformation.

---

[57] Jones, *Trauma and Grace*, 227.
[58] Rambo, *Spirit and Trauma*, 143.
[59] Baldwin, *Trauma-Sensitive Theology*, 157.
[60] Jones, *Trauma and Grace*, 225.

2

Critical Reflections on the Discourse on a "Traumatized Church"

Jennifer E. Beste

A common refrain among Catholics in informal conversations, media, and scholarly discussions and publications is that Catholic clergy, laity, and/or the church are in a traumatized state as a result of clergy sexual abuse and church officials' systemic cover-up. In this chapter I raise ethical and theological concerns about applying the designation of trauma and traumatization so broadly within this particular context. Such sweeping claims function to distort our understanding of these events and cloud our discernment about what constitutes authentic Christian discipleship in response. As I will argue, taking a strong presumptive stance against the idea of a "traumatized church" has far-reaching ethical and theological implications that will make it easier to pursue justice and healing effectively through solidarity with clergy-perpetrated child sexual abuse survivors (CPCSA) and Catholic children globally who currently remain at high risk for clergy sexual abuse.

TRAUMA AND ITS EFFECTS

Trauma research indicates that CPCSA constitutes a unique form of trauma usually resulting in negative spiritual effects that are persistent throughout adulthood.[1] According to the American Psychiatric Association's DSM-V,[2] trauma constitutes exposure to death, threatened death, actual or threatened serious injury, or actual or threatened sexual violence. Experiencing a traumatic event can occur through (1) direct exposure, (2) witnessing the trauma, (3) learning that a relative or close friend was exposed to a trauma, or (4) indirect exposure to aversive details of the trauma, usually in the course of professional duties (for example, first responders, medics). Traumatization occurs when persons experience the following criteria for post-traumatic stress disorder (PTSD): (1) persistent intrusive symptoms like unwanted upsetting memories, flashbacks, nightmares, dissociative reactions, and/or physiological, physical, and emotional reactivity after exposure to traumatic-related stimuli; (2) avoidance of trauma-related stimuli; (3) negative alterations in cognitions and mood; (4) alterations in arousal and reactivity (such as the vicious cycle between hyper-arousal and emotional numbing); and (5) duration of symptoms lasting more than a month that create social and occupational impairment.[3] While the mechanisms for traumatic reenactment are not fully understood, traumatized victims experience a compulsion to reenact the trauma by behaving self-destructively, harming others, and/or becoming revictimized.

Interpersonal trauma destroys a sense of self-protection, personal invulnerability, safety, and trust in others in a world that has lost all predictability. An especially sinister side of trauma is that, even when the event has ended, one's key assumptions about oneself and one's relations to others in the world have been

---

[1] While this section analyzes the traumatic effects of clergy sexual abuse survivors abused as children (persons under eighteen), such effects are also often experienced by survivors abused as adults.

[2] Diagnostic and Statistical Manual of Mental Disorders, 5th ed. (Arlington, VA: American Psychiatric Association, 2013). This is the handbook used by healthcare professionals in the United States and much of the world as the authoritative guide to the diagnosis of mental disorders.

[3] DSM-V, 271–77.

shattered. Such disintegration of one's perception of self and world disrupts one's normal pattern of functioning.

The most immediate traumatic response among children being sexually groomed and abused by clergy is dissociation. Dissociation refers to separating and splitting off elements of the traumatic experience—emotions, thoughts, sensation, location, time, and meaning—into shattered fragments that defy conscious integration. In addition, victims of sexual abuse frequently experience depersonalization (the experience of being an outside observer) and derealization (the experience that things are not real).[4] For most children who are sexually abused, dissociation as a sole coping mechanism will not be effective in consistently denying or ignoring the reality of the abuse.[5] Such victims also react to the loss of control experienced during abuse by experiencing self-blame, guilt, shame, and self-denigration on subconscious and/ or conscious levels. These often cause victims to struggle with a persistent sense of low self-esteem, self-loathing, worthlessness, and inferiority. While dissociation and self-blame function to help sexually abused children survive the abuse, these responses usually create debilitating post-traumatic stress symptoms and other negative effects that can pervade or resurface throughout survivors' lives.

In addition to post-traumatic stress symptoms, child sexual abuse also creates debilitating long-term physical and emotional effects, and has a negative impact on victims' physiological, neurological, and endocrine systems.[6] Child sexual abuse survivors are at increased risk for alcohol and drug addiction, sexual dysfunction, compulsive sexual risk-taking, chronic diseases, eating disorders, obesity, and substance abuse disorders. Psychologically, they are at much higher risk for anxiety and panic disorders, emotional dysregulation, major depressive disorder, suicidal ideation, and

---

[4] DSM-V, 302–5.

[5] Judith Herman, *Trauma and Recovery* (New York: Basic Books, 1992), 103.

[6] Debra Wilson, "Health Consequences of Child Sexual Abuse," *Perspectives in Psychiatric Care* 46, no. 1 (January 2010): 56–64.

suicide. Child sexual abuse and subsequent traumatization disrupt victimized children's construction of a coherent sense of self and can "catastrophically alter the trajectory of cognitive, psychosocial, sexual, and spiritual development."[7] Survivors often have trouble with cognitive function and development, flexible and abstract thinking, and with accurately assessing their situation.[8] These things obviously affect survivors' academic performance as well, narrowing future career opportunities.

Such lack of a coherent sense of self impedes the development of agency, a sense that one has control over one's actions and emotions, particularly the ability to deliberate and choose actions that cohere with a life plan consisting of beliefs, values, and goals that make life meaningful.[9] Persistent negative effects of child sexual abuse can be so debilitating that it prevents them from functioning well enough to maintain employment.

Furthermore, child sexual abuse undermines survivors' capacity to trust and form healthy relationships and experience a sense of belonging in their communities. Many survivors also report difficulty in forming and maintaining healthy sexual relationships. Child sexual abuse survivors report greater degrees of spiritual harm than child sexual survivors abused by non-clergy.[10] When

---

[7] Jason M. Fogler, Jillian C. Shipherd, Stephanie Clark, Jennifer Jensen, and Eron Rowe, "The Impact of Clergy-Perpetrated Sexual Abuse: The Role of Gender, Development, and Posttraumatic Stress," *Journal of Child Sexual Abuse* 17, nos. 3–4 (2008): 330.

[8] Kathleen M. Palm and Victoria M. Follette, "The Roles of Cognitive Flexibility and Experiential Avoidance in Explaining Psychological Distress in Survivors of Interpersonal Victimization," *Journal of Psychopathology and Behavioral Assessment* 33, no. 1 (2011): 79–86.

[9] Susan Harter, "The Effects of Child Abuse on the Self-System," in *Multiple Victimization of Children: Conceptual, Developmental, Research, and Treatment Issues*, ed. B. B. Robbie Rossman and Mindy S. Rosenberg (New York: Haworth Maltreatment and Trauma Press, 1998), 156; James Childress, *Who Should Decide?* (Oxford: Oxford University Press, 1982), 61.

[10] Sylvia A. Marotta-Walters, "Spiritual Meaning Making Following Clergy-Perpetrated Sexual Abuse," *Traumatology* 21, no. 2 (2015): 64–70.

a perpetrator is a member of the Catholic clergy who represents God, victims' concept of and faith in God, their Catholic identity, and sense of spiritual security can be eviscerated.[11]

THE DISCOURSE OF TRAUMATIZATION IN THE CATHOLIC CLERGY SEXUAL ABUSE CRISIS

In addition to acknowledging victims' traumatization and suffering, some Catholic clergy, scholars, psychologists, and organizations have made broader claims that Catholic clergy, the laity, and/or the church itself also have been traumatized. For instance, theologian Adam DeVille laments that the "sins of [clergy sexual] abuse traumatize us all in the Body Christ, albeit to different degrees and in different ways."[12] In *Abuse and Cover-up,* Gerald Arbuckle asserts that the culture of the church is in trauma: "The church is in a paralyzing state of unspoken grief, chaos, and trauma. Its hierarchy, priests, and religious—finally, as a consequence of the overwhelmingly tragic findings of the sexual scandals and cover-up—have largely been discredited and demoralized."[13] Psychologist Mary Frawley-O'Dea also claims that the church has been traumatized by CPCSA. She asserts that all Catholics can become traumatized when victims disclose abuse:

> When ACEs [adverse childhood experiences] are exposed, perpetrators, abusive or neglectful families, enabling institutions and others are often traumatized. . . . Even a perpetrator can be traumatized when she/he is exposed for victimizing another. Life is changed forever. Shock, anger,

---

[11] Thomas P. Doyle, "The Spiritual Trauma Experienced by Victims of Sexual Abuse by Catholic Clergy," *Pastoral Psychology* 58 (2009): 244–45.

[12] Adam DeVille, "Abuse, Trauma, and the Body of Christ," *Catholic World Report,* January 9, 2020.

[13] Gerald Arbuckle, *Abuse and Cover-up: Refounding the Catholic Church in Trauma* (Maryknoll, NY: Orbis Books, 2019), 109.

fear and other post-traumatic symptoms may ensue, including minimization, denial and dissociation.[14]

Frawley-O'Dea asserts it is possible to differentiate the meaning of being traumatized versus victimized:

> Victimization occurs when a person or group exerts destructive power over an innocent person or group. Trauma is a response to an experience, including but not limited to one that is victimizing. Even a perpetrator can be traumatized when she/he is exposed for victimizing another. Life is changed forever. Shock, anger, fear and other post-traumatic symptoms may ensue, including minimization, denial and dissociation.[15]

Similarly, Fr. Hans Zollner, president of the Institute for Anthropology: Interdisciplinary Studies on Human Dignity and Care, formerly the Center for Child Protection at the Pontifical Gregorian University in Rome, has asserted that the church is suffering from institutional trauma as a result of CPCSA. In multiple lectures he has compared the church as an institution to an individual suffering from a traumatic event:

> The trauma is split off in the brain so that it doesn't intervene in your day to day functioning. So it is cut off and you build a wall around it so that it doesn't continuously break up and make you dysfunctional. The cost is that part of your brain is split off and part of your experience of the world is split off, and my thesis is that the same has happened for the whole church.[16]

---

[14] Mary Gail Frawley-O'Dea, "Trauma Can Bring About Growth," *National Catholic Reporter,* June 6, 2016.

[15] Frawley-O'Dea.

[16] Fr. Hans Zollner, SJ, "Global Perspectives on the Sex Abuse Crisis," Villanova University, February 14, 2020.

Michelle Martin reports that Fr. Zollner notes that eventually the wall develops cracks: "The trauma bleeds through, and the person suffers flashbacks, reliving rather than simply remembering the traumatic event."[17] He asserts that these dynamics are presently playing out in the Catholic Church: "What has been hidden is coming out now, but that brings out the whole history. When people read news of an abuse that happened fifty years ago, they read it like it happened yesterday."[18] Zollner claims that church officials' "incapability for decades of dealing properly with perpetrators and the paralysis that many church leaders go through when they are confronted with media reports of clergy abuse is a result of this dissociation and splitting divisions that are rooted in trauma."[19] The splitting of parishes, dioceses, and school communities where abuse has happened is "some kind of consequence of a traumatic experience."[20] When public disclosures of abuse occur, Catholic clergy experience institutional traumatization and react to such disclosures as though they were an existential threat for the institution itself. This in turn triggers a traumatic reaction and leads to paralysis—a sense that there is nothing one can do to resolve this crisis.[21]

> I've seen this ten years ago when the scandal was unfolding in Germany and you could see how the Bishops Conference was overwhelmed by the news that broke day after day after

---

[17] In Michelle Martin, "Leading Clergy-abuse Expert Addresses Impact the Crisis on Global Catholic Church," *Chicago Catholic*, March 2, 2020.

[18] In Martin.

[19] Fr. Hans Zollner, SJ, "Catholicity and Sexual Abuse," Cambridge University, November 12, 2019.

[20] Zollner.

[21] Some Catholic scholars object to the word *crisis* for many reasons. I am simply using the term to collectively refer to CPCSA, subsequent cover-up, and continued resistance in some dioceses globally to be fully transparent, responsible, and accountable for abuse and to do all that is possible to prevent further CPCSA.

day. It created a climate of shock and paralysis and that leads in a systemic view to the splitting off of the traumatic event. What does such a traumatization bring about? The undermining of institutional self-perception, an existential threat, the avoidance of responsibility, and the sense of institutional powerlessness. You can see and you can touch this paralysis with your hands. People have no creativity anymore. They are in a tunnel with no way out.[22]

Zollner acknowledges that the church as a traumatized institution often reacts to public disclosures of abuse defensively, perceiving and presenting itself as the victim who is being attacked. He argues that the church literally "cuts off" documentation of the trauma:

You don't poke the documents in the archives, or you don't write the proper documents, you don't produce the reports or you don't keep them. You destroy them. Again, let us forget more or less consciously. Then you refuse to cooperate in detecting abuse because it would add to the harm, add to the pain, add to the anger, and add to the hopelessness.[23]

Fr. Zollner emphasizes that Catholic priests especially are in a state of great fatigue and burnout. Recounting a talk he delivered to priests about the crisis in one Australian archdiocese where they already had had five talks on this topic, he states: "They can't hear it anymore, but it won't go away and we have to deal with the situation in a different way."[24] For Fr. Zollner, this new way must include directly confronting and responding to CPCSA with transparency and full moral accountability as well as empathetic listening to and supporting survivors.

---

[22] Zollner, "Global Perspectives on the Sex Abuse Crisis," Villanova University, February 14, 2020.

[23] Fr. Hans Zollner, SJ, "Global Perspectives on the Sex Abuse Crisis," Villanova University, January 29, 2021.

[24] Fr. Hans Zollner, SJ, "Catholicity and Sexual Abuse," Cambridge, November 12, 2019.

ETHICAL AND THEOLOGICAL IMPLICATIONS OF THE "TRAUMATIZED CHURCH" DISCOURSE

The claim that the people of God—Catholics ranging from clergy and laity to particular priest perpetrators and their victims—are traumatized by CPCSA deserves critical scrutiny because of the ways it influences our ethical assessment of those involved in the crisis and our theological reflection on sin, the body of Christ, our image of God, the workings of grace, and Christian discipleship. To begin, this discourse suggests erroneously that trauma's defining characteristics (debilitating PTSD symptoms like dissociation, denial, minimization, and anger) apply to the church's enormous constituency. If these symptoms are the price that bishops, priests, and lay Catholics pay for becoming aware of CPCSA, it is reasonable to conclude that Catholics en masse are operating with emotional dysregulation, compromised ability to relate constructively to others, and impaired moral agency. We may then find it compelling to interpret leaders' decades of denial of the scope and depth of clergy abuse and failure to remove priest perpetrators from ministry to be rooted in trauma and resulting post-traumatic stress impairments. Likewise, many bishops' lack of empathy and support for abuse survivors and aggressive legal tactics (countersuits and other intimidation tactics to discourage lawsuits) could be attributed to alternating PTSD states of hyper-arousal and emotional constriction and fight-or-flight responses. The paralysis and fatigue of coping with constant allegations of CPCSA would not only begin to explain but partially exonerate the Vatican and many bishops around the globe for their sluggish response since 2002 to prioritize resources to respond justly and do everything possible to prevent further abuse.

Through this lens of a traumatized church, we are also likely to ease our critical assessment of lay Catholics' moral culpability when they knew or suspected priests of clergy sexual abuse and chose not to intervene, stop the abuse, or warn others in their parishes. A reprieve of moral responsibility would extend likewise to (1) Catholics who have reacted to victims' allegations of CPCSA by siding with perpetrators and advocating for them to be reinstated after credible allegations were made, and (2) unsupportive Catholics who have disbelieved and even maligned victims and their families.

Embracing the idea of an entire church impaired by its PTSD symptoms would also influence our theological interpretations of the clergy sexual abuse crisis. If clergy or lay members' acts of wrongdoing arose in part due to lack of understanding and emotional dysregulations resulting from PTSD, the sins of all who abused or enabled abuse are mitigated. According to both Catholicism and the legal system, cognitive impairments and lack of knowledge are mitigating circumstances that lessen, and in some cases remove, moral responsibility and legal sanctions. According to the *Catechism of the Catholic Church* serious sins require grave matter, full knowledge, and deliberate choice: "Serious sins presupposes knowledge of the sinful character of the act, of its opposition to God's law. It also implies a consent sufficiently deliberate to be a personal choice."[25]

Furthermore, if we adopt the "traumatized church" discourse, it becomes easier to view the people of God as representing the broken and traumatized body of Christ. If we are collectively traumatized, we are likely to imagine Christ compassionately suffering in solidarity not only with clergy sexual abuse survivors and their families, but also with sexually abusive or negligent bishops, priests, and laity who knew of CPCSA and failed to intervene. It is problematic, too, that our hope for healing and justice in this scenario becomes more rooted in an image of a sovereign God who can choose (or not) to have mercy and infuse us with grace, and less rooted on activism and concrete actions to resolve the crisis effectively. Moreover, if we perceive that a "traumatized people of God" represent the broken body of Christ, the primary emphasis of Christian discipleship also shifts toward prayers to God for forgiveness, prayers of repentance, and petitions for divine grace to heal us from traumatic impairment and paralysis.

---

[25] *Catechism of the Catholic Church*, 2nd ed. (Washington, DC: United States Catholic Conference, 2000), no. 1859.

THE NEED TO REJECT SWEEPING CLAIMS OF A "TRAUMATIZED CHURCH"

The narrative of a "traumatized church" can be compelling because the vivid language and images connected with trauma can resonate with many people's sense of horror at the reality of clergy sexual abuse. As we have seen, it also invites hope for a solution that does not require much time and energy from us—hope that, given our traumatic paralysis, God will respond to our prayers to heal and redeem the body of Christ so that the church can restore its good name, integrity, and positive influence in the world.

However, is such a narrative true? Does it accurately reflect the dynamics at work in Catholics' responses to clergy sexual abuse? After studying more than three decades of research on the Catholic CPCSA crisis and traumatized groups who have experienced violence (war, genocide, and sexual violence), I am hermeneutically suspicious and ethically wary of extending claims of traumatization so broadly in this context. This discourse is not only morally imprecise but carries significant ethical and theological fallout that undermines genuine reforms needed for a just response. Five reasons in particular lead me to conclude that Catholics ought to take a strong presumptive stance[26] against claiming that people beyond victims and their loved ones have been traumatized by CPCSA.

First, this discourse radically departs from decades of trauma research that led to the revisions in the American Psychological

---

[26] A presumptive stance does not entail an absolutist position that rules out the possibility that non-abused individuals cannot become traumatized. Instead, it requires sound evidence before accepting such a claim. Research indicates that therapists and others who listen to sexual abuse survivors' accounts of sexual violence and empathize with them can experience vicarious traumatization. It is also possible, of course, for Catholics who have counselled survivors or listened repeatedly to first-hand accounts to suffer from secondary traumatization. It also happens that some Catholics experience knowledge of the abuse and cover-up as a spiritual death if it has robbed them of belief in God, church, and community.

Association's concept of trauma and traumatization as well as research on bystanders' typical responses to trauma resulting from moral evil. It is true, of course, that many lay Catholics and clergy members have suffered as a result of this crisis. Catholic bishops have likely felt overwhelmed, fatigued, and burned out by having to address allegations. Many—if not all—non-offending priests have also experienced embarrassment and shame about other priests' sexual crimes. They may even have experienced harassment and disrespect as a result of being unfairly associated with priest perpetrators or the cover-up. Also, many lay Catholics have certainly experienced disgust, anger, and grief over the sexual abuse of children by clergy. They have felt painfully betrayed by Catholic leaders. Some have lost their religious identity and community because they could no longer support a church that enabled and covered up one of the worst crimes against children imaginable.

While these forms of suffering and harm are undeniable, they cannot accurately be conflated to traumatization. No research studies indicate that, collectively, Catholic leaders and non-abused Catholic clergy or lay Catholics experience PTSD symptoms needed to meet criteria for a PTSD diagnosis. Confronting revelations of CPCSA does not constitute a serious injury, a threat to one's life, or sexual violence. The vast majority of Catholics who have not been sexually abused or not had a loved one abused by clergy have not become so impaired by the crisis that they experienced a shattering of their sense of self, could not remain employed, and/or became unable to maintain regular social interactions and relationships. In contrast, much evidence on bishops' reactions to victims' disclosures indicates the opposite occurred. Rather than having their identity and cognitive capacities shattered and their agency compromised by traumatic paralysis, many bishops developed highly effective strategies to keep victims silent about the abuse and to protect the church's reputations and assets. For instance, many victims kept their abuse secret because church officials falsely promised them the perpetrators would be removed from active ministry. If that tactic was not sufficient, many also quietly offered nondisclosure settlements to survivors. Bishops hired lawyers who engaged in aggressive legal tactics that revictimized survivors.

Trauma research on non-complicit bystanders' responses to moral evil also undermines the notion that non-abused Catholics have been traumatized by knowledge of clergy sexual abuse. Historical studies have found that while many bystanders react empathetically and altruistically to victims of trauma caused by natural disasters, they tend to deny, minimize, and blame victims of trauma caused by moral evil. According to trauma theorists, such reactions result from a self-interested desire to avoid the reality of evil, fear, and discomfort. As Bessel van der Kolk explains:

> Society becomes resentful about having its illusions of safety and predictability ruffled by people who remind them of how fragile security can be. . . . Society's reactions seem to be primarily conservative impulses in the service of maintaining the beliefs that the world is fundamentally just and that "good" people can be in charge of their lives.[27]

Recognizing the full reality of clergy sexual abuse and institutional cover-up threatens our illusory sense of safety, control, and trust in humanity, society, and the church. This may begin to explain why a significant number of Catholics have sided with priest-perpetrators over victims when knowledge of the abuse becomes known. It is emotionally easier to avoid or minimize the degree of harm victims have experienced than confront the reality that a priest whom they like and consider a spiritual friend or mentor has committed the kind of evil disclosed by victims. Ultimately, trauma studies indicate that, rather than becoming traumatized through empathetic identification with victims, Catholic bystanders are

---

[27] Bessel van der Kolk and Alexander C. McFarlane, "The Black Hole of Trauma," in *Traumatic Stress: The Effects of Overwhelming Experience on Mind, Body, and Society*, ed. Bessel van der Kolk, Alexander C. McFarlane, and Lars Weisaeth (New York: Guilford Press, 2007), 27.

more likely to react to clergy sexual abuse by denying or minimizing the trauma in order to preserve their mental well-being.

Second, extending claims of traumatization beyond victims and their families to include perpetrators and complicit bystanders ultimately functions to coopt the suffering of those who have been victimized for one's own benefit and agenda. There is something horrifically wrong with perpetrators and enablers causing such extreme trauma to children and then inserting themselves into the expanding circle of those who claim to be traumatized. Catholic leaders' complaints that the church was being targeted by secular media in their coverage of clergy sexual abuse exemplifies how leaders can coopt the concepts of victimization and traumatization to divert attention from themselves and avoid being fully responsible for enabling and covering up clergy sexual abuse.

Concept creep[28] facilitates such misappropriation of victims' suffering in various ways. Associating trauma with stressors that are less violent and intense than the American Psychological Association definition dilutes the meaning of trauma and risks emptying the concept of significance. This ought to raise ethical concerns for Catholics because it minimizes and trivializes the extreme suffering from traumas like genocide, imminent threat to one's life, and sexual violence. Catholic scholars and psychologists are, of course, not alone in making such claims. There has been a tendency, both in the academy and in popular culture, to expand the concept of trauma to include less severe stressful events such that the vast majority of persons qualify as traumatized. Some researchers, for instance, have proposed that any stressful event (including childbirth, sexual harassment, infidelity, emotional

---

[28] The term *concept creep* describes how the use of trauma can be stretched so that its meaning "becomes less stringent, extending to quantitatively milder variants of the phenomenon to which it originally referred." Nick Haslam, "Concept Creep: Psychology's Concepts of Harm and Pathology, " *Psychological Inquiry* 27 (2016): 1–17. See also Richard McNally, "The Expanding Empire of Psychopathology: The Case of PTSD, *Psychological Inquiry* 27 (2016): 46–49.

losses, or any experience that is judged by people to be harmful and have lasting effects) can qualify as trauma.[29]

As Richard McNally notes, significant concept creep occurred in psychiatry when the DSM-III was revised. In the DSM-IV (1994), trauma was expanded to include persons who learn about others' experience of a violent death or serious threat of life; however, the DSM-IV failed to specify that learning of death or serious threats to others requires some personal connection to those threatened. Such expansion of the concept of trauma made 89.6% of Americans eligible to be assessed for PTSD.[30] As psychiatric historian Ben Shepherd points out, "Any unit of classification that simultaneously encompasses the experience of surviving Auschwitz and that of being told rude jokes at work must, by any reasonable lay standard, be nonsense, a patent absurdity."[31] The DSM-V (2013) has corrected this omission and now specifies that one must be personally connected to the trauma victim's experience of a violent death, serious threat to life, or sexual violence. However, the concept creep that occurred among psychologists and the general public is not easily undone.

An articulate critic of concept creep is historian Wulf Kansteiner, who identifies a trend among humanities scholars of abstracting from historical traumatic events and instead focusing on philosophical and psychological sources to create the concept of cultural trauma. They have utilized the concept as a metaphor, for instance, to describe the postmodern condition, the problem of human communication, and/or any form of real or symbolic violence that one perpetrates, experiences, or observes in person or virtually:

---

[29] Haslam, 6–7.

[30] Naomi Breslau and Ronald C. Kessler, "The Stressor Criterion in DSM-IV Posttraumatic Stress Disorder: An Empirical Investigation," *Biological Psychiatry* 50 (November 1, 2001): 701.

[31] Ben Shephard, "Risk Factors and PTSD: A Historian's Perspective," in *Posttraumatic Stress Disorder: Issues and Controversies*, ed. Gerald M. Rosen (London: Wiley, 2004), 57.

Dominant schools of thought in trauma research tend to conflate the traumatic and non-traumatic, the exceptional and the everyday, and even to obfuscate the essential difference between the victims and perpetrators of extreme violence.[32]

Portraying trauma as ubiquitous has the unintended consequence of disrespecting victims of extreme violence:

Moral honesty and conceptual and historical precision demand that trauma be first and foremost read from the perspective of the victim and only then carefully expanded to explore other borderline phenomena.[33]

The fact that it is even plausible in the Catholic social imaginary for scholars, clergy, and laity to lump CPCSA victims together with perpetrators and the bishops who tolerated, enabled, and covered up abuse itself reflects a subconscious minimization and trivialization of the degree of moral evil and suffering of children sexually abused by clergy. To expose the minimization and trivialization of moral evil and suffering of children sexually abused by clergy, it might be helpful to ask whether Catholics would accept an analogous claim in other contexts like the Holocaust or racist America. How would they react to a contemporary German scholar who claims that Hitler, sadistic SS soldiers, non-Jewish German bystanders, and Jewish children in concentration camps were all traumatized during the Third Reich and thus unable to register the gravity of the moment and respond as moral agents? How would they respond to a white Catholic theologian who argues that white Americans who raped African slave children, cheered at lynchings during the Jim Crow era, or witnessed the death of George Floyd on social media have all been traumatized and are unable due to traumatic paralysis to respond justly to

---

[32] Wulf Kansteiner, "Genealogy of a Category Mistake: A Critical Intellectual History of the Cultural Trauma Metaphor, *Rethinking History* 8, no. 2 (June 2004): 194.

[33] Kansteiner, 214.

racism? Such a position would be summarily denounced. Critics would quickly point out that such claims constitute an unacceptable mockery of the degree of evil and trauma suffered by Jews and African Americans. There would be a public outcry that such a discourse enables guilty parties to not only harm and traumatize a marginalized group, but then turn around and coopt the suffering of victims by seizing the label of traumatization and victimization for themselves. Scholars espousing such claims would almost certainly pay a price in their personal and professional lives. Why, then, does this claim that everyone is traumatized not elicit the same negative visceral response when the context is the sexual torture and abuse of children by bishops and priests?

I asked myself this question a long time ago when I stared uncomprehendingly at a 2002 Gallup Poll asking US Catholics this question: "As a result of the recent news about sexual abuse of young people by priests, have you, personally, questioned whether you would remain in the Catholic church, or not?" By 2002, it was well known that Catholic clergy sexual abuse was a global phenomenon and that the causes of clergy sexual abuse were more complex than simply a problem of a "few bad apples" fooling their superiors and getting away with abuse. Only 22 percent of Catholics indicated that they had considered the question about whether they would remain Catholic.[34] Over the next sixteen years of ongoing global media coverage of bishops' and cardinals' abusive and negligent behavior toward survivors, increased disclosures of priest-perpetrators, and survivors' accounts of clergy sexual abuse, the number increased to 37 percent. These low percentages deeply unsettle me because Catholics were not being asked whether they might leave the church but only whether the idea of leaving crossed their minds. While I have been tempted to dismiss these results as mistaken or unrepresentative, the possibility that 63 percent of US Catholics have not even asked themselves whether it is morally problematic to support a church that has systemically sexually abused children—and continues to place

---

[34] Jeffrey M. Jones, "Many US Catholics Question Their Membership Amid Scandal," *Gallup*, March 13, 2019.

children at high risk for abuse—makes me wonder to what extent Catholics still avoid, deny, minimize, and trivialize the moral evil and trauma of CPCSA.

Third, because the terms *church* and *people of God* encompass all Catholics, imprecise and ambiguous, Catholics are more easily able to conflate important distinctions that exist between those who harm and those who are harmed, and thus buy into the notion that the church's response mirrors CPCSA survivors' traumatization and recovery. However, this analogy breaks down when we consider important psychological and moral distinctions between causing harm and being harmed. The causes and motivations underlying the stress reactions of perpetrators greatly differ from the reaction of victims to CPCSA. As noted above, victims experience dissociation, denial, and the full range of PTSD symptoms because such sexual abuse by a priest defies conscious integration. Dissociation, denial, and avoidance function as defense mechanisms to make basic survival possible. In contrast, when one's secret of perpetrating, tolerating, enabling, or failing to report CPCSA is disclosed publicly, ordinary stress reactions like denial and avoidance stem from embarrassment, shame, and/or a desire to avoid guilt and protect one's ego and positive self-concept, reputation, and status. Such differences in the reactions of those perpetrating and those perpetrated against give rise to very different experiences that cannot adequately fall under the same umbrella concept.

Widening the circle of the traumatized to include perpetrators, complicit church leaders and other bystanders, and victims also results in a forced conflation of what constitutes healing and growth, which likely results in negative consequences for survivors. Besides asserting that all of these groups—perpetrators, enabling bishops, complicit bystanders, and victims—are traumatized, Frawley-O'Dea also claims that all of these groups can experience post-traumatic growth. Based on her clinical practice, Frawley-O'Dea has observed that some clients who suffered from adverse childhood experiences have been able to heal and experience post-traumatic growth. She draws on psychologists Lawrence Calhoun and Richard Tedeschi's definition of post-traumatic growth as "positive psychological change experienced as a result of the struggle with highly challenging life circumstances." These clients exhibit resiliency, deep empathy for others, and generous altruism. Frawley-O'Dea argues that, just as survivors of adverse childhood experiences can experience post-traumatic growth, so too can the Catholic Church. In its traumatized state, the church reacted to CPCSA in a defensive manner, seeking above all else to preserve its reputation: "Church officials lied, denied and projected blame on victims, parents of victims, a sexually liberated and sexualized culture, bad apple priests, the '60s, the media. They had seen the enemy and it was not them."[35] Frawley-O'Dea argues that steps toward post-traumatic growth require honest and rigorous self-examination to identify and then examine the root causes of clergy sexual abuse. In order to do this, all in the church need to let go of defensiveness, arrogance, and clericalism. The next step is to mourn, grieve, and repent enough for all the suffering and harm the people of God have been made to suffer through clergy sexual abuse of minors.

The problem with this recipe for post-traumatic growth is that it in no way resembles what is needed to foster survivors' healing process and prospects for post-traumatic growth. One of the key insights of trauma research is that, in order to break the cycle of traumatization and obsessive PTSD re-enactments of the trauma, supportive relationships are necessary to offer survivors a safe space to remember and piece together the traumatic events into a conscious narrative and then mourn and grieve the losses resulting from trauma. Catholics who read Frawley-O'Dea could very well receive the impression that it is simply a matter of the will for traumatized CPCSA victims to recover, move on from the trauma, and experience post-traumatic growth. Applying Frawley-O'Dea's account of steps needed for the church to heal and grow to individual CPCSA survivors can easily fuel our already strong cultural tendencies to blame victims for their traumatization and inability to "just get over it."

---

[35] Frawley-O'Dea, "Trauma Can Bring About Growth."

Fourth, as I articulated earlier, claims that the institutional church is traumatized by clergy sexual abuse and is mired in traumatic paralysis lessen our assessment of the moral responsibility and culpability of clergy perpetrators, complicit leaders, and bystanders. In the field of moral psychology, moral typecasting research indicates that an inverse relationship exists between moral patency (perceiving oneself as a target of harm) and agency.[36] Concept creep, then, can lead to a tendency for more people to view themselves as victims who are defined by their suffering and innocence and have diminished agency. Research also indicates that persons who understand their problems as psychiatric illnesses tend to be more pessimistic about recovery and less confident in their capacity to exert control over their struggles. Thus, if Catholic bishops, clergy, and lay members perceive themselves as suffering from a psychiatric diagnosis of PTSD as a result of this crisis, then their sense of moral agency and expectations about effectively enacting reform likely decrease. Such decreased sense of moral agency can subtly fuel an unspoken complacency about the slow and inconsistent progress toward genuine change.[37] Thus, Fr. Zollner's claim that Catholic leaders' tepid and ineffective responses to clergy sexual abuse are rooted in traumatization and result in traumatic paralysis has an unintended consequence of lessening their sense of moral responsibility that he himself would abhor. It undercuts his own tireless efforts to create a Catholic culture that fully supports survivors and is fully transparent, responsible, and accountable for clergy sexual abuse.

Fifth, and most important, Catholics should take the presumptive stance I have been considering because following Christ as his disciples requires that we direct our focus and energy on those

---

[36] Kurt Gray and Daniel Wegner, "Moral Typecasting: Divergent Perceptions of Moral Agents and Moral Patients," *Journal of Personality and Social Psychology* 96, no. 3 (2009).

[37] Karen Terry, "Reckoning and Reform: New Horizons on the Clergy Abuse Crisis," *Fordham Center on Religion and Culture*, 2019 Russo Family Lecture, March 26, 2019.

who are most vulnerable, marginalized, and powerless (such as CPCSA survivors and children). Christian discipleship requires courageous activism and resistance against those who create laws, structures, and policies that create culture where Catholic children continue to be at high risk for clergy sexual abuse.[38] The lived example, teachings, and commands of Jesus demand this focus and commitment. In the Gospels, Jesus consistently expresses that nurturing and protecting children's well-being constitute an essential priority of Christian discipleship. In the Greco-Roman culture of his time, children were considered property of their parents and possessed low status and rights. It is thus remarkable that Jesus includes children so often in his teaching and healing. Mark, Matthew, and Luke all include the story of the apostles trying to prevent children from drawing near to Jesus. According to Mark's Gospel, when Jesus notices the disciples rebuking them, he is indignant, and says, "Let the children come to me; do not stop them, for it is to such as these that the kingdom of God belongs. Truly I tell you, whoever does not receive the kingdom of God as a little child will never enter it" (Mk 10:14-15).[39] As New Testament scholar Judith Gundry-Volf notes:

> Jesus raises the stakes. Not only is welcoming children a mark of the great; it is a mark of welcoming Jesus himself. . . . Welcoming children thus has ultimate significance. It is a way of receiving and serving Jesus and thus also the God who sent him. Conversely, failing to welcome children is a way of rejecting Jesus and God.[40]

Jesus's anger at the disciples' rebuke of children is also significant because it is one of two references to Jesus's anger in the New

---

[38] Terry.

[39] Zollner, "Catholicity and Sexual Abuse," Cambridge, November 12, 2019.

[40] Judith Gundry-Volf, "To Such as These Belongs the Reign of GOD": Jesus and Children, *Theology Today* 56, no. 4 (January 2000): 476.

Testament. Gundry-Volf argues that this indicates the seriousness of the teaching.[41]

Furthermore, by affirming that his apostles must become like children to enter the kingdom of heaven, Christ subverts the values of the kingdom of the world (with its obsession on hierarchy, status, competition, and power over others), and identifies/celebrates/lauds the opposite values of the kingdom of heaven. Jesus also expresses his fierce protection of children by issuing a warning to anyone who would harm a child:

> "Whoever welcomes one such child in my name welcomes me. If any of you cause one of these little ones who believe in me to sin, it would be better for you if a great millstone were fastened around your neck and you were drowned in the depth of the sea. . . . And if your eye causes you to sin, tear it out and throw it away; it is better for you to enter life with one eye than to have two eyes and to be thrown into the hell of fire. Take care that you do not despise one of these little ones, for I tell you, in heaven their angels continually see the face of my Father in heaven." (Mt 18:5-11)

Scripture scholars such as Lorne Zelyck suggests 18:6 is best translated as "Whoever scandalizes one of these little ones who believe in me."[42] When analyzing the Greek word for scandalize elsewhere in the New Testament and outside the New Testament, he argues that it is clearly associated with sexual sin and refers in Matthew 8:6 to the sexual abuse or exposure of children.[43] Jesus's promise of divine retribution, which will be worse than drowning in the depths of the sea, communicates divine judgment about the severity of moral evil present in the sexual abuse of children.

---

[41] Judith M. Gundry-Volf, "The Least and the Greatest: Children in the New Testament" in *The Child in Christian Thought*, ed. Marcia J. Bunge (Grand Rapids, MI: Eerdmans, 2001), 44.

[42] Lorne Zelyck, "Matthew 18:1–14 and the Exposure and Sexual Abuse of Children in the Roman World," *Biblica* 98 (2017): 39.

[43] Zelyck, 40–45.

Jesus's (and the Matthean community's) concern about sex with children is consistent with Judaism's and early Christianity's critique and condemnation of this practice, which is not uncommon in Roman and Greek culture.[44] Condemnation and repudiation of priests who have sex with children are likewise a consistent thread through the Catholic tradition.

The Gospels' emphasis on Jesus's special care and concern for the poor and marginalized provides further warrant to attend to the traumatization of survivors and do everything possible to create child-safe cultures in every parish. Strong scriptural warrants indicate that Jesus would promptly overturn and eradicate any Catholic beliefs, teachings, laws, traditions, and church structures that marginalize victims and create risk factors for all forms of abuse. Such preferential option for the marginalized and powerless is also a thread throughout the Catholic tradition, finding its most explicit expression and development in Catholic social thought. Connecting humanity's creation in God's image, the dignity of the human person, solidarity, the preferential option for the poor and vulnerable, and other key themes of Catholic social thought, church writings since *Rerum Novarum* (1891) have decried social injustices rooted in abuses of power. Within the context of clergy abuse, Catholics need to practice and implement these beliefs and values by finding authentic ways to be in solidarity with survivors, ensure that everything possible is done to prevent clergy child sexual abuse, and implement a just response to this crisis.

THEOLOGICAL IMPLICATIONS OF REJECTING THE "TRAUMATIZED CHURCH" DISCOURSE

If we fully acknowledge that complicit clergy and laity cannot be let off the hook by claims of traumatic impairment and that they are fully morally culpable, our theological understanding of sin in this context is altered and becomes more complex. We can more easily see through perpetrators' individual and collective

---

[44] Zelyck, 44–48.

self-deception and grasp the depth of moral evil and sinfulness present in CPCSA abuse, cover-up, and secondary victimization of survivors. Rejecting this discourse allows Catholics to identify leaders' reassignment of priests to uninformed parishes, subsequent cover-up, and unsupportive responses to victims as reflecting social and structural sins of clerical entitlement and abuse of power. Lay Catholics are similarly morally responsible for unsupportive or apathetic responses to victims and their tendencies to become complacent about clergy child sexual abuse as media headlines of clergy abuse fade away.

Becoming fully accountable for past and present responses to clergy sexual abuse also alters theological reflections on the church as the body of Christ. Rather than perceiving all Catholics as traumatized members of Christ's body, acknowledging that non-abused Catholics possessed full moral agency fosters honest recognition of how Catholics' sins of commission and omission have broken and continue to break Christ's own body. Instead of placing the onus and responsibility on God to magically infuse Catholics with grace in a top-down manner to heal our collective traumatic impairments, Catholics will more clearly see the onus for resolving the crisis themselves. Since healing and recovery from traumatization occur in the presence of supportive relationships, Catholics are more likely to view themselves as collaborators with God to enact healing and justice.

Furthermore, acknowledging our moral responsibility to be collaborators with God and becoming grounded in Christ's values and priorities transform our understanding of what it means to follow Christ faithfully in response to this crisis. Christ's preferential option for and identification with "the least of my brothers and sisters" calls us to place the needs of children and safety of children and victims first. Christian discipleship entails courageous solidarity with clergy sexual victims and all children who currently remain at high risk of clergy sexual abuse. Solidarity involves reaching out to survivors, asking for their perspectives in order to understand the dynamics of this crisis, and listening and witnessing to their accounts of sexual violence. It also involves identifying and reforming the Catholic beliefs, attitudes, practices, laws, and ecclesiastical structures within Catholic culture that enable clergy sexual abuse and cover-up.

CONCLUSION

Taking a strong presumptive stance against the narrative of a "traumatized church" has important positive theological and ethical implications that foster authentic Christian discipleship. Research findings that traumatization requires personal exposure to a trauma or personal connection to a trauma victim, coupled with findings that bystanders tend to deny, minimize, and trivialize trauma caused by moral evil, undermine the acceptability of imprecise notions that the church or the people of God have been traumatized by knowledge of clergy sexual abuse and subsequent cover-up. It discredits the claim that church leaders' response to public disclosures of clergy sexual abuse accurately mirrors the dynamics of traumatization experienced by an individual's experience of sexual violence. Church officials' global inability for decades to deal properly with perpetrators, and to respond effectively to prevent clergy sexual abuse, cannot be attributed to traumatic dissociation and paralysis, but to other systemic cultural and structural factors.

3.

What Is Redemption?

John N. Sheveland

This chapter argues that child abuse prevention efforts in the Catholic church need to be supplemented by a thorough communal approach to the healing of direct and indirect victims of clergy sexual abuse, and this amounts to a change in the culture of the church away from patterns of clericalism and narcissism in which both clerical and lay members participate, toward a victims-first approach marked by deep listening to the voices and insights of survivors themselves, new attention to the theology of redemption, an embrace of the principles of high reliability organizations, and the renewal of communal prayer through the liturgy of the mass as one liturgical pattern of accompaniment.

To date, the Roman Catholic Church's developing response to clergy sexual abuse has been confined largely to the domain of prevention and less well developed in the domain of a communal culture and practices that facilitate, through a range of relationships, the processing of sexual abuse trauma occurring within the church and beyond it. Facing it, processing it, and doing so amid wise and sensitive relationships is a prerequisite for healing. This distinction between prevention and healing remains meaningful and points, on the one hand, to undeniable organizational improvement at the level of prevention in the context of the US church: safe environment training for adults and children, annual audits of diocesan implementation of the "Charter for the Protection of Children and Young People,"[1] enhanced screening for human development and psychosexual integration among candidates to the priesthood, and active diocesan review boards are all consequential examples of progress since 2002, as the recent *2019 Annual Report* and the *2020 Annual Report* demonstrate.[2]

On the other hand, despite the significant and often unseen work of diocesan victim assistance coordinators and other members of their safe environment team, persistent neglect at the level of survivor and communal healing, which hang more on emotional intelligence and spiritual capacity within affected relationships and community, driven by the macro context of the culture within the institution, continues to hold back the community from a more direct and authentic engagement in healing in response to the church's crimes and sins of abuse.[3] As crucial as prevention is, it is one side of the needed response. What is needed also is a deeper personal, spiritual, and communal reckoning with what it means to be constructive members of this church, this body, as a post-traumatic body affiliated with those harmed directly and indirectly by abuse. What is the nature of the harm done, both to survivors and to the community affected by traumatic wounding? Do we recognize our solidarity in suffering within this distorted and distorting web of child sexual abuse traumatic wounding?[4]

---

[1] United States Conference of Catholic Bishops, "Charter for the Protection of Children and Young People" (2002, 2011, 2018).

[2] United States Conference of Catholic Bishops' Secretariat for Child and Youth Protection, *2019 Annual Report: Findings and Recommendations*; *2020 Annual Report: Findings and Recommendations*.

[3] United States Conference of Catholic Bishops' Secretariat for Child and Youth Protection, *2019 Annual Report: Findings and Recommendations*, esp. vi–vii, 3–4. See also Richard Gaillardetz, "A Church in Crisis," *Worship* 93 (2019): 206.

[4] John N. Sheveland, "Redeeming Trauma: An Agenda for Theology Fifteen Years On," in *American Catholicism in the 21st Century: Crossroads, Crisis, or Renewal?* College Theology Society Annual, ed. Benjamin T. Peters and Nicholas Rademacher (Maryknoll, NY: Orbis Books, 2018): 137–48.

This concern pertains to the capacity of the culture of a church community to facilitate or impede healing. In her November 2019 address to the US Bishops Committee for the Protection of Children and Young People, Karen Terry, principal researcher for the *Nature and Scope* study and the *Causes and Contexts* study, told the US Bishops' Committee for the Protection of Children and Young People that children remained at high risk of abuse in the Catholic Church.[5] Her warning was founded upon a distinction between policies and procedures, on the one hand, and the culture of the church that affects the people who follow through with policies and procedures, on the other. That is, Terry invited the bishops to contemplate the distinction between micro-level efforts of prevention and macro-level changes still needed in the church's *culture* of protection in order to secure the necessary attention and effort for prevention. For Terry, while the church's complex hierarchy and structure coupled with its decentralization from diocese to diocese and parish to parish are risk factors, so is a lack of buy-in within the existing culture implementing prevention policies. The lack of buy-in includes problematic evidence of ongoing behaviors of protecting church reputation, assets, and a priest's canonical right to his own good name, concealing abuse or accusations, and transfer of priests with allegations, all happening alongside insufficient attention paid to the harm caused to victims. This is recent news in Cincinnati, West Virginia, Buffalo, and elsewhere. Her assessment in November 2019 is that macro-level changes in the culture of the church are still needed in order to secure more universal buy-in to the church's prevention policies. Macro-level changes will render the church more authentic to its own mission and identity while animating the micro-level prevention efforts with even more strength.

---

[5] John Jay College of Criminal Justice, *The Nature and Scope of Sexual Abuse of Minors by Catholic Priests and Deacons in the United States 1950–2002* (Washington, DC: United States Conference of Catholic Bishops, 2004); John Jay College Research Team, *The Causes and Context of Sexual Abuse of Minors by Catholic Priests in the United States, 1950–2011* (Washington, DC: United States Conference of Catholic Bishops, 2011).

A direct way of speaking to this necessary cultural shift is through a victims-first approach. This approach, sorely lacking even in the years after 2002, gathers the entire church as the people of God to focus upon and to listen deeply to the experience of victim-survivors. A victims-first approach prioritizes the ecclesial conditions for the possibility of their healing and embraces an ecclesial commitment toward those ends as constitutive of the church's mission and identity. Somewhat more pointedly, a victims-first approach necessarily inverts power dynamics so that the experience of victim-survivors becomes authoritative with respect to how we perceive the scope of the problem and the community's opportunities for redress, and authoritative also with respect to the criterion around which authentic listening and accompaniment are determined. Child protection policies must be more than procedures; they must become the spontaneous expressions of a church—a *people*—that has embraced the ethos of protection and healing organizationally, spiritually, personally, and relationally. This means that, in an appropriate manner, the pattern of focusing on abusers and on the church's institutional reputation needs to be purified by a more earnest culture of attunement to global and ecclesial child vulnerability, healing of direct and indirect trauma wounds, and the flourishing of survivors.

Once people learn about the dynamics of traumatic wounding, it is really no surprise that an institution will let languish the far more difficult task of healing and sizing up the scope and scale of the harms in need of redemption. Reformed theologian Deborah van Deusen Hunsinger notes that "traumatic events are extraordinary not because they occur rarely but rather because they overwhelm the ordinary human adaptations to life."[6] "The subjective experience," she writes, "of feeling overwhelmed uniquely characterizes trauma and differentiates it from those situations that are experienced perhaps as exceptionally stressful but not as

---

[6] Deborah van Deusen Hunsinger, "Bearing the Unbearable: Trauma, Gospel, and Pastoral Care," *Theology Today* 68, no. 1 (2011): 11. See also Deborah van Deusen Hunsinger, *Bearing the Unbearable: Trauma, Gospel, and Pastoral Care* (Grand Rapids, MI: Eerdmans, 2015).

traumatic."[7] Similarly, Jennifer Beste isolates the distinctive spiritual harm that some describe as "soul murder" attending clergy child sexual abuse. "Trauma by definition," she writes, "is a state of being negatively overwhelmed physically and psychologically: it is the experience of terror, loss of control, and utter helplessness during a stressful event that threatens one's physical and/or psychological integrity."[8] That deeply felt loss or annihilation causes many survivors to dissociate during experiences of abuse, and this dissociation is a fracture of the self that often correlates with debilitating post-traumatic stress symptoms, the effects of which often derail the future of human subjectivity, including the reexperiencing of the traumatic event in flashbacks, nightmares, intense bodily or emotional sensations, and behavioral reenactments whether directed inwardly or outwardly toward others. Beste notes that "many clergy sexual abuse survivors also suffer from extreme shame, self-blaming, self-loathing, damaged self-esteem, lack of trust, social isolation, suppressed rage, impaired ability for intimacy, sexual dysfunction, anxiety, depression, and addictions."[9]

Hunsinger exposes the dynamics of abandonment and isolation that attend abuse itself but also the behaviors of well-intended allies captured by the problematic advice to "get over it" or an array of other inadvertent minimizations or denials of survivor experience that reflect the discomfort and unpreparedness of the one trying to help.[10] Those who suffer from traumatic wounding are treated to a steady diet of verbal and behavioral patterns that minimize, deflect, and even blame and intimidate. Beste's trauma research finds that the dynamics of traumatization render an individual incapable—on one's own—of transcending the totalizing effects of trauma and its post-traumatic stress symptoms. Acceptance, accompaniment, and support from trusted others

---

[7] Hunsinger, "Bearing the Unbearable," 12.

[8] Jennifer Beste, "Mediating God's Grace in the Context of Trauma: Implications for a Christian Response to Clergy Sexual Abuse," *Review and Expositor* 105 (2008): 248.

[9] Beste, 248.

[10] Hunsinger, "Bearing the Unbearable," 12.

are therefore crucial to break the traumatic cycle. For Beste, the incarnational and sacramental thrust of the Catholic tradition speak to the relationship of God's grace and redemptive activity in the Christ event playing out through ongoing historical and social mediation, interpersonally. For Beste, Karl Rahner's pastoral writings emphasize that the church depends on all members to use their gifts bestowed by the Holy Spirit to advance prospects for human liberation and salvation. For Rahner, she notes approvingly, "every member in the body of Christ can and must serve as a channel of salvation for all others."[11]

The communal response to persons undergoing traumatic wounding is a telling variable for the prospects of healing. Deborah van Deusen Hunsinger does not mince words here: "Understanding becomes a part of the holding environment that contains anxiety and increases a sense of empowerment."[12] As Rahner attested in his own way, and as trauma studies attest in theirs, individual traumatic wounding is never merely individual but situated in community and determined significantly by the health of that community. "Severe emotional pain cannot be endured if it does not have a relational home, someone to hold what cannot be borne."[13] For Hunsinger, a pastoral theologian who trains seminarians at Princeton Theological Seminary, this call certainly constitutes part of her own vocation as a minister and teacher of ministers. Transposed into the Catholic context, her call for a "relational home" or "holding environment" presents a challenge and opportunity for both ordained leaders and the laity in Catholic communities.

As victim assistance coordinators from diocese to diocese understand well, a core ingredient of what Hunsinger refers to as a

---

[11] Beste, "Mediating God's Grace in the Context of Trauma," 247. See also Pope Francis, "Letter of His Holiness Pope Francis to the People of God," August 20, 2018; John N. Sheveland, *Piety and Responsibility: Patterns of Unity in Karl Rahner, Karl Barth, and Vedanta Desika* (London: Routledge, 2018), 44–57, 183–91.

[12] Hunsinger, "Bearing the Unbearable," 18.

[13] Hunsinger, 23.

"relational home" or "holding environment" is the capacity and willingness of trusted persons to listen deeply. Duane Bidwell has written of deep listening from the perspective of practical theology, counseling, and Buddhist-Christian multiple religious belonging. Deep listening is a relational practice in which caregivers suspend their own self-orientation and reactive thinking in favor of becoming receptive to what is unknown and unexpected in the other. Bidwell describes deep listening as "receptivity to doubt, mystery, and ambiguity without reaching for concepts, facts or reason. . . . It moves beyond the five senses to incorporate imagination, intuition, subconscious awareness, and nonlinear thinking; this type of listening can be largely pre-conceptual...[it] qualifies as heart knowledge."[14] Such capacity for deep listening might become a lofty goal for local Catholic communities to help repair the macro context of prevention efforts Karen Terry found wanting.

It is no secret that pathological narcissism has been a repetitive personality trait among situational clergy offenders and also the much smaller subset who specialized as pedophiles in the predatory abuse of prepubescent children. Narcissistic personality traits would mitigate against what Bidwell refers to as "deep listening" and Hunsinger as a "holding environment," and as such must be disqualifying for any seeking holy orders. There can be no question that among many clergy there is an unhealthy subculture of clericalism, in which they feel superior in their psychology or as uniquely called by God and set apart to serve, as unaccountable to others, to laity, or to the expectations to which all are held.[15] They suffer, as do some bishops, from a lack of self-awareness, callousness, low empathy, self-deception and self-justification, addictive behaviors, and an abiding focus upon

---

[14] Duane Bidwell, "Deep Listening and Virtuous Friendship: Spiritual Care in the Context of Religious Multiplicity," *Buddhist-Christian Studies* 35 (2015): 3–13.

[15] Mark Francis, CSV, "Reflections on Clericalism and the Liturgy," *Worship* 93 (2019): 201. See also Gaillardetz, "A Church in Crisis," 207 (esp. note 9), 209–11.

their own needs.[16] These narcissistic personality traits might seek out and benefit from cultural or institutional enablers of the same. Clericalism as an institutional culture that promotes exceptionalism of some and subordination of others, aids and abets the individual psychology of a narcissist. In a liturgical setting, for example, writes Mark Francis, "Any action or attitude of the priest at worship that disregards or minimalizes the role of the whole body of Christ at worship is a manifestation of clericalism," rendering the assembly passive consumers of locutions and movements.[17]

The role of narcissism in the clergy abuse crisis is not limited to clergy abusers or to clergy callously indifferent to a community's need for healing.[18] Those narcissistic traits of callousness, low empathy, self-deception, and lack of remorse can be found among others in the community who remain silent or indifferent, who merely defer to authority at the expense of their own baptismal dignity, voice, and contribution to the body, or among those who feel the church has already done enough to prevent abuse, or that the church's responsibility is to prevent abuse whereas healing is a private matter, or that a generalized focus on the abuse crisis distracts from the church's mission. Perhaps not as grave as full-blown narcissism, a number of common remarks or sentiments have narcissistic features and are ingredient to the macro cultural problem still hindering institutional and communal response. These sentiments include feelings that the church needs to move on from this issue; that victims and the issue of abuse itself pose an inconvenience or a discomfort; that the church already dealt with this problem in previous years or in previous bankruptcies or in previous court cases; that victims frequently leave the church

---

[16] Fernando Ortiz, "Seminary Formation: Lessons from the *Causes and Context of Sexual Abuse* Study," *Seminary Journal* 19, no. 2 (2013): 10–19.

[17] Francis, "Reflections on Clericalism and the Liturgy," 199–200.

[18] Thomas P. Doyle, "Clericalism: Enabler of Clergy Sexual Abuse," *Pastoral Psychology* 54, no. 3 (2006): 197–99.

and so there need be no urgency to design liturgies with their healing in mind; that we seem unable to hold enough liturgies of lament or listening sessions to satisfy our critics and so why bother to offer any; or that the secular culture or media have placed their figurative foot on our throats and will not let us get off the ground, as if to assume a victim identity and substitute oneself for actual victims.[19]

So, too, institutional structures that continue to manage the role, visibility, and impact of lay professionals qualified to assist and redirect the church's response, especially lay women professionals, imply a callous affect and may reveal self-deception concerning the causes and conditions of abuse and the opportunities for remediating the crisis and healing those harmed. The inability to feel rightly—to feel empathetically as one member to another of the body of Christ, whose plights are one's own plights, whose joys are one's own joys, whose redeeming is one's own redeeming and to perceive ourselves as a *people*—frustrates the church's own call and mission in and to the world. It is not merely the inability or struggle to feel rightly that frustrates the work of the church in this moment. It is that this inability frequently remains unconscious, unexamined, and mutually reinforced by others who share it, whether clerical or lay.[20]

It can be audacious to ask what redemption is for victim survivors of abuse. If redemption is a theological way to speak of how God pulls people back from repetitive experiences of annihilation or conditions that threaten or overwhelm, such redemption will always be specific and correlated to the person's experience of harm and the available holding environment of care, or the lack thereof.[21] To be sure, even the language and model of redemption may need to be inspected. As one prominent survivor of clergy sexual abuse told me in a private conversation, the very notion of redemption, if it means some divine force from outside oneself

---

[19] Doyle, 200, 203–4.

[20] Gaillardetz, "A Church in Crisis," 208.

[21] David H. Kelsey, *Imagining Redemption* (Louisville: Westminster John Knox, 2005).

stepping in to fix the person harmed as an extrinsic power, "does not sit very well." Even as there cannot be any one model for the experience of God actively relating to persons so as to redeem them, we can learn from ethnographic scholarship modeling a victim-first approach by asking, *what have survivors undergone when they heal or find their wounds transformed?* The church as the body of Christ would ask this question in order to come alongside others in patterns of deep listening and accompaniment, to learn from the authority of victims' experience and their ways of encountering transformation or redemption.

A decisive contribution comes from Susan Shooter of the United Kingdom and her book *How Survivors of Abuse Relate to God.*[22] Shooter interviews nine women who underwent different kinds of sexual abuse traumatic wounding and who, over the course of years and decades, found those wounds to be encountered transformatively by a God who remained and made all the difference. From their witness, Shooter codes three "higher concepts" that may help us to see from their faith perspective what better practices might look like. Those higher concepts include: first, "God's timeless presence"; second, "transformation"; and third, "knowing ministry." Together, they capture what Shooter calls the "core category"—*Knowing God's Timeless Presence Transforms*—which emerged from the data and provides glimpses into the processes by which these women encountered healing.[23]

For Shooter, the core category "Knowing God's Timeless Presence Transforms" bears an intentional grammatical ambiguity.

---

[22] Susan Shooter, *How Survivors of Abuse Relate to God: The Authentic Spirituality of the Annihilated Soul* (London: Routledge, 2016). For a summary statement of the book's findings, see Susan Shooter, "How Survivors of Abuse Relate to God: A Qualitative Study," in *The Faith Lives of Women and Girls: Qualitative Research Perspectives,* ed. Nicola Slee, Fran Porter, and Anne Phillips (London: Routledge, 2013): 221–31. For a discussion of Shooter's ethnographic insights, see John N. Sheveland, "Redeeming Trauma: An Agenda for Theology Fifteen Years On," in Peters and Rademacher, *American Catholicism in the 21st Century*, 137–48.

[23] Shooter, *How Survivors of Abuse Relate to God*, 76.

One meaning of this phrase captures the survivor's own inner dynamics, while another meaning captures her contributions to and among the people of God. Of the first, Shooter writes, "The survivors know God's timeless presence in their lives and this has transformed them and healed the effects of abuse, and continues to heal them and transform the effects of abuse." Of the second intended meaning, Shooter writes, "Because they know and have experienced transformation by God's presence in their lives, this awareness equips and enables them to become God's agents for the transformation of others."[24] The second intended meaning begins to highlight a worry of Shooter's, namely, that "pastoral theology has been concerned almost exclusively with ministering *to* survivors, not what ministry should be accomplished *by* survivors."[25] To perceive survivors—to listen deeply to them—for the potential wisdom, insight, right affect, and ministry they might offer to their communities represents one way that a church might embrace a victims-first approach. Priests and bishops, likewise, can become learners before they perform as teachers.

The first higher concept, *God's timeless presence,* captures a complex developmental process within the lives of those survivors for whom core memories of abandonment by others and by God over time are modulated, supplemented, and eventually healed by a spiritual realization of God always having been with them in their "pain-sharing."[26] The survivor's core spiritual insight knows God now as actively loving and caring beyond all harm, in a personally intimate and dynamically active way. In connection, the survivor undergoes a palpable reconception of her past and of herself as the dear, lovable one to whom God drew near and actively continues to draw near, before, during, and beyond all harm. This was not the belief at the time of abuse but rather became an unfolding spiritual realization over time that reconfigured core memories of abuse. This experience of God's active and abiding intimate love heals memories of the past, specifically

---

[24] Shooter, 76.
[25] Shooter, 76.
[26] Shooter, 56.

memories when there had been no personal connection with God and God was perceived to have "allowed" bad things to happen.[27]

The second higher concept, *transformation,* includes the transformation of three painful beliefs typical of clergy sexual abuse traumatic wounding. First, whereas God had been thought of previously as permitting the abuse or being indifferent to it, that belief becomes transformed in a manner that repairs the God-relation. The agency of the abuser who abused in freedom becomes clearer now. God was present not in stopping or preventing abuse, but in providing resources to endure it and, with an eye on the future, helping the survivor to face struggles to come over the process of healing. In this awareness not only is the God-relation repaired, but the survivor palpably experiences God as actively relating to her in love and accompaniment in the past, present, and into the future. Second, the survivor realizes a seismic shift or sea change in her self-worth and self-love, undoing the dynamics of self-hatred frequently attending abuse, dynamics that had expropriated her from her own irrevocable dignity and goodness. Against those distortions of self-worth, a transformation or conversion to her own irrevocable dignity and goodness stems from the revivified God-relation. Third, the pain and evil the survivor underwent, while not undone, forgotten, or taken away, has been transformed nonetheless in some tangible way toward a good, such as renewed and meaningful friendships, contributions to the healing of others, or a sustaining relationship with the God who never left. To be sure, the ethnographic interviews do not represent these goods as justifiable reasons for the abuse happening. Rather, the interviews demonstrate a newfound agency on the part of these women, wherein they separate abuse from the will of God and live with greater self-worth and self-determination as survivors rather than merely as victims constrained and dominated by an aggressor.[28]

Finally, the third higher concept Shooter coded from her ethnographic data, *knowing ministry,* is itself a grateful expression of healing expressed through a desire to offer concrete acts of healing

---

[27] Shooter, "How Survivors of Abuse Relate to God," 224.

[28] Shooter, *How Survivors of Abuse Relate to God,* 62–63.

service to others. Knowing ministry witnesses to the manner in which God's sustaining relationship funds the survivor's new and creative ministry toward others made to suffer similar crimes and sins. In its recovery of survivor agency and on the strength of the new forms of knowledge gained from "God's timeless presence" and "transformation," this third core category, "knowing ministry," is an observation about who in our communities is most capable of rendering pastoral care and ministry to those wounded. Shooter's interviewees "now appear to be active in service in a way that clearly reflects what they have experienced of God's care for them."[29] One sees edifying examples of this dynamic playing out in survivor-based organizations like Spirit Fire.[30]

The benefit of Shooter's bottom-up approach, where she conducts and codes oral histories, is that we begin to see what better practices actually look like for real people; we begin to acknowledge skillsets and pastoral approaches that are victim-centric and are capable of being healing for some, even many; and we begin to recognize who among us embodies the skillsets needed to follow through with this work of the church. In short, these women whose experiences had been transformed possess authentic experience and knowledge about God's love and unconditional positive regard, and, crucially, they know how to relate and minister to others so affected. Such spiritual potential and authority notwithstanding, these women repeatedly experienced institutional structures and interpersonal power dynamics restricting their agency and the pastoral opportunity their agency affords others wounded by abuse, mitigating an otherwise astonishing pastoral potential.[31] Shooter's ethnographic research presents to religious leaders and authority figures, especially in hierarchical

---

[29] Shooter, "How Survivors of Abuse Relate to God," 228.

[30] According to its website, spiritfirelive.wordpress.com, "Spirit Fire is a fellowship of survivors of abuse within the Church who share, as part of our ongoing recovery, a spiritual practice which permits us to offer our wisdom, experience, and faith to all others who seek healing, growth, and reconciliation in the wake of the abuse of children and vulnerable adults in a faith setting—in particular in the Catholic Church."

[31] Shooter, *How Survivors of Abuse Relate to God*, 74–76.

and masculine contexts, the uncomfortable finding that they may not be the ones best equipped to lead pastorally in this context; in some instances their role in part may be to get out of the way while simultaneously empowering others to undertake the church's healing work.[32] The constructive form of this insight would lead leaders to recognize, celebrate, and promote the contributions of survivors as members of the body of Christ for the healing sake of all members of this body, whether direct or indirect victims of abuse or the indifferent. In the context of a post-traumatic church, such an insight would be an appropriate application of Paul's theology of the body of Christ, with its many gifts and charisms, its mutuality and interdependence.

A decisive feature of the three higher concepts and the core category from Susan Shooter's ethnographical research is that, first, they center the voices and spiritual processes of nine women. While there is no implication that these voices and spiritual processes should become a model or expectation for the healing and transformation of other survivors of abuse, they do illustrate, for these women, how multifaceted healing did develop. These voices also provide pastoral caregivers and the church as a whole some literacy in survivor experience and a set of possible opportunities by way of healing that could be relevant for others. Second, they create space for hope and allowance for a lengthy developmental process over a lifespan. These core categories depend on a healthy relational home or holding environment within the community to fund or enable the capacity of these women to recognize God's timeless presence, to undergo various kinds of transformation, and to reengage their own agency by offering their own redemptive ministry alongside others who suffer. While not imposing the experiences of these nine women or this model onto others, Shooter's concrete research supplies the church with at least a partial vision for how the church can cultivate itself as a relational

---

[32] On "getting out of the way," see Daniel Horan, OFM, "A Spirituality of Resistance: Thomas Merton on the Violence of Structural Racism in America," in Peters and Rademacher, *American Catholicism in the 21st Century*, 198.

home or holding environment for the sake of its own members and its own integrity. Crucially, the fact that these nine women faced a variety of institutional and gender-based obstructions to their own healing and to their ability to render authentic pastoral ministry to others serves as a sign of what we see confirmed too often as endemic to the church. The ethnographic research should motivate people up and down the hierarchical structures of a community to check for overt as well as unconscious expressions of asymmetrical power dynamics that function to diminish the voices, lamentations, and wisdom of survivors, or the advocacy of those seeking to accompany survivors.

Checking for power imbalances and unhealthy asymmetrical relationships is a sign of health for any organization and must become a prerequisite for the church's handling of its own abuse crisis and its potential prophetic role in bringing the resources of the church to bear upon child vulnerability and abuse beyond the church. The United States Conference of Catholic Bishops' Secretariat for Child and Youth Protection has adapted and embraced the approach of high reliability organizations. At the time of this writing, 23 of 176 Roman Catholic dioceses in the United States have accepted the opportunity to be trained in the principles of high reliability made available to them by the Secretariat for Child and Youth Protection.[33]

High reliability organizations confront the challenges of working in high-risk environments through their organization-specific application of the principles of high reliability to generate low rates of harm throughout the organization. In the context of the US Church, the principles of high reliability fall under two headings: anticipation and containment. *Anticipation* involves, first, a "preoccupation with failure" in the sense of habitually directing one's organizational assets and attention to focus upon organizational weaknesses and to address immediate failures to protect and to heal when they occur. As well, high reliability organizations support an organization culture of fixation upon possible

---

[33] United States Conference of Catholic Bishops, "HRO Principles Summary," 2020.

failures, even if these have not occurred. Second, "reluctance to simplify" signals a preference to generate a more nuanced picture of organizational risk factors and a willingness to generate a root cause analysis of failures and the role of long-held beliefs in those failures. Third, "sensitivity to operations" is an ability to become aware of risks at all levels of an organization and to foster front-line conditions among staff to promote communication and openness.

The second set of principles concerns *containment* of the damage caused by an event of harm after it occurs. First, the "commitment to resilience" signals an ability to innovate new solutions in a dynamic environment, often by working with multidisciplinary teams and removing barriers to collaboration. Second, "deference to expertise" is the organizational ability to respond to events of harm based on the best available information from subject-matter experts. Deference to expertise stands in contrast to the mere reliance upon established or presumptive authority and to a reluctance to keep staff trained, competent, and responsible for child protection.

These principles address some of the roadblocks to ministry that Susan Shooter's interview subjects faced from institutional powerbrokers. Deference to expertise, for example, if embraced organizationally and culturally, would create conditions and space for survivor witness, testimony, and wisdom to take hold among the community and especially in competent ministry to those harmed.

The ecclesiology of the Second Vatican Council supports these moves. In particular, a metaphor for the church in the council's *Dogmatic Constitution on the Church (Lumen Gentium)*, as the people of God being a pilgrim people already anticipates the need to remain vigilant, self-aware, and preoccupied with sin. Jason King argues that the pilgrim-church model of the church in *Lumen Gentium* implies four characteristics of the church applicable to addressing clergy abuse. A pilgrim church is marked by (1) its own imperfection, (2) its striving for perfection, (3) its sense of solidarity, and (4) its accountability to Christ. With regard to

the imperfection of the pilgrim church, King acknowledges that
Lumen Gentium speaks of a real yet imperfect holiness marking
the church. Not only are specific people imperfect, King argues,
but the church as a social body is imperfect.[34] King underscores
the salutary effect of this recognition:

> By acknowledging that the church is imperfect, the church
> hierarchy would be more willing and ready to seek out
> weakness and breakdowns [read: preoccupation with fail-
> ure]. The hierarchy would not be so constrained by fear that
> the revelation of failures would necessarily bring scandal.
> Rather, it would be more open to those who discover or
> point out failings in the life of the church. On the other
> hand, acceptance by the faithful of an imperfect church
> might prepare them in a more realistic way for addressing
> church deficiencies.[35]

How might such practices become part of a community's
emotional intelligence and way of proceeding? How might a
community be schooled in practices of deep listening to survivor
experience and in high reliability principles?

Heather Banis, an author in this volume, offered the US bishops
some indications at their November 2018 general assembly in
Baltimore.[36] In her capacity as the victim assistance coordinator
for the Archdiocese of Los Angeles, she was invited to speak to
the full gathering of bishops short months after the Pennsylvania
grand jury report and the allegations against Theodore McCarrick,
a former cardinal in the US church. Some of her advice pertains to
the bishops in their particular role, but other advice can pertain to

---

[34] Jason King, "Vatican II's Ecclesiology and the Sexual Abuse Scandal,"
in *Vatican II: Forty Years Later,* College Theology Society Annual 51, ed.
William Madges (Maryknoll, NY: Orbis Books, 2006), 154.

[35] King, 155. On the force of pilgrim church vis-à-vis abuse, see Gerald Arbuckle, *Abuse and Cover-up: Refounding the Catholic Church in
Trauma* (Maryknoll, NY: Orbis Books, 2019).

[36] Heather Banis, Address to the General Assembly of US Bishops,
November 13, 2018.

all, such as the recommendation to pray liturgically (not merely privately) for victims at every mass, and to talk about what we have learned publicly and openly, modeling the belief that we can talk about this and that "our God and our church are big enough." She instructed the bishops to be victim-centric, and pointed out that liturgical ways of doing so would be to pray for victims at every mass, to hold liturgies of lament, and to offer apology meetings when new reports surface. These and other activities would demonstrate to victim-survivors that they are part of the church; these practices would also raise the emotional intelligence of the entire body of the church. Not unlike Susan Shooter, Heather Banis impresses upon the bishops that they *need* the victims in order to learn how to make the necessary changes. The bishops must become learners.[37]

It is difficult to know to what extent her comments made an impact, but Banis underscores that same transformation of the culture of the church, or the macro culture of the church, that Karen Terry rightly regards as a liability. How does a church challenge itself from within its own often unexamined flows of culture? What resources do we have from within to break in upon those complicit cultural customs and artifacts?

One resource might be the liturgy itself. Some may perceive Banis's advice to pray for victims at every mass to be quaint or ineffectual, even misplaced. But for those of us who struggle with low empathy or even narcissism, the liturgy might be a way the church's tradition works upon our interior spiritual landscape like a mind-training exercise. The change in culture will not happen through the mere exchange of ideas and intellectual assent. Instead, it is our affect, our capacity to accompany and to love and to love at cost, that is found to be wanting and in need of conversion, with ongoing cost to direct and indirect victims of clerical abuse.

In response to Banis's call to pray for victims at mass as a communal and shared practice, liturgical prayers were written for the

---

[37] John N. Sheveland, "Receptive Theological Learning in and from the Asian Bishops," *Asian Horizons* 10, no. 3 (2016): 545–60.

website of the Center for Child Protection at the Pontifical Gregorian University in Rome.[38] Renamed in 2021, the IADC is one of the best institutional drivers of change in the Catholic Church today. Some prayers of the faithful can be victim-centric, others might focus on an ecclesial lament and ecclesial repentance. Learning how to pray differently now appears to be an important way to raise spiritual awareness of the various experiences of victim-survivors and to grow a community's range of affect or feeling. In terms of designing specific prayers attentive and responsive to the experiences of traumatic wounding in our church, the principle of subsidiarity helps us to understand that the people of God in each local environment bear the responsibility for discerning prayers with maximal impact for their place and time. They must emerge from the concrete particulars of time, place, and culture, not be dictated or handed down from the outside. They may be designed by presiders, other priests, deacons, liturgists, music directors, teachers, or laity.

There is no obvious reason why victims cannot be held in prayer at every mass; nor are there persuasive reasons why a presider should consistently neglect to include such prayers, especially in his own voice. Such neglect implies an unacceptable indifference either to survivors or those wishing to accompany them, stemming from a probable clericalism. Liturgical prayer can be healing for victims and their allies by establishing truth-telling as an ecclesial and liturgical practice occurring before God, one which can reestablish trust through repeated communal action. In such prayers survivors and their allies may experience themselves as seen, heard, and even presented with opportunities to reconfigure their own specific wounding and memories. So, too, in tone and style, prayers can communicate words of comfort to those harmed

---

[38] John N. Sheveland, "How Do We Pray in a Post-Traumatic Church?" guest contributor, Center for Child Protection, October 16, 2019. The center remains at the Pontifical Gregorian University in Rome but was expanded and renamed in September 2021 as the Institute of Anthropology: Interdisciplinary Studies on Human Dignity and Care (IADC) in order "to expand its scope, to award academic degrees, and to develop its own academic faculty."

or prophetic words of ecclesial self-examination and confession of ecclesial sin.

A victim-centered prayer of the faithful, which also acknowledges the violence that abuse of a child renders to entire communities, might read like this:

> We pray for all victims of abuse around the world, within the church and beyond, and especially for all children everywhere, that the healing Spirit of God move within and among them. And that the church—the people of God—be filled with the same healing spirit. *We pray to the Lord.*

A somewhat more strenuous and confessional prayer, which acknowledges clerical and institutional responsibility, might read more like this:

> We the church pray for its leaders, that they would practice new leadership by recognizing and repenting of sin and its consequences within the church, especially those sins that cause innocent children, families, and communities to suffer unjustly. *We pray to the Lord.*

Both prayers reflect different dimensions of the one reality, and it can be useful to separate them and give spiritual attention to each. In all cases the prayer should reflect the clarity of a victims-first approach, which in turn may open victim-survivors anew to the redemptive power of the liturgy. The prayer and its liturgical placement may welcome the wounded into a new and personally meaningful spiritual realization of the ways in which God acts as Lord and redeemer of even these experiences. Such fresh encounter, however, is contingent upon tangible liturgical openings and possibilities. None of this is a matter of course.

While likely too long for liturgies other than masses of healing or liturgies of lament, other forms of prayer like the one below invite the congregation into a more extended contemplative practice. As a contemplative practice, a prayer could be exploratory, filled with petition yet also gratitude, drawing congregants into new vistas of hope and possibility. It can also employ different theological structures, including creedal, trinitarian, and eucharistic structures. One such extended example might read like this:

> Good and gracious God, we come before you because you first came alongside us. You are the God who has drawn near and remains near. Fashion us into a grateful people. Lord we are grateful for the painstaking efforts of those working for child protection and child flourishing at this crucial time. May they be joined by all in the church. Bless them, be with them, comfort them, and empower them. Help us to model your will for the church according to St. Paul, united in Christ and therefore disinterested in factionalism and party spirit.
>
> Lord, create within us clean and cleaner hearts to see the world, the church, and all of your children everywhere as you see them, as you know them, as you relate to them as God and redeemer. Draw closer still, especially to all those made to suffer from the crime and sin of abuse, and restore for them the power of your purifying love. May they know your unfailing gaze of love as their deepest truth, before, within, and beyond all harm.
>
> Creator God, you are father and mother to us all, your children. You have made us one family and you draw us into your own life. Help us, and help us to help others, when we no longer feel your loving gaze. Come to us once more and make our hearts ready.
>
> Lord God, in the humanity of your son Jesus Christ you assumed all that is human, took it up into your divine life, and healed it from all that was broken and self-contradictory. And so now in you and therefore in us, shame has no power. Grant us the wisdom of your Word to live into this new life, and help us to breathe new life into a church where shame is given no place, bears no impediment, gives way to a boundless precious love for all and a self-love among all. This is now, for us, the love beyond imagining which is the mission of your church because it was the mission of your Son.

Lord God, breathe into us the fire and connective energy of your Holy Spirit, which binds us together in the church as pilgrims and friends and redeemed sinners. May your spirit move once more to renew the face of this Earth so that there is no child vulnerability. Be with all children everywhere, even in this moment those who are threatened, insecure, or unloved. In the unrestricted power of your Spirit, may they know themselves as dear and lovable, not alone; as whole and complete, not vulnerable; as known and cherished and in communion, not abandoned. Give to them and to all who need it your Holy Spirit of resiliency.

Lord, may we your pilgrim church muster courage and truth to confess sins where they are present. Forgive us our sins. For your sake and for the sake of all those you love beyond imagining—especially your children—redeem us. Redeem the church called to preach your good news. May its vocation to protect children be fully realized, so that the people of God become for the world a sacrament of salvation, a sign of child protection and child flourishing. *Amen.*[39]

As Heather Banis instructs the leadership of the US church about the importance of regular liturgical opportunities for congregations to pray for victims in the shared space of the mass and its liturgy, Eileen Dombo and Cathleen Gray recommend spiritual practices like prayer, meditation, attending religious services, or spiritual reading as restorative practices for clinical caregivers harmed vicariously or indirectly by exposure to traumatic wounding. They write for, and from the perspective of, clinical social workers and other caregivers who professionally take in the experience of their clients and can become exposed to vicarious wounding.[40] In their self-care model, the spiritual practices of Buddhism can become practical aids to develop capacity to sense the

---

[39] Sheveland. Used with permission of the IADC.

[40] Eileen A. Dombo and Cathleen Gray, "Engaging Spirituality in Addressing Vicarious Trauma in Clinical Social Workers," *Social Work and Christianity* 40, no. 1 (2013): 90.

dignity of each client, to listen without judgment, and to regard the interpersonal space in which they work as sacred. Meditation as a spiritual practice for such professionals can facilitate awareness of internal processes and build capacity to choose whether and how "to respond to specific thoughts, sensations, and feelings."[41]

Dombo and Gray work with meditations upon the *brahma-viharas* or divine abodes of Buddhism to access breath control, awareness of mental thoughts and reactions, concentration, and compassion. For the clinical worker engaged in this difficult work, Dombo and Gray translate meditation upon the divine abodes of love, joy, compassion, and equanimity into simple but profound practices for clinical professionals. Compassion meditations might simply be: "May I be gentle with myself in my work," or "May I be attuned to those I help." Letting-go meditations could be: "May my client know peace," or "May I let go of my reactions to my client's pain." Reflection meditations might simply be: "May I heal from my own pain and suffering," or "May I give thanks for being able to do this work."[42]

Liturgical rituals, liturgical prayer, and other forms of spiritual practice may help to heal survivors' bodies and spirits more effectively than direct forms of communication in counseling settings while providing tangible, public means for an entire community to tell the truth and process its own wounds and the wounds of others.[43] They can help to heal the minds and bodies of those throughout the body of Christ who choose in various ways to accompany their harmed sisters and brothers. Readiness to do so, and reliance upon the wisdom and spiritual practices from traditions, will surely factor into the extent to which the Catholic Church—the people of God, a pilgrim people, the body of Christ—is able to effect the necessary change in culture to address and heal these self-inflicted wounds.

---

[41] Dombo and Gray, 96.
[42] Dombo and Gray, 99.
[43] Beste, "Mediating God's Grace in the Context of Trauma," 256.

4.

What Can Make Churches Unsafe?

The Catholic Church
as Total Institution

Cristina Lledo Gomez

This chapter explores the organizational culture of the church, which lends to abuses of power and, consequently, abuse of vulnerable persons. It argues that, while legislation, training, and systems have been put in place to communicate zero tolerance for child abuse in churches, church authorities can continue to spiritually abuse members given that the systems and culture supporting child sexual abuse can remain largely unexamined. The chapter utilizes the work of Palmer, Feldman, and McKibbin on total institutions from their analysis of cases in volume 16 of the *Final Report* of the Australian Royal Commission into Institutional Responses to Child Sexual Abuse (hereafter referred to simply as Royal Commission) and applies their findings to the Catholic Church from a Catholic theologian's point of view.

In the 1950s, psychology professor Solomon Asch conducted his famous conformity experiments to demonstrate that under social pressure, individuals conform, even against their own better judgment.[1] Results were mixed, showing 5 percent of participants conforming with the majority in all eighteen trials while 25 percent defied majority opinion. The rest conformed in at least one out of the eighteen trials.[2] Before the study Asch had already been concerned about the impact of Hitler's regime during WWII upon individuals, such that otherwise ordinary good-willed citizens could be convinced to kill, torture, experiment on, and become blind to the violence toward fellow human beings and even take no personal responsibility, as the Eichmann "just following orders" defence showed.[3] For Asch, the concerning question was whether a person "possesses the freedom to act independently, or whether he characteristically submits to group pressures."[4] Asch's study, even if flawed, might provide some provisional insight into how a culture of secrecy and cover-ups over child sexual abuse in the Catholic Church and many other institutions was accepted as the norm in the 1960s, 1970s, 1980s and even into the 2000s, after allegations of clerical abuse of children had already been brought to light by the "Spotlight" team of the *Boston Globe* newspaper.[5]

---

[1] S. E. Asch, "Effects of Group Pressure upon the Modification and Distortion of Judgements," in *Groups, Leadership, and Men: Research in Human Relations,* 177–90 (Pittsburgh, PA: Carnegie Press, 1951).

[2] Asch's study was later critiqued not only for its unethical method according to today's American Psychological Association standards, but also because Asch treated conformity as a singular type when there are several forms. See Kevin Wren, "Solomon Asch and Normative Social Influences," in *Social Influences* (London: Routledge, 1999), 26.

[3] "Letter by Adolf Eichmann to President Yitzhak Ben-Zvi of Israel," English translation, *The New York Times,* January 27, 2016. In the letter Holocaust organizer Adolf Eichmann, as a last plea for clemency from his war crimes, argues that like fellow war criminals he was "forced to serve as mere instruments in the hands of the leaders."

[4] Asch, "Effects of Group Pressure upon the Modification and Distortion of Judgements," 177.

[5] "Church Allowed Abuse by Priest for Years," Part 1 of 2, *Boston Globe,* January 6, 2002.

A decade on, in 1961, Stanley Milgram, inspired by Asch's conformity experiments, conducted his famous obedience to authority figures experiment.[6] The results of the experiment showed a minority who refused to follow the commands of the authority figure, the "experimenter" in the white lab coat, standing next to the volunteer participant, who was the "teacher," and who was meant to administer electric shocks to a "learner" if that person got a wrong answer or was silent. Yet a majority (65 percent) showed they were willing to administer the maximum voltage of electric shocks to the learner (450 volts) despite hearing requests from the learner to be released from 150 volts, agonizing screams at 285 volts, complaints of heart pain, refusal to answer questions and ultimately silence at 330 volts. Milgram's experiment might explain how people can become desensitized to violence, silence their own consciences, and relegate responsibility to an authority figure, even if it involves inflicting pain and possible death upon another human being. More pointedly, regarding clerical abuse of children, Milgram's experiment could provide insight into how a church could create a culture where people showed adherence to canon law (including the law of keeping the church away from scandal) rather than the natural law within themselves, and civil law, which would highlight that sexual abuse of minors was a crime to be reported to civil authorities.

A third study of interest, the Stanford Prison experiment, was conducted by Phillip Zimbardo a decade on from Milgram's experiment. In the study Zimbardo utilized college students to simulate a prison setting where half of the students played the role of guard and the other half, prisoner. Initially, the students did not take their roles seriously. But once they settled into them, the volunteers executed their roles at the extreme: guards abused their power of authority while prisoners experienced mental breakdown because of the abuse. While this study was critiqued especially for its unethical methods, it points nonetheless to the

---

[6] S. Milgram, "Behavioural Study of Obedience," *Journal of Abnormal and Social Psychology* 67 (1963): 371–78.

capabilities for violence and abuse of power even among good-willed, mentally healthy individuals. In psychology, this is what is called the powerful situation.[7]

In highlighting these three studies, I wish to highlight my current concern that, while legislation, training, and systems have been put in place to communicate zero tolerance for child abuse in churches, the propensity for abuse in the church in its other forms, particularly in the form of spiritual abuse, remains. Accountability, transparency, clericalism, and governance issues connected to abuse of power and child abuse in the church remain issues for the Australian Catholic Church, as evidenced in submissions to the 2020–22 Australian plenary council and in commentary and reports on the plenary and abuse in the church.[8] Given that sexual abuse in the church has often been about the abuse of power rather than simply sex, I argue that the focus upon child protection must also include vulnerability to abuse of power, in the church's culture and its systems.

As someone who has worked in various areas and levels of the church, from parishioner, parish youth minister, reader, senior server, and extraordinary minister of holy communion to chair of the Australian Catholic Bishops Commission for Social Justice, from pastoral associate for staff at a Catholic university to Catholic theology lecturer and high-school religion teacher, from the mother of children attending Catholic primary and high schools,

---

[7] C. Haney, C. Banks, and P. G. Zimbardo, "Interpersonal Dynamics in a Simulated Prison," *International Journal of Criminology and Penology* 1 (1973): 69–97. See also, Wayne Weiten, *Psychology: Themes and Variations,* 10th ed. (North Ryde: Cengage Learning, 2016), 443.

[8] Australian Catholic Bishops Conference, *Continuing the Journey: Instrumentum Laboris for the Fifth Plenary Council,* January 2021; Implementation Advisory Group and the Governance Review Project Team, *Light from the Southern Cross: Promoting Co-Responsible Governance in the Catholic Church in Australia,* May 2020; Peter Johnstone, "Catholics Want Reform," *Pearls and Irritations: John Menadue's Public Policy Journal,* June 30, 2020; Gail Freyne, "A Plenary of Broken Promises?," *Pearls and Irritations: John Menadue's Public Policy Journal,* June 17, 2020.

to wife of a permanent deacon, I have seen and experienced from various viewpoints how churches can support people but also use and abuse, traumatize and re-traumatize them as volunteers and/or paid workers. A range of research has already shown that abuse from the church can range from sexual abuse to spiritual abuse.[9] The research by Lisa Oakley shows that even adults not considered at risk or vulnerable have had their share of spiritual abuse in the church.[10]

This chapter begins by exploring the concept of persons made vulnerable because of abuse, particularly those who experience complex post-traumatic stress disorder (CPTSD). These include adults who have experienced childhood sexual abuse inside and outside of churches. This first section argues that persons experiencing CPTSD are present in the church and, thus, safeguarding for adult vulnerable persons and not just children should be the agenda for church institutions. It also argues that even non-vulnerable persons are in need of safety due to the possibility of being subjected to spiritual abuse, as shown in the decade-long research of Oakley.[11] The second and main part of this chapter investigates organizational cultures of abuse, particularly the total institution, and compares its characteristics to the Catholic Church's power structures and

---

[9] See Lisa Oakley, Kathryn Kinmond, and Justin Humphreys, "Spiritual Abuse in Christian Faith Settings: Definition, Policy and Practice Guidance," *The Journal of Adult Protection* 20, no. 3/4 (2018): 144–54; see also, Lisa Oakley, Lee-Ann Fenge, Simon Bass, and Justin Humphreys, "Exploring the Complexities of Understanding Vulnerability and Adult Safeguarding within Christian Faith Organisations," *The Journal of Adult Protection* 18, no. 3 (2016): 172–83; Royal Commission, *Final Report— Volume 16, Religious Institutions,* Commonwealth of Australia (2017); Kathleen McPhillips, "'Soul Murder': Investigating Spiritual Trauma at the Royal Commission," *Journal of Australian Studies* 42, no. 2 (2018): 231–42.

[10] Oakley, Kimmond, and Humphreys, "Spiritual Abuse in Christian Faith Settings," 152.

[11] Lisa Oakley and Kathryn Kimmond, *Breaking the Silence on Spiritual Abuse* (Basingstoke: Palgrave Macmillan, 2013); Lisa Oakley and Justin Humphrey, *Escaping the Maze of Spiritual Abuse: Creating Healthy Christian Cultures* (London: SPCK, 2019).

systems. It largely utilizes the work of Palmer, Feldman, and McKibbin on total institutions as found in the *Final Report* of the Royal Commission. Finally, given the church's vulnerability to abuse of power, the chapter proposes a trauma-informed approach that prioritizes care of vulnerable persons.

CHURCH ABUSE OF VULNERABLE AND NON-VULNERABLE PERSONS

According to the Australian Government, *abuse*

> will often violate a person's human rights. Where it results in death, abuse will violate a person's right to life. More commonly, abuse will violate a person's right not to be subject to cruel or degrading treatment, which is considered an absolute right.[12]

In Australia, the research on abuse of children shows its prevalence, based on several studies, as ranging from 5–18 percent (physical), 6–17 percent (emotional), 4–23 percent (exposure to family violence), and 1.6–4 percent (neglect).[13] Sexual abuse ranges up to 45 percent of females when a broader definition was incorporated (for example, "flashing by a stranger").[14] For the Australian Institute of Criminology, child sexual abuse is more commonly perpetrated by "a male relative (other than the victim's father or stepfather; 30.2 percent), a family friend (16.3 percent), an acquaintance or neighbor (15.6 percent), another known person (15.3 percent), or the father or stepfather (13.5 percent)."[15] These findings are consistent with the 2016

---

[12] Australian Government Australian Law Reform Commission, "Adult Safeguarding Laws," June 8, 2017, §14.13.

[13] Australian Institute of Family Studies, *The Prevalence of Child Abuse and Neglect,* Child Family Community Australia Resource Sheet, April 2017 (2021).

[14] Australian Institute of Family Studies.

[15] Kelly Richards, "Misperceptions about Child Sex Offenders," *Trends and Issues in Crime and Criminal Justice* 429 (Canberra: Australian Institute of Criminology).

Australian Bureau of Statistics Personal Safety Survey results, which state that

> about 2.5 million Australian adults (13%) experienced physical and/or sexual abuse during childhood. The majority of adults who reported childhood physical abuse only (97%) and sexual abuse only (86%) knew the perpetrator, with 81% of those who experienced physical abuse only being abused by a family member.[16]

Australia's National Research Organisation for Women's Safety Limited also points out that some groups are disproportionately affected by sexual violence, namely, culturally and linguistically diverse women, Aboriginal and Torres Strait Islander women or native women, women with a disability, LGBTQ women, women living in rural or remote areas, and women in prison.[17] These groups are disproportionately affected by sexual violence due to the greater rates of sexual violence they experience compared to the Australian average, and/or due to the additional barriers they face when seeking support and justice. Meanwhile, in 2017 the Royal Commission recorded it had "heard from 6,875 survivors in private sessions, of whom 4,029 (58.6 percent) told us about child sexual abuse in religious institutions"; 2,489 survivors, or two-thirds of that population, stated that the sexual abuse occurred in Catholic institutions.[18]

Clearly, childhood sexual abuse in Australia occurs more often in the home than in any other setting, by someone known to the victim. And, if children are not physically or sexually abused, they can be abused simply by their exposure to abuse and violence

---

[16] Australian Bureau of Statistics, "Characteristics and Outcomes of Childhood Abuse," *Personal Safety* (Australia, 2016).

[17] ANROWS, Australia's National Research Organisation for Women's Safety to Reduce Violence against Women and Their Children, *Invisible Women, Invisible Violence: Understanding and Improving Data on the Experiences of Domestic and Family Violence and Sexual Assault for Diverse Groups of Women: State of Knowledge Paper* (Sydney: Australia's National Research Organisation for Women's Safety, December 2016).

[18] Royal Commission, *Final Report.*

in the home or through the neglect of their needs. But as is well known, abuse is often underreported. Some researchers would agree, for example, that "many adult problems might be 'the logical consequences of childhood maltreatment.'"[19] Others would argue that the culture of silence surrounding childhood abuse implies its true prevalence can hardly be known, since it would "raise questions of complicity and comprise grounds for deep national shame."[20] The implication for church institutions is that a number of their population will have experienced childhood abuse, and those persons would be considered vulnerable persons, where *vulnerable person* is defined as:

a) a child or children; or
b) an individual aged 18 years and above who is or may be unable to take care of themselves, or is unable to protect themselves against harm or exploitation by reason of age, illness, trauma or disability, or any other reason.[21]

Adult child abuse survivors can be considered vulnerable persons given that they can suffer from CPTSD, which includes the symptoms of core post-traumatic stress disorder (PTSD) as well as:

1. severe and pervasive problems in affect regulation;

2. persistent beliefs about oneself as diminished, defeated or worthless, accompanied by deep and pervasive feelings of shame, guilt or failure related to the traumatic event; and

3. persistent difficulties in sustaining relationships and in feeling close to others. The disturbance causes significant

---

[19] Lucy Berliner, "Foreword," in John N. Briere, *Child Abuse Trauma: Theory and Treatment of the Lasting Effects* (Newbury Park, CA: Sage, 1992), in Blue Knot Foundation, *"The Last Frontier": Practice Guidelines for Treatment of Complex Trauma and Trauma Informed Care and Service Delivery"* (Sydney: Blue Knot Foundation, 2019), 38.

[20] Blue Knot Foundation, *"The Last Frontier,"* 40.

[21] Australian Government Department of Social Services, "Vulnerable Persons, Police Checks, and Criminal Offences," July 29, 2014.

impairment in personal, family, social, educational, occupational or other important areas of functioning.[22]

A key concern for church institutions is that those who experience CPTSD have difficulties with affect regulation. This means that in response to even a minutia of stress, they can operate outside of their "window of tolerance"—that is, "the threshold at which they can tolerate emotion without becoming either agitated and anxious (hyperaroused) or 'shut down' and numb (hypoaroused)."[23] Examples of hyperarousal activity include sudden outbursts of anger, irritability, paranoia, and an inability to focus. On the opposite end, hypoarousal activity appears as dissociation and withdrawal, the "freeze" in the fight-flight-freeze-fawn human defensive response.

But complex trauma is "not always the result of childhood trauma."[24] As the Blue Knot Foundation states, complex trauma could also come from "adults' experience of violence in the community . . . domestic and family violence, civil unrest, war trauma or genocide, refugee and asylum seeker trauma, sexual exploitation and trafficking, extreme medical trauma and/or retraumatisation."[25] The implication for church institutions is that not only are there possibly child sexual abuse survivors in their midst but also persons experiencing complex post-traumatic stress resulting from other experiences of trauma and violence. Therefore, when a church member or employee, for example, exhibits behavior associated with hyper- or hypoactivity, as described above, there is a chance the person is experiencing CPTSD and can be considered a vulnerable adult. And, if the church desires to live its belief in the "preferential option for the poor," it must find a way to help such individuals to

---

[22] World Health Organization, "Complex Post-traumatic Stress Disorder" (6B41), in International Classification of Diseases, 11th rev. (ICD-11) v2022-02.

[23] Blue Knot Foundation, *"The Last Frontier,"* 72.

[24] Blue Knot Foundation, *Living with and Healing from Complex Trauma* (Sydney: Blue Knot Foundation, 2021), 7.

[25] Blue Knot Foundation.

find safety in a space where they are clearly not feeling safe whether the threat is real or not.

While some church leaders and/or staff might consider the removal of the person experiencing CPTSD from the church environment as a solution to the problem, this is not only unsustainable but also unethical given it can send a message of rejection of a person for the state of mental health. Unfortunately, as the Royal Commission has shown, church leaders can prioritize their own reputations, self-interests, and self-protection above the safety and care of vulnerable persons.

My experience of psychological abuse as a church employee and a survivor of childhood sexual abuse supports the Royal Commission's judgment. A former supervisor took adverse legal action against me and may not have had any understanding of CPTSD or hyper/hypo arousal. One can only guess that my behavior appeared to this supervisor as insubordination rather than the behavior of a frightened person who was in freeze mode and afraid to be alone together in a room for fear of further emotional abuse. When my psychologist sent the supervisor several letters confirming my CPTSD and requesting finding collaborative solutions, the supervisor ignored the requests and instead sent me home, stating I could only return to work once I had been cured of my trauma and I could be alone in a room with this individual, given this was what the same individual chose to require of me in my job. This supervisor instructed fellow colleagues not to speak with me and blocked me from speaking with any other authorities within the organization and threatened legal action if I told my husband, who was also working for the same organization, of the abuse. These actions against me led to several episodes of panic attacks and eventually I needed intensive trauma treatment to overcome the ordeal. Retrospectively, I can see this was not just psychological abuse but also spiritual abuse given it was executed by a church authority and I was accused of harming the organization by promoting women's priestly ordination, which is considered against church teaching. In truth I had not engaged in such promotion but was advocating the leadership of women in the church. Yet in my view, my abuser was not interested in the truth.

A recent conference presentation by PhD candidate Tracy McEwan, researching the experiences of Gen X women in Australia, claims that a considerable number of Gen X women experience everyday spiritual abuse from the Catholic Church.[26] She describes the spiritual abuse expressed as controlling behaviors centered around the Gen X women's reproductive capabilities, including being made to feel shame for accessing IVF because of difficulties with childbearing or for using contraception because they couldn't handle more children but wished to be intimate with their spouse. Such accounts are not new, given the extent of pain women have experienced in the Australian church, as recorded in the historic study commissioned by the Australian Catholic Bishops Conference called *Woman and Man: One in Christ Jesus,* published in 1999.[27] To date, the thirty-one recommendations from the report to address the pain of women in the church remain to be seen in most if not all Australian Catholic parishes.[28]

---

[26] Tracy McEwan, "Everyday Spiritual Abuse in Roman Catholicism: Gen X Australian Women's Experiences," Spiritual Abuse: Coercive Control in Religions Conference, University of Chester, England, September 3–4, 2021. See also Tracy McEwan, "Changing Patterns of Religious Practice and Belief among Church-attending Catholic Women in Australia," *Journal for the Academic Study of Religion* 31, no. 3 (2019): 186–215.

[27] Research Management Group, *Woman and Man: One in Christ Jesus*, Report on the Participation of Women in the Catholic Church in Australia (Sydney: Harper Collins Religious, 1999). For context on the report, see Sonia Wagner, SGS, *Woman and Man: One in Christ Jesus: A Retrospective* (September 20, 2009). See also Maryanne Confoy, "All for One (Article on Woman and Man: One in Christ Jesus. Report on the Participation of Women in the Catholic Church in Australia (1999)," *Eureka Street* 9, no. 8: 10–11. For recent reflections on the *Woman and Man* report, see Sandie Cornish, ed., *Still Listening to the Spirit: Woman and Man Twenty Years Later* (Alexandria, NSW: Australian Catholic Bishops Conference Office for Social Justice, 2019).

[28] For more stories of global women's painful experiences in the church context, see The Catholic Women Speak Network; see also *Catholic Women Speak: Bringing Our Gifts to the Table* (New York: Paulist Press, 2015). See also, The Catholic Women Speak Network, Tina Beattie, and Diana Culbertson, *Visions and Vocations* (Mahwah, NJ: Paulist Press, 2018).

At the same spiritual abuse conference, "Pastor P.," who wished to remain anonymous to self-protect against further spiritual abuse from his former Chinese church (since he continued to receive abuse after he had left), demonstrated that abuse does not sit outside of culture.[29] In his case the spiritual abuse occurred in the context of what he called Confucian Chinese culture, which is marked by a shame and honor system that prioritizes filial piety. Pastor P. explained that in his Chinese culture elders are to be obeyed without question and that they have free reign in the execution of their authority; there are no boundaries or accountability structures except accountability to an older person than the elder. Concepts of shame and loyalty to family and the Chinese culture are used to control church members. Moreover, God is used to justify the spiritual abuse by elders. An example of such controlling behavior is when Pastor P. was told that he was dishonoring God by wearing jeans on the altar.[30]

The stories above demonstrate the need to attend to the under-examined notion of spiritual abuse of vulnerable persons, whether children or adults, in Christian Churches. Psychologist and research expert on spiritual abuse, Lisa Oakley, defines spiritual abuse as:

> a form of emotional and psychological abuse. It is characterized by a systematic pattern of coercive and controlling behavior in a religious context. Spiritual abuse can have a deeply damaging impact on those who experience it. . . . This abuse may include: manipulation and exploitation, enforced accountability, censorship of decision making, requirements

---

[29] Pastor P., "Experience-based Narrative: The Hidden Spiritual Abuse in Chinese Churches," conference paper, Spiritual Abuse: Coercive Control in Religions Conference, University of Chester, England, September 3–4, 2021.

[30] See Katie Cross, "'I Have the Power in My Body to Make People Sin': The Trauma of Purity Culture and the Concept of 'Body Theodicy,'" in Karen O'Donnell and Katie Cross, *Feminist Trauma Theologies: Body, Scripture and Church in Critical Perspective* (London: SCM Press, 2020). Cross speaks similarly of how the women of her survey recall stories of being made to feel shame because they did not exhibit enough faith.

for secrecy and silence, coercion to conform, control through the use of sacred texts or teaching, requirement of obedience to the abuser, the suggestion that the abuser has a "divine" position, isolation as a means of punishment, and superiority and elitism.[31]

Oakley further presents the ways in which censorship can be applied in spiritual abuse:

- Inability to ask questions
- Inability to disagree
- Inability to raise concerns
- Inability to discuss the topic of spiritual abuse both individually and collectively.[32]

For Oakley, the impact of spiritual abuse can lead to several questions—showcasing the extent of damage done to an individual because of this form of abuse:

- Who can I trust?
    o Can I trust myself?
    o Should I build relationships with others?
- Who am I?
- How do I cope with the fear?
- What do I believe?
    o What do I believe about God, church, faith, and the Bible?
- How long does the impact last?
- Who is there to support me?
    o Will they understand spiritual abuse?[33]

A key impact of spiritual abuse is the loss of trust in oneself and others because what one judged to be safe was proven to be, ultimately, unsafe. This leads to a reluctance to form new relationships

---

[31] Oakley and Humphrey, *Escaping the Maze of Spiritual Abuse*, 30–31.
[32] Oakley and Humphrey, 64.
[33] Oakley and Humphrey, 84.

or to be wary of new ones. Other key impacts are the reassessing of beliefs, living constantly with fear and the memory of the abuse, and the feeling of not being understood and unsupported because of the spiritual abuse.

What makes spiritual abuse a cause for concern is that people who do not present as at-risk or vulnerable persons who might even work in safeguarding roles for the church, can themselves experience spiritual abuse, as the following account shows:

> In my view the silence surrounding spiritual abuse allows it to continue. It is very difficult to challenge somebody who tells you they have the authority of God on their side. You risk appearing ungodly and uncommitted. My husband and I suffered spiritual abuse. We were not believed—we were cut off from the community that we had been part of our whole lives. Lies were told about us after we left. The level of controlling leadership was like nothing I've seen anywhere else. I have worked in safeguarding and child protection for my whole working life yet even I suffered in this way—such is the power of somebody who says they know the will of God for your life and uses threats and intimidation as a form of control.[34]

As evidenced here, establishing safety for all persons, vulnerable or not, should be a priority for churches. While it would be impossible and unreasonable to have all personnel of church institutions trained in a psychological degree specializing in abuse, the Blue Knot Foundation believes it is not unreasonable for them to be trauma-informed—an approach that focuses on the first principle of "do no harm" and which seek ways to make institutions safer for all. To apply this approach in Catholic churches, we must first explore what can make churches unsafe; that is, we must explore what makes churches vulnerable to abuses of power and consequently the abuse of individuals, whether it is in the form of sexual, physical, psychological, or spiritual abuse.

---

[34] Respondent, "Understanding Spiritual Abuse in Christian Communities," in Oakley and Humphrey, 65.

ORGANIZATIONAL CULTURE AND
ABUSE VULNERABILITY IN CHURCHES

Donald Palmer, Valerie Feldman, and Gemma McKibbin authored *Final Report: The Role of Organisational Culture in Child Sexual Abuse in Institutional Contexts* for the Royal Commission.[35] Jennifer Martin and Matthew Ricketson accurately summarized the report and argued that "the first thing their report makes clear is how little academic attention has been given to examining why institutions fail children."[36] Scanning for the number of academic literature on child abuse, Palmer, Feldman, and McKibbin found that, among forty-four-hundred articles, just forty-one, or only 1 percent, were dedicated to the investigation of "role of culture in child sexual abuse in institutional contexts."[37]

For Palmer, Feldman, and McKibbin, the formal organization as a *total institution,* using a concept from Erving Goffman,[38] was a major focus of their research report. They describe the total institution as an "'ideal type' of formal organisation that envelops its members more comprehensively than other types."[39] They list its four characteristics: first, consisting of "staff and 'inmates,'" of which there are many types, including boarding-school residents, prisoners, and children's home residents; second, "staff in total institutions exert nearly total control over all aspects of inmates' lives," "conducted within a confined physical space," and "senior staff indirectly control inmates' lives through supervisory staff"; third, staff control inmates' lives "via impersonal formalised rules and procedures"; and last, "their principal objective is the transformation of human beings."

---

[35] Donald Palmer, Valerie Feldman, and Gemma McKibbin, *Final Report: The Role of Organisational Culture in Child Sexual Abuse in Institutional Contexts* (Sydney: Commonwealth of Australia, 2016).

[36] Jennifer Martin and Matthew Ricketson, "Why Do Institutions Fail to Protect Children?" *Inside Story*, February 26, 2019.

[37] Palmer, Feldman, and McKibbin, *Final Report*, 19.

[38] Erving Goffman, "On the Characteristics of Total Institutions," in *Asylums,* 1–124 (New York: Anchor Books, 1961).

[39] Palmer, Feldman, and McKibbin, 36.

According to Goffman, "total institutions 'are forcing houses for changing persons; each is a natural experiment on what can be done to the self.'"[40] Palmer, Feldman, and McKibbin argue that it is important to examine the ways in which the culture of total institutions relates to the perpetration and detection of child sexual abuse and responses to it because "a good number of the organisations the Royal Commission investigated" are either "quintessential total institutions," or "have key attributes of the total institution ideal type," or "some of the cultural forces operating in total institutions can be found in other organisations the Royal Commission investigated that do not correspond to the total institution ideal type."[41]

The Catholic Diocese of Wollongong in case study no. 14 of the Royal Commission report was viewed by Palmer, Feldman, and McKibbin as "resembl[ing] a total institution in several respects relating to priests," not because they are physically confined but because their "lives are constrained by their role in the priesthood" and they live in almost a bubble, where their homes are on church property, their entire career is pursued within the church, their "dress and appearance, personal property, work assignments and interpersonal relationships (in particular, sexual relationships)" must fall in accordance with canon law and church doctrine.[42]

Moreover, Palmer, Feldman, and McKibbin argue the Catholic Church itself presents elements of the total institution ideal type. Using the work of Goffman (1961), Zimbardo (2010), and Haney, Banks, and Zimbardo (1973), they undertook six key points of analysis of the total institutions exhibited in the Royal Commission's *Final Report*,[43] including the Catholic Church cases. The key points are these:

---

[40] Goffman, "On the Characteristics of Total Institutions," 12.

[41] Palmer, Feldman, and McKibbin, *Final Report*, 38.

[42] Palmer, Feldman, and McKibbin, 37.

[43] Goffman, "On the Characteristics of Total Institutions"; P. G. Zimbardo, *The Lucifer Effect: Understanding How Good People Turn Evil* (New York: Random House, 2010); Haney, Banks, and Zimbardo, "Interpersonal Dynamics in a Simulated Prison"; Royal Commission, *Final Report*.

- Total institutions constitute alternative moral universes
- Total institutions employ theories of human transformation and embrace assumptions about human nature
- Total institutions extinguish their members' previous identities
- Total institutions promote secrecy
- Total institutions exhibit unique power structures
- Total institutions exhibit unique informal group dynamics.

Below, I explore the key points of analysis and apply them to my knowledge as a Catholic theologian as well as my experiences of working for the Catholic Church.[44]

The Catholic Church as Alternative Moral Universe

Palmer, Feldman, and McKibbin argue that the nature of total institutions is to have "near total control" of its members in their "alternative moral universe."[45] That is, what makes them total institutions is that "they possess an internal apparatus for labelling and responding to deviant behaviour that is independent of civil society" and they "tend to exhibit cultural content that supports and shapes the expression of the internal apparatus."[46] Given this description, Palmer, Feldman, and McKibbin argue the Catholic Church "exhibits elements of the total institution ideal type," not only in the way canon law regulates priests' behavior but also in the way that it is seen as divinely inspired.[47] I personally know of several priests and religious who consider canon law as being above civil law. The whole controversy about laws on child abuse disclosure,

---

[44] Note that what Palmer, Feldman, and McKibbin describe as "total institution" applied to the Catholic Church would for sociologist, Christie Davies, be in fact the "greedy institution," since a greedy institution requires "total commitment" while the total institution requires "total residence." See Christie Davis, "Goffman's Concept of the Total Institution: Criticisms and Revisions," *Human Studies* 12, no. 1–2 (1989): 84.

[45] Palmer, Feldman, and McKibbin, *Final Report,* 38.

[46] Palmer, Feldman, and McKibbin, 38.

[47] Palmer, Feldman, and McKibbin, 38–39.

particularly within the confessional, evidences this, and it has seen priests declare that they are prepared to go to jail rather than disclose content obtained in the confessional.[48] This is a difficult and complex matter.[49] Interestingly, Palmer, Feldman, and McKibbin did not recognize that seminaries, where priests are trained, clearly fulfill the criteria for total institutions. Thus, the ordained leaders of the church have been formed in these alternative moral universes in which their behavior and thinking are shaped by their "formators"—the staff in control of their lives and training.

Palmer, Feldman, and McKibbin also point out that churches conducted their own investigations, made their own judgments regarding the innocence or guilt of perpetrators and victims, and then executed their own consequences for the perpetrator.[50] The creation of Catholic Professional Standards Limited, the national office of safeguarding in the Catholic Church in Australia, in response to the *Final Report* of the Royal Commission, sought to foster a culture of safety for children and other vulnerable persons in churches. But considering what has been discussed, it appears as simply another "internal apparatus for labelling and responding to deviant behaviour," given that it is funded by the Australian Catholic Church and thus beholden to its funders as well as canon law.[51]

---

[48] See, for example, Stephanie Smail, "Melbourne's Catholic Archbishop vows he would go to jail rather than break the confessional seal," *PM on the ABC,* August 14, 2019; Catholic News Agency, "Australian Priests 'Willing to Go to Jail' Rather than Break Confessional Seal," *Crux: Taking the Catholic Pulse,* June 18, 2018.

[49] I discuss this in greater detail in Cristina Lledo Gomez, "The Conducive Situation in Abuse and the Catholic Church: Exploring Integral Theories of Sexual Violence and Ecclesiologies Supporting Clerical Abuse," *Buddhist-Christian Studies* 41 (2021): 127–47.

[50] Palmer, Feldman, and McKibbin, *Final Report,* 39.

[51] See Catholic Professional Standards Ltd, *National Catholic Safeguarding Standards,* ed. 1 (2019). See also Kathleen McPhillips, who similarly argues that the setting up of CPSL does not meet the Royal Commission recommendation of setting up an external body that can make the church accountable. Kathleen McPhillips, "Religion after the Royal Commission: Challenges to Religion–State Relations," *Religions* 11, no. 44 (2020): 1–13.

Altogether, these amount to the setup of an alternative moral universe by the Catholic Church, independent of civil authorities. While the very foundation of Christianity is built on promoting an alternative reality, God's kingdom, which is meant to bring good news to the poor, marginalized, vulnerable, and powerless, the systems and structures built to service this alternative reality have also enabled abuse and protected perpetrators while leaving the very people it was meant to serve vulnerable to abuse and re-traumatization. Churches must come to terms with this truth and strive to find better ways to keep all people safe. That means questioning long-held beliefs, systems, and structures, and being prepared to change them, particularly if results present the very antithesis to God's kingdom.

Catholic Churches and Human Nature and Transformation

Palmer, Feldman, and McKibbin reason that the Catholic Church resembles total institutions in that it "operates according to an elaborate system of beliefs about the fundamental nature of human beings and the ways that nature can be developed," expressed in a body of doctrine (the magisterium) and canon law.[52] They suggest that, by beginning with the premise of humanity as sinful (flawed or broken), this gives reason for human transformation. In the Catholic Church this transformation occurs mainly through participation in the sacraments, including the sacrament of reconciliation, which communicates forgiveness of any sin and consequently communicates salvation of the soul. Palmer, Feldman, and McKibbin believe that it is through sincere efforts by individuals at contrition and repentance through confession and penance that they may earn this salvation.

Palmer, Feldman, and McKibbin note further that priests have special access to this forgiveness, given their commitment to service and the celibate life. I add that, as the administrator of absolution from sin, bishops (and priests delegated with this role by bishops)

---

[52] Palmer, Feldman, and McKibbin, *Final Report*, 40.

are given a particular power that, from the penitent's perspective, puts them in the place of God. In addition, Catholic teaching states that the Eucharist contains elements for the forgiveness of sin, including the penitential rite at the introductory section of the mass, and the reception of holy communion. In celebrating the mass on their own, priests can believe themselves to have been forgiven without having to undergo the same serious processes of repentance and reparation as lay persons, especially since it can be viewed that living the celibate life is already a participation in lifelong mortification and transformation.

Nevertheless, viewing perpetration of child sexual abuse as a moral flaw that can be forgiven permits perpetrators to believe that their soul is saved even when they have committed such abuse. Additionally, given that only bishops and priests can consecrate the Eucharist, a power differential between priests and the laity is liturgically reinforced. Ultimately, the asymmetric relationship in total institutions is paralleled in the Catholic liturgical system with the minority group, priests, set up as the "gatekeepers" to the sacraments, and the majority, the laity, taught to access the sacraments for their salvation.

The Catholic Church and Total Institutions' Extinguishing of Member Identities

Palmer, Feldman, and McKibbin do not use the Catholic Church as an example of total institutions' tendency to extinguish their members' identities. In total institutions, "inmates" are isolated from anything that ties them to their previous identities, which includes family, friends, possessions, clothing, memorabilia, even locations. In contrast, the Catholic Church encourages the fostering of loving and healthy relationships with one's family and friends. It teaches unity in diversity and thus, in principle, fosters diversity and the fostering of individual identity and gifts for self and the common good.

But, if one believes that there are essentially two groups within the church—the ordained and the non-ordained (laity)—and that the ordained have the superior roles of teaching, governing, and sanctifying, then individual identity ultimately becomes unimportant. Rather, position in the church hierarchy determines how people are identified. Sadly, many priests lament that many people see them as religious authorities rather than as persons first. Inversely, many lay people with their gifts and talents, and as adults who can make their own decisions, complain of being unheard, underutilized, and infantilized because they are not part of the church hierarchy.

Infantilization in the church is the treatment of laity as infants who cannot make adult decisions for themselves and are expected to follow and not question authority. Moreover, they are not encouraged to follow their own informed consciences, to question church teachings and canon law, or to think critically about them. Meanwhile, the continued use of titles for the ordained (Reverend, Father, Bishop, Grace and Eminence) and not the laity (who can possess titles of distinction such as Dr., Professor, Captain, or Judge) in both daily and formal settings, and the use of metaphors to describe the laity as "sheep" or the "children of God" while priests are "pastors" or "fathers" who act *in persona Christi*—all are examples of clericalism used alongside infantilization of the laity.[53]

Palmer, Feldman, and McKibbin note that "the more people see others as inferior and themselves as superior, the less they feel obliged to respect the rights and needs of those others."[54] Citing David Kipnis, an expert on the social psychology of power, they state that "the possession and wielding of power can corrupt people's views of themselves and others."[55] Citing Lee-Chai, Chen, and Chartrand, they point out that research exists linking "the possession and use of power to sexual aggression."[56] It is evident that, by

---

[53] For more discussion on the infantilization of the laity, see Cristina Lledo Gomez, "From Infants to Mothers: Recovering the Call to the People of God to Become Mother Church in *Lumen Gentium*," *Ecclesiology* 11, no. 1 (Jan 2015): 32–62. Clericalism is extensively discussed by my other colleagues in this book. Thus I have refrained from this here and have not provided further references on clericalism.

[54] Palmer, Feldman, and McKibbin, *Final Report*, 44.

[55] Palmer, Feldman, and McKibbin, 44.

[56] Palmer, Feldman, and McKibbin, 44.

putting a church member essentially into one of two groups, laity or ordained, or leadership or employee, without systems to recognize, respect, and protect individual dignity, rights, and needs, the church enables those in power, the "superior" group, to justify and even deny or cover up abuse of power. Mindful that, in Zimbardo's prison experiment, good-willed and mentally healthy people can fall into roles of guard/superior/authority and prisoner/inferior/victim, the church needs to find a way to move from this tendency toward the two-tier hierarchical model of church, that lends itself to asymmetric power differential and abusive relationships.

The Catholic Church and Promoting Secrecy

Palmer, Feldman, and McKibbin point out what is commonly known about the responses of Catholic Church institutions whose authorities have abused. That is, they point out the shroud of secrecy laid upon disclosures and situations.[57] For Palmer, Feldman, and McKibbin, "total institutions tend to be opaque from the vantage point of their members and the larger society" as a way of controlling "their attitudes and behaviour," to prevent external scrutiny and accountability, and "to slow detection and impede responses to child sexual abuse."[58] But they also explain that institutions that do not exhibit the characteristics of total institutions can present as "closed systems"—thus facilitating abuse, impeding detection and undermining "an appropriate response when it occurs."[59]

The concept of the closed system is common in sociology, management theory, and organizational behavior. It derives from physics, which states "that a closed system does not involve any mass flow across its boundaries."[60] In other words, in closed systems there is no interaction between a system and its environment,

---

[57] See Royal Commission, *Final Report*.

[58] Palmer, Feldman, and McKibbin, *Final Report*, 45.

[59] Palmer, Feldman, and McKibbin, 46.

[60] Ibrahim Dincer and Yunus A. Cengel, "Energy, Entropy and Exergy Concepts and Their Roles in Thermal Engineering," *Entropy* 3, no.3 (2001): 116–49.

and thus the system is not affected by the environment and vice versa. Schools, churches, and hospitals have been labeled closed systems by researchers such as Hartill who posit that they "all offer opportunities for child abuse."[61]

In my experience of seeing psychological or spiritual abuse of those who worked in a bishop's office or curia, secrecy is used to buy victims' silence, to threaten victims and their colleagues with lawsuits if they speak to one another about the circumstances of being pushed out of their employment by a Catholic institution. Church staff are instructed to believe church leaders unreservedly over victims. No other logic or common sense is permitted into the scenario except the logic of keeping the leader, the institution, and their reputation in a position of authority, even at the cost of the dignity and rights of the employee being abused.

Secrecy can also be used regarding decision-making processes, affecting one's employment. Those affected were not consulted or prepared, for example, to receive a reduction of their salary or the termination of their job. I have seen lay persons who worked for at least a decade to build up a Catholic institution be informed that the Catholic Church no longer has any money for the work of the institution, or the institution itself is to be subsumed under another institution. In one case I know of, the head of a Catholic institution participated in a process that he thought would revamp his organization, address money concerns, and ensure its longevity. Yet, in the end, it was a facade to facilitate the termination of his employment and the organization he had helped to build up over his lifetime. Overall, in situations of abuse in the Catholic Church where secrecy is applied to employment situations, the highest priority has been about protecting dwindling funds and reputations. The trauma caused to individuals is viewed as unfortunate but nevertheless necessary collateral damage.

In resembling both total institutions or closed systems, the Catholic Church must become wary of its nontransparent or

---

[61] Hartill, in Palmer, Feldman, and McKibbin, *Final Report,* 46. See M. Hartill, "Sport and the Sexually Abused Male Child," *Sport Education and Society* 10, no. 3 (2005): 287–304.

secretive processes, which can appear harmless or taken for granted as the norm but are, in fact, fostering a culture that normalizes hiding abuse and abusers and encouraging abuses of power. While church members may currently have a heightened sensitivity toward the protection of children because of the establishment of child safety legislation, churches cannot be complacent about the harm they may be causing adults in the form of psychological or spiritual abuse and retraumatization.

The Catholic Church and Unique Power Structures

In total institutions a pyramid-like hierarchy operates in which a single superior governs subordinates, who in turn govern lower-level subordinates, requiring "subordinates to engage in or refrain from a relatively narrow range of mainly work-related behaviours."[62] The dynamic between management and staff follows the bureaucratic model of deferring to the more senior figure. In principle, this dynamic is not compatible with the nature of the church since the church teaches all are made equal in God as the *imago Dei,* but also since in Christ "there is no longer Jew or Greek, there is no longer slave or free, there is no longer male and female; for all of you are one in Christ Jesus" (Gal 3:28). No one can be made inferior to another in the church understood as the body of Christ or in God's reign.

But the church is structured in that similar pyramid hierarchy as the total institution (pope—bishop—priest—deacon—laity). Theologies of ministry, of the church, and of the people of God might explain that those on the lower and wider end of the pyramid are not subordinates but rather are equals through their baptism with different roles in the church, just as the hands and feet perform different roles in the body, as in 1 Corinthians 12:12–20. Yet in practice, the two-tier system that separates the ordained and the laity operates in churches. The voice of the ordained carries greater

---

[62] Palmer, Feldman, and McKibbin, *Final Report,* 47.

weight in the church than that of lay persons, including in crucial decision-making matters for the community.

A further point of consideration is the role of obedience in total institutions. "The norm of obedience to authority tends to be very strong in total institutions. Further, the rewards allocated tend to be minimal and the punishments dispensed tend to be severe in such contexts."[63] In the Catholic Church obedience to authority is a promise or vow undertaken alongside the vow of celibacy at ordination. In *Pastores Dabo Vobis (On the Formation of Priests in the Circumstances of the Present Day)*, a post-synodal exhortation written in 1992, John Paul II describes obedience in the priestly life:

> There can be no genuine priestly ministry except in communion with the supreme pontiff and the episcopal college, especially with one's own diocesan bishop, who deserves that "filial respect and obedience" promised during the rite of ordination. (no. 28)

The parent-child relationship encouraged here is a cause of concern because of its resemblance to asymmetric relationships in total institutions. However, John Paul II appears to suggest correctives so that obedience is not misused for abuse. The priest's obedience must be seen as assisting him to "exercise in accordance with the Gospel the authority entrusted to him for his work with the People of God: an authority free from authoritarianism or demagoguery." Further, "it is not the obedience of an individual who alone relates to authority, but rather an obedience which is deeply a part of the unity of the presbyterate" (no. 28).

As the priests are "children" to their bishops, so are the laity to the priests in *Pastores Dabo Vobis*:

> The priest must live and give witness to his profound communion with all. As Pope Paul VI wrote: "We must become brothers to all at the very same time as we wish to be their

---

[63] Palmer, Feldman, and McKibbin, 47.

shepherds, fathers and teachers. The climate of dialogue is
friendship. Indeed, it is service." (no. 74)

Several underlying questions regarding these principles on obedience are important to pose: What structures are put in place in the
Catholic institution to ensure that the parent-child relationship is
not an opportunity for abuse? Is the promotion of parent-child
relationship between the ordained and the laity healthy? Are there
better metaphors to view the relationship, given we already know
asymmetric relationships without accountability are the basis for
the abuse of power and abuse of individuals?

In contrast, Catholic teaching on the authority of the informed
conscience says one's conscience can override any other authority
figure or text. In practice, the informed conscience is an under-
emphasized and underutilized teaching in the Catholic Church.
It is the ultimate law that trumps all other Catholic teaching,
even if the dictates of one's conscience run contrary to church
teaching. *Dignitatis Humanae* (1965) explains that "a man . . .
is not to be forced to act in a manner contrary to his conscience.
Nor . . . is he to be restrained from acting in accordance with
his conscience, especially in matters religious" (no. 3).[64] Here I
highlight the neglect of Catholic authority figures to teach or
highlight the authority of an informed conscience. Without the
development of this ability and with the promotion of absolute
obedience to authority in churches, it becomes the norm to listen
to church authority rather than one's own conscience. The result
is relegation of responsibility to an authority figure on important
decisions that can affect fellow human beings. Like Milgram's
experiment and Eichmann's defense, people can close their eyes
to abuse as they place their trust in superiors who they believe
are in control. The authority of men in white coats is here paralleled by the men in clerical vestments. Without structures put in
place to reinforce that all are the *imago Dei* and equal in dignity
and respect to one another, dangerous asymmetric relationships

---

[64] See also Paul VI, *Gaudium et Spes* (1965).

are reinforced through clericalism and infantilization of the laity, leading to cultures of abuse of power found in total institutions.

Unique Informal Group Dynamics in the Catholic Church

A total institution's unique informal group dynamics could be summarized in the mentality of an "us and them." Palmer, Feldman, and McKibbin state that group members of total institutions create this essentialist binary relationship by forming "negative stereotypes of outsiders."[65] They also distinguish themselves from outsiders by creating a separate ethic of behavior and thinking and then enforcing them as norms through "sanctions that range in severity from subtle cues and verbal recriminations to physical harm."[66] At the end of the day, "support [of] fellow group members, especially from attacks by non-group members," becomes the highest priority for the group, over any other priority or value.[67]

A chilling feature of group dynamics in total institutions is "the 'denial of victim' technique of neutralisation" explained below:

> The cultural milieu in which staff members in total institutions are immersed tends to feature the "denial of victim" technique of neutralisation. In this milieu, inmates are viewed as not deserving of ethical treatment and, perhaps, as deserving of unethical treatment. This technique of neutralisation immunises staff members from the guilt they may otherwise experience after abusing a child or young person, failing to report a fellow staff member's abuse or failing to respond to disclosures of abuse.[68]

---

[65] Palmer, Feldman, and McKibbin, *Final Report*, 49.

[66] Palmer, Feldman, and McKibbin, 49.

[67] Palmer, Feldman, and McKibbin, 49.

[68] Palmer, Feldman, and McKibbin, 49.

Overall, in total institutions, staff members tend "to view inmates in stereotypically negative ways—in particular as morally inferior," creating a culture that facilitates perpetration, impedes detection of abuse, and undermines responses to abuse.[69]

Given the view of "inmates" in total institutions as inferior, they are not believed by staff and are seen as "untrustworthy and possibly vindictive."[70] In conjunction, inmates neither trust staff nor their concern for the inmates' well-being. Thus, abuse by of inmates by staff tends to be unreported by victims. If the abuse was caused by a peer, inmates also do not report because of the obligation to "support their peers."[71] Further, peers who observe another peer abusing one of their own also do not report the observed abuse for fear of "castigation by fellow inmates."[72] Furthermore, Palmer, Feldman, and McKibbin describe the propensity of the abused child in total institutions to become child abusers themselves in "extreme circumstances" due to the nature of informal group dynamics in total institutions. That is, "informal groups develop norms that group members, especially group leaders, enforce."[73]

In the Catholic Church these concerning features of unique informal group dynamics of total institutions can be seen when clericalism and infantilization of the laity dominate. While the foundation of the church was built upon an "us and them" mentality captured in the infamous phrase by the early church fathers—*extra ecclesiam nulla salus* (outside the church, there is no salvation)—this is no longer the church's stance.[74] As Vatican II's *Gaudium et Spes* suggests in its famous opening sentence, there is no longer an "us and them" mentality between the church and the world:

---

[69] Palmer, Feldman, and McKibbin, 49.

[70] Palmer, Feldman, and McKibbin, 49.

[71] Palmer, Feldman, and McKibbin, 50.

[72] Palmer, Feldman, and McKibbin, 50.

[73] Palmer, Feldman, and McKibbin, 50.

[74] On the early church fathers, see Cristina Lledo Gomez, *The Church as Woman and Mother: Historical and Theological Foundations* (Mahwah, NJ: Paulist Press, 2018).

The joys and the hopes, the griefs and the anxieties of the men of this age, especially those who are poor or in any way afflicted, these are the joys and hopes, the griefs and anxieties of the followers of Christ. (no. 1)

CONCLUSION: FROM ABUSE-VULNERABLE TO TRAUMA-INFORMED CHURCHES

Psychological research has clearly demonstrated the power of social pressure in compelling conformity (Solomon Asch), obedience to authority figures (Stanley Milgram), and the power of roles to shape abusive behavior in institutions (Phillip Zimbardo). Sociology builds upon these insights with models of the total institution and the closed system. While Catholic Church institutions are not total institutions—people are free to enter or leave church spaces and not every aspect of their lives are controlled by those in leadership—many features of church institutions resemble features of total institutions. A way forward for churches is to understand what systems, mindsets, and practices create a culture of abuse in organizations. If churches claim to be serious about safeguarding children, then the pursuit of safeguarding must be broadened to include all people—not only because we cannot know who in the community is experiencing CPTSD, but also because the structures, thinking, and practices that enabled child abuse can remain and abuse would simply be expressed in forms other than the sexual abuse of minors, that is, expressed in the form of psychological or, more particularly, spiritual abuse.

For the Blue Knot Foundation, a way to help trauma survivors is to become best-practice trauma aware organizations, where the personnel of the institution use five key principles: (1) establishing safety first and foremost by personnel within the organization but also in the physical spaces of institutions; (2) promoting trustworthy practices among all people in the organization; (3) providing choice especially to the traumatized person; (4) using collaboration to find solutions and ways forward; and finally (5) instead of rescuing or worse, being paternalistic, finding ways to empower traumatized persons, which is vital to their processes of healing. In short, the principles of a trauma-informed approach are safety, trust, choice, collaboration, and empowerment.

Most notable about these five principles from an Australian Catholic theological point of view is not only their alignment with the submissions sent in by Australian church communities to the 2020–22 plenary council. These principles of a trauma-informed approach also align with the idea of a synodal church, as promoted by Pope Francis—a welcoming, inclusive, healing-focused, "field hospital" type of church. There is no room to explore these associations in this chapter. Suffice it to say that theology and the sociology and psychology of organizational behaviors can help Catholic churches to move from being abuse-vulnerable to safe, trauma-informed churches. In applying the Blue Knot Foundation's checklist for trauma-informed care and practice for organizations, the Catholic Church appears not to come close to being trauma-informed in its care and practices for its people, even though many people in the church are good-willed and have good intentions. The Catholic Church has a long way to go toward being safe. The test of integrity for those who claim to be committed to safeguarding in the church will be the commitment to reexamining long-held beliefs, practices, and what is taken for granted as the norm; being prepared to take responsibility for change; and accepting that there will be personal and communal costs to this journey.

5.

Visions of Survivor Healing and Empowerment in Response to Trauma

Scott R. A. Starbuck

Survivors of ecclesial sexual violence may reach for tangible anchors for accompaniment and hope within religious traditions when their trust in leadership and church structure have been betrayed. In the context of healing and pastoral care, it is important for survivors and surviving communities to have the depth and specificity of the scriptural witness available as a possible anchor that embraces survivors and holds perpetrators and complicit systems accountable. Key scriptural passages are well suited to provide both accompaniment and hope since survivors and surviving communities may find some experiential continuity with the compositional community of the text. Increasingly, scholars recognize that postexilic generations that gathered and organized the burgeoning scriptural text did so in response to generational trauma. Survivors of the two-year siege of Jerusalem (587–586 BCE), exile to Babylon, and eventual return to a destroyed and devastated Judah (538–515 BCE) undoubtedly carried deep shame and other trauma reactions like the lack of dignity, objectification, and exploitation associated with war and displacement.

This chapter views two key passages from the Book of Isaiah (55:1–13 and 61:1–11) that offer visions of healing that support

117

individual action and self-agency (reclaiming power, choice, and an ability to engage for others) for the post-traumatic. These biblical texts demonstrate that the healing of trauma depends upon lay empowerment and a new or recovered sense of personal agency sourced by the will and work of God. At the same time, these prophetic texts stand as a dire warning to any form of clericalism that curtails or is unwelcoming to the agency, empowerment, and healing of persons. These crucial biblical voices may help victims of clergy abuse find their own empowerment, dignity, healing, and hope in their relationship with God.

PASTORAL CONTEXT

In her pastoral reflections on trauma and healing within church contexts, Deborah van Deusen Hunsiger observes, "When human trust has eluded them, the traumatized desperately need an anchor, a point of reference, something reliable in which to place their trust."[1] This chapter explores two anchors in the scriptural text that may prove helpful to survivors of clergy sexual abuse as they eventually turn to the excruciatingly difficult and complex task of reconstituting their faith.[2] Although the exegetical content of this chapter emerges from the results of traditional biblical scholarship, its intention is pastoral. The chapter hopes to support theologically, pastorally, and psychologically the spiritual agency of survivors by drawing attention to key theological movements

---

[1] Deborah van Deusen Hunsinger, *Bearing the Unbearable: Trauma, Gospel, and Pastoral Care* (Grand Rapids, MI: Eerdmans, 2015), 16.

[2] If trauma recovery might be generalized as encompassing three stages (the establishment of safety, remembrance and mourning, and then eventually reconnection with ordinary life), the reconstitution of faith, though likely an issue of crisis in each stage, is most appropriate to the third stage of recovery. Lament, also thoroughly supported by the biblical text, will likely be helpful in the second stage of recovery. For the three general stages, see Judith L. Herman, "Recovery from Psychological Trauma," *Psychiatry and Clinical Neurosciences* 52 Suppl. (1998): 145–50.

in the prophetic corpus that seek to preserve the individual and the community by envisioning a healing alternative to clergy-centered spirituality.

A crucial pastoral step toward healing in a post-traumatic church is privileging the heart of God for God's people rather than protecting or exonerating ecclesial structures that have been complicit in abuse. Although this should be obvious morally, it is essential in terms of the pastoral call to participate with the traumatized in their healing. Theological critique is necessary because "trauma destroys the social systems of care, protection, and meaning that support human life"[3] and because "the recovery process requires the reconstruction of these systems."[4] It is with survivors of trauma, not the institutions and structures themselves, that redemptive and reconstructive healing is eventually fueled. It is important for those accompanying to understand that the biblical texts not only support this task but privilege it.

PROPHETIC CRITIQUE

Far from being a modern secular critique of a "holy" structure, the biblical texts are replete with prophetic critique of the very structures that might commonly hold a validation of divine sponsorship (temple, priest, king, sacrifice, prayer).[5] The prophet Jeremiah exposes God's deep love for his common people by expressing divine rage over the sanctioned leaders and assumed holy structures of the Judean Temple:

> Woe to the shepherds who destroy and scatter the sheep of my pasture!" says the LORD. Therefore thus says the LORD, the God of Israel, concerning the shepherds who shepherd my people: It is you who have scattered my flock, and have

---

[3] Herman, 145.

[4] Herman, 145.

[5] For example, Isaiah 3:12, "O my people, your leaders mislead you, and confuse the course of your paths."

driven them away, and you have not attended to them. So I
will attend to you for your evil doings, says the Lord. Then
I myself will gather the remnant of my flock out of all the
lands where I have driven them, and I will bring them back
to their fold, and they shall be fruitful and multiply. I will
raise up shepherds over them who will shepherd them, and
they shall not fear any longer, or be dismayed, nor shall any
be missing, says the Lord. (Jer 23:1–4)[6]

In this passage the "shepherds" are those among the Judean royal-
priestly elite who exploit the people under royal rule, or in our
terms, the laity under their charge.[7] Through the prophet Jeremiah
God confronts them, promises to hold them accountable, and
promises to intervene on behalf of victims to restore their broken
lives as well as to provide new leadership—new shepherds—so
that the victims no longer fear or suffer cognitively or relationally.
In other words, Jeremiah promises thoroughgoing divine healing
for the victims of traumatic exploitation.

In Jeremiah's mind new shepherds will occupy the traditional
structures of religious authority. In fact, the very next verses look
forward to a new Davidic king who will bring renewal and healing righteousness.[8]

---

[6] Unless otherwise indicated, all biblical translations are taken from the
NRSV. This passage is assigned in the lectionary to Proper 11B/Ordinary
16B/Pentecost 9.

[7] Jack R. Lundbom, *Jeremiah 21–36: A New Translation with Intro-
duction and Commentary*, vol. 21B, Anchor Yale Bible (New Haven,
CT: Yale University Press, 2008), 167; and Karen C. Sapio, "Exegetical
Perspective on Jeremiah 23:1–6," in *Feasting on the Word: Preaching the
Revised Common Lectionary: Year B*, ed. David L. Bartlett and Barbara
Brown Taylor, vol. 3 (Louisville: Westminster John Knox Press, 2009),
3245; and F. B. Huey, *Jeremiah, Lamentations*, vol. 16, The New American
Commentary (Nashville: Broadman and Holman Publishers, 1993), 210.

[8] See Walter Brueggemann, *A Commentary on Jeremiah: Exile and
Homecoming* (Grand Rapids, MI; Eerdmans, 1998), 207; and Leslie C.
Allen, *Jeremiah: A Commentary*, ed. William P. Brown, Carol A. Newsom,
and David L. Petersen, The Old Testament Library (Louisville: Westminster John Knox Press, 2008), 259.

> The days are surely coming, says the LORD, when I will raise
> up for David a righteous Branch, and he shall reign as king
> and deal wisely, and shall execute justice and righteousness
> in the land. In his days Judah will be saved and Israel will
> live in safety. And this is the name by which he will be called:
> "The Lord is our righteousness." (Jer 23:5–6)

Yet this hope never materialized.[9] Judah will never again see a
Davidic king reign over them. This hope that was still possible in
Jeremiah's time proved itself to be, at a minimum, unworkable
because of the Babylonian exile and following period of Persian
restoration. Where it was theoretically and theologically possible
that a new David within essentially old theology and structures
could bring righteousness and healing from a practical standpoint,
realistically the royal-priestly structure had to give way for a new
form of healing and right relationship with God and one another.

The twin observations that the most straightforward reading
of Jeremiah 23:5–6 created irresolvable cognitive dissonance and
that the old hierarchical structures of priest and king historically
necessitated new forms of divine-human organization and connection are pastorally significant in our present context. Despite a
theoretical hope that survivors of clergy abuse might heal within
the very structures that were either silent before or complicit in
their abuse, it is most often that victims will need to, understandably, abandon these particular places and structures to heal fully
as well as to participate in the justice and right relationship God
offers. Jennifer Beste speaks to this powerfully:

> The vast majority of clergy abuse survivors also report that
> such abuse severely debilitated or destroyed their faith and
> trust in God and/or their Church; many experience a complete

---

[9] J. J. M. Roberts, "The Old Testament's Contribution to Messianic Expectations," in *The First Princeton Symposium on Judaism and Christian
Origins: The Messiah*, Developments in Earliest Judaism and Christianity, ed. James Hamilton Charlesworth and J. Brownson (Minneapolis:
Fortress Press, 1992), 49.

loss of spiritual sustenance, comfort, and support. Many survivors express anger, a sense of betrayal and an inability to forgive God for allowing the sexual abuse. The vast majority of clergy abuse survivors report that such abuse severely debilitated or destroyed their faith and trust in God and/or their Church. These clergy abuse victims often have no one to help them work through these fears because the prospect of talking to a priest, entering a Catholic Church, receiving Communion or the Sacrament of Reconciliation evokes too much anxiety and fear. Thus, most survivors are deprived of key sources of experiencing God's grace—the Church community, Mass, and sacraments—because these sources are inextricably linked to the very source of their victimization.[10]

Understandably, even if the perpetrators of abuse have been removed, the place(s) of abuse, the ecclesial structures, and even the form of clergy-led spirituality can be triggering and re-traumatizing. Survivors can experience significant cognitive dissonance: how did the structures that promised loving connection between divine and human become a place of violence, betrayal, exploitation, and dehumanizing? In the first stage of the healing of trauma, establishing the safety of survivors is of paramount importance, and so removal from, anger toward, and critique of traditional leadership and ecclesial structure are both appropriate and redemptively necessary. Often the twin paths of healing and spiritual development will need to step outside of the ecclesial norm structurally and theologically. Exploring new modalities will help to avoid re-traumatization and may facilitate a survivor's integrated experience of living more deeply into an owned and self-embodied relationship with God.

---

[10] Jennifer Beste, "Mediating God's Grace within the Context of Trauma: Implications for a Christian Response to Clergy Sexual Abuse," *Review and Expositor* 105 (Spring 2008): 248–49. See also Kerry Fater and Jo Ann Mullaney, "The Lived Experience of Adult Male Survivors Who Allege Childhood Sexual Abuse by Clergy," *Issues in Mental Health Nursing* 221, no. 3 (2000): 290.

It is vitally important for abuse victims, those supporting them, and our communities of faith to know that stepping outside a modern or even traditional ecclesial norm is not stepping outside a biblically validated path. In fact, in one of the most heavily referenced sections of the Old Testament text in the New Testament, Isaiah 40—66, the ecclesial vision of the prophetic collection fully supports the survivor's need for self-agency and a revisioning of sacral leadership structures that reduce "othering" and shaming.

ISAIAH 40—66

The Book of Isaiah was written, collected, and compiled over many years. Some of the material is authentic to the eighth-century prophet, Isaiah of Jerusalem. Since this prophet also had disciples who recorded his prophetic oracles, most scholars view the entire Book of Isaiah as a multigenerational work that was not completed until, at the earliest, the sixth century BCE.[11] This means that the various oracles now found in the Book of Isaiah represent the thought of an Isaianic tradition that eventually produced a scroll for study and engagement among the literate in Jerusalem during the Persian Restoration. Oracles found in chapters 40—66 date to either the period of the Babylonian exile (587–538 BCE) or to the Persian Restoration (538–333 BCE).[12] The book, however, first functioned as a scriptural text in a period when the survivors of the exile struggled to find a way forward in life and faith. Would they rebuild the old known structures supported by old theological beliefs, such as those espoused by Jeremiah? Or might God be opening new paths for healing and agency requiring new forms and revised theology?

---

[11] See Robert A. Kugler and P. J. Hartin, *An Introduction to the Bible* (Grand Rapids, MI: Eerdmans, 2009), 14–15.

[12] Raymond E. Brown, Joseph A. Fitzmyer, and Roland E. Murphy, *The New Jerome Biblical Commentary* (London: New Bloomsbury, 2014), 280, 329–30.

Since the Book of Isaiah first functioned as scripture in the period of the Persian Restoration, and because most of Isaiah 40—66 dates either to the exile or the restoration, it is appropriate to situate this content within the genre of trauma literature. It was a literature that "appropriated with communal contexts as a means of shaping collective identity, particularly in relations to disasters that may have fragmented the community."[13] The precipitating disaster was the Babylonian annihilation of the nation of Judah. Kathleen O'Connor explains that the Babylonians "deported leadership, destroyed much of the capital city of Jerusalem, removed the king, burned down the temple, undermined the economy, and occupied the land."[14] Not only did these actions bring death and physical destruction, but previously stable theological foundations and structures proved impotent when confronted by Babylonian coercive power. As victims of hegemonic violence, the survivors lived with lingering effects including the loss of "faith and trust in institutions, traditions, and in God. After disaster beliefs that once supported life breakdown in a vacuum devoid of meaning."[15] While the precipitating violence traumatizing the community was forced migration and not religious abuse as defined in modern contexts, the theological resources that emerged from the multifaceted trauma of the Babylonian exile offer potential spiritual anchors and divine hope.

ISAIAH 55:1–13

Survivors may be familiar with this text from the Book of Isaiah because it occurs in the Roman Catholic lectionary on several

---

[13] Christopher G. Frechette and Elizabeth Boase, "Defining 'Trauma' as a Useful Lens for Biblical Interpretation," in *Bible through the Lens of Trauma*, ed. Elizabeth Boase and Christopher G. Frechette (Atlanta: SBL Press, 2016), 15.

[14] Kathleen M. O'Connor, *Genesis 1–25A* (Macon, GA: Smyth and Helwys, 2018), 5.

[15] Kathleen O'Connor, "How Trauma Studies Can Contribute to Old Testament Studies," in *Trauma and Traumatization in Individual and Collective Dimensions: Insights from Biblical Studies and Beyond*, ed. Eve-Marie Becker, Jan Dochhorn, and Else K. Hold (Gottingen: Vandenhoeck and Ruprecht, 2014), 213.

Sundays and holy days.[16] At first glance Isaiah 55:1–5 appears to invite the exilic community, which is poor, metaphorically parched, and distraught,[17] to a deep sustaining water source: "Hear, everyone who thirsts, come to the waters." One might even recall a dialogue between Jesus and the Samaritan woman in which Jesus offers "a spring of water gushing up to eternal life" (Jn 4:14) and suspect that the invitation is for more than hydration. Indeed, the Isaian text continues by shifting in a surprising direction:

> and you that have no money,
>   come, *buy* and eat!
> Come, *buy* wine and milk
>   without money and without price.
>   (Isa 55:1, emphasis added)

On a literal level, the text seems impossible: how does anyone buy anything without money and without a set price? This incongruity, however, is key for understanding the promise of this passage to be given not only to a desperately poor community, but to a traumatized community that needs more than a handout, more than charity.[18] It must find its own agency and self-direction. Even without money it must buy for itself without cost: survivors must discover agency.

In fact, personal agency is the interpretive key to the entire passage. Not only are exilic survivors commanded to come and buy, but they are also commanded to listen, eat, and delight because God is giving them, the post-traumatic community, something they could have never anticipated or hoped for.

---

[16] Proper 10A / Ordinary 15 A, Proper 13A / Ordinary 18A, Proper 20A / Ordinary 25A, Baptism B, and Easter Vigil ABC.

[17] "An unusual invitation is extended. The list of those to be included is not limited to people of social standing, not even to people of sufficient means to come properly attired." Paul D. Hanson, *Isaiah 40—66*, Interpretation, a Bible Commentary for Teaching and Preaching (Louisville: John Knox Press, 1995), 177.

[18] See John N. Sheveland, "Without Price," *The Expository Times* 131, no. 10 (2020): 447–48.

Listen carefully to me, and eat what is good,
   and delight yourselves in rich food.
Incline your ear, and come to me;
   listen, so that you may live.
I will make with you *an everlasting covenant,*
   my steadfast, sure love for David.
                (Isa 55:2–3, emphasis added)

Through the prophetic voice of Isaiah 55, God invites the post-traumatic community—the beleaguered, dislocated, and poor—to enter an everlasting covenant.[19] This is not a newly minted covenant. Rather, it was originally given to none other than King David in 2 Samuel 7. The covenant of leadership and divine blessing that was given to David and his descendants, the long line of kings of Judah, is now being transferred to the post-traumatic community itself. Although this is a gift of grace, it is better understood as a gift of empowerment and accompaniment. The covenantal work that the descendants of David were to do but failed to do (and because of that failure the post-traumatic community suffered due to their neglect, incompetence, selfishness, and false piety), the survivors of the exile are now invited to claim and are empowered to accomplish:

See, I made him a witness to the peoples,
   a leader and commander for the peoples.
See, you shall call nations that you do not know,
   and nations that do not know you shall run to you,
because of the Lord your God, the Holy One of Israel,
   for he has glorified you.

God "glorifies" (the meaning in Hebrew is "invests divine weightiness in") the post-traumatic community. The old structures and

---

[19] For a discussion of the communalization of the royal office in Isaiah 55 and the royal psalms, see Scott R. A. Starbuck, "Theological Anthropology at a Fulcrum: Isaiah 55:1–5, Psalm 89, and Second Stage Traditio in the Royal Psalms, in *David and Zion: Biblical Studies in Honor of J. J. M. Roberts,* ed. Bernard F. Batto, Kathryn L. Roberts, and J. J. M. Roberts (Winona Lake, IN: Eisenbrauns, 2004), 247–65.

old leaders will no longer be the sole locus of God's truth, grace, redemption, and glory. These divine attributes are not to be embodied in a better and more trustworthy hierarchical kingship but in the authenticity of a living, healing, empowering, justice-centered, healing-directed relationship between God and the post-traumatic community, and through them extended to the entire world.

This deep theological movement will strike readers as counterintuitive. Rather than restoring the old religious structures so that they become trustworthy and competent, God moves in a completely new, nonhierarchical communalized direction. In other words, the prophet's message is that betrayal and abuse were not at the hands of a "few bad apples," but that God will honor and redeem the experience of the exiled and abused to forge a new and better justice-oriented human/divine connection. Survivors who have been accustomed to believing that God's grace and purpose are forever wedded to the hierarchical structure of the church may miss the radical vision of the prophet.

Even within the scriptural text, resistance and opposition toward the prophetic revisions are anticipated, and so the divine voice doubles down and makes clear:

> For my thoughts are not your thoughts,
>   nor are your ways my ways, says the LORD.
> For as the heavens are higher than the earth,
>   so are my ways higher than your ways
>   and my thoughts than your thoughts. (Isa 5:8–9)

Pastorally, Isaiah 55:1–13 opens a vision for healing and empowerment through the discovery of divine invitation, self-agency, and shared blessing for survivors of self-shattering trauma. Rather than blaming the victim or minimizing trauma, the prophetic text puts forth a vision that God will work alongside the traumatized and they do not have to await the emergence of a future "good shepherd" or structural cleansing. They are themselves enough. They, along with other survivors, are invited to a covenantal banquet. This banquet signals covenant making from God that is eternally valid and freely given. The covenant is made between God and each survivor, at least the survivors who take up the invitation. God's deep and wonderful purposes will be accomplished through covenantal partnership of the entire called post-traumatic community and God.

In other words, this passage offers a radically healing and empowering picture of the new organization through which God will work. Paul Hanson says it well:

> In the name of the same God who invited *all* to the banquet, Second Isaiah announced that God's plan had not been defeated by the ruin of the royal house of David but rather that the everlasting covenant was now to be expanded beyond the privileged elite to embrace the entire community of those obedient to God's word. The connection with the Servant Songs is evident here, for the covenant people "shall call nations that you do not know" (55:5a). The vocation of being "a witness to the peoples" assigned to David would now pass to the entire community of those faithful to God.[20]

Indeed, the vision of a gathered community of survivors blessed, empowered, and sustained by God can be useful pastorally in several ways.

For example, the work of D. S. Martsolf and J. R. Mickley suggests that the spiritual dimension of healing in general can be observed through five key attributes:

1. Meaning - the ontological significance of life; making sense of life situations; deriving purpose in existence.

2. Value - beliefs and standards that are cherished; having to do with the truth, beauty, worth of a thought, object, or behavior; often discussed as "ultimate values."

3. Transcendence - experience and appreciation of a dimension beyond the self; expanding self-boundaries.

4. Connecting - relationships with self, others, God/Higher Power, and the environment.

---

[20] Hanson, *Isaiah 40—66*, 179.

5. Becoming - an unfolding of life that demands reflection and experience; includes a sense of who one is and how one knows among other things.[21]

Utilizing the above rubric, researchers discovered that the most salient attribute for survivors of childhood sexual abuse was *connecting* rather than value or transcendence. "Among the aspects of connecting that were important to survivors of sexual violence were: (a) getting together with others in settings that were seen to be spiritual in nature, (b) connecting to others in very deep and spiritual ways, and (c) connecting with God."[22] Spiritual support groups and participation in shared leadership groups like Alcoholics Anonymous and other twelve-step programs were of particular significance.

Often clergy receive praise for content delivery in terms of meaning and value and are expected to be facilitators of transcendence or guides of becoming. Yet for survivors of sexual abuse, unmediated connecting with God and others is the primary conduit of spiritual nurture. This fits the poetry of Isaiah 55:1–5, in which theological content is invitational ("come to the waters . . . come, buy and eat!"), rigorously honest ("everyone who thirsts . . . you that have no money . . . Why do you spend your money for that which is not bread, and your labor for that which does not satisfy?"), upholds deep health and recovery ("eat what is good . . . delight yourselves in rich food . . . so that you may live"), and communalized ("I will make with you [plural] an everlasting covenant"). In other words, the way forward in and beyond the Babylonian exile necessitated a shift from hierarchical performative leadership to communalized shared leadership, and specifically shared leadership emerging from post-traumatic survivors.

---

[21] D. S. Martsolf and J. R. Mickley, "The Concept of Spirituality in Nursing Theories: Differing World-Views and Extent of Focus," *Journal of Advanced Nursing* 27 (1998): 294–95.

[22] Gregory Knapik, Donna S. Martsolf, Claire Draucker, Karen D. Strickland, "Attributes of Spirituality Described by Survivors of Sexual Violence," *The Qualitative Report* 15, no. 3 (2010): 652.

That is, to use Martsolf and Mickley's categories, *meaning, value, transcendence,* and *becoming* would be discovered through *connecting* to members of the community and connecting unmediated to God, not through the hierarchy of the Temple.

There is strong scriptural support, then, for the healing and engagement away from traditional structures, especially structures that may privilege meaning, value, and transcendence over healthy and healing connection. If one is to take the prophetic text seriously, communalized structures of healing, agency, and empowerment are, in fact, *the chosen structures* through which God will also facilitate meaning, value, transcendence, and becoming. Is that not precisely illustrated in the life and teachings of Jesus of Nazareth? This being the case, any ecclesial structure and leadership that might be open to such prophetic biblical transformation would be imbued with deeper meaning and more effective ministry. Yet primarily, Isaiah 55:1–13 stands with and for survivors of clergy sexual abuse by inviting all survivors and all who will stand with survivors into honest, healthy, responsible, and transformative community unmediated by hierarchical structure, wherever it might be found.

ISAIAH 61:1–11

Whereas Isaiah 55:1–13 transforms and communalizes the royal covenant, Isaiah 61:1–11 expands the biblical conception of priesthood to be embodied by the same community invited to the royal covenantal feast. This passage falls on Advent 3B in the lectionary and may be familiar. However, it might also be overshadowed with the gospel reading for the day, Luke 1:39–56, also known as the Magnificat. Rather than the full text of Isaiah 61:1–11, selected verses are read:

> The spirit of the Lord GOD is upon me,
>   because the LORD has anointed me;
> he has sent me to bring good news to the oppressed,
>   to bind up the brokenhearted,

to proclaim liberty to the captives,
    and release to the prisoners,
to proclaim the year of the LORD's favor,
    and the day of vengeance of our God,
    to comfort all who mourn.

. . . .

I will greatly rejoice in the LORD,
    my whole being shall exult in my God;
for he has *clothed me with the garments of salvation,*
    he has *covered me with the robe of righteousness,*
as a bridegroom decks himself with a garland,
    and as a bride adorns herself with her jewels.
For as the earth brings forth its shoots
    and as a garden causes what is sown in it to
    spring up,
so the Lord GOD will cause righteousness and praise
    to spring up before all the nations. (Isa 61:1–2,
       10–11, emphasis added)

Occurring in Advent and read in anticipation of the birth of Jesus Christ, it would be easy for a worshiping community to miss a post-traumatic historical and contextual reading of the text. So too, the theological force suggested by the metaphorical clothing of a post-traumatic surviving community with the garments of salvation and the robe of righteousness is blunted by the lectionary's selective inclusion of only verses 1–2 and 10–11 in the lectionary passage.[23]

Critical content for understanding the passage occurs in verse 6a: "You [plural] shall be called priests of the LORD, you [plural] shall be named ministers of our God." In this verse a collective group receives the divine commission to be called priests and

----

[23] For an exegetical treatment of the clothing metaphor, see Scott R. A. Starbuck, "Disrobing an Isaianic Metaphor (Robe of Righteousness) as Power Transfer in Isaiah 61:10," in *Dress and Clothing in the Hebrew Bible: "For All Her Household Are Clothed in Crimson,"* ed. Antonios Finitsis (London: Bloomsbury, 2019), 143–59.

named ministers. Who is this collective group? Within Isaiah 40—66 it is the same community that is invited to the royal feast and given the eternal royal covenant in Isaiah 55. It comprises the oppressed, the brokenhearted, those freed from captivity and released from prison (v. 1). In verses 10–11, one reads the expressed joy of one such member from that collective group. The voice cries out with rejoicing and exultation because he has been metaphorically clothed with the garments of salvation (priestly garb) and covered with the robe of righteousness (v. 10). Similar to the everlasting covenant offered to the post-traumatic survivors in Isaiah 55:3, in verse 8 God extends another everlasting covenant. Although this covenant shares similarities with the royal transfer from king to the post-traumatic community, here it is extended to include not only the royal hierarchy but also that of the priests.

In Isaiah 61 the shift in religious structure and personnel from the hierarchical models of king and priest to the communalized model of nonhierarchical relationship emerges from divine concerns for justice: "For I the LORD love justice, I hate robbery and wrongdoing; I will faithfully give them their recompense, and I will make an everlasting covenant with them" (v. 8). Significantly, the postexilic community had suffered injustice from many powers—previous Judean rulers and priests, their Babylonian overlords, and even from Jewish leaders sponsored by the Persians who worked for restoration in Jerusalem along Persian transactional models. All these experiences were traumatizing. The way forward, signaled by the text, is for the post-traumatic community to claim agency and serve in priestly capacities themselves, though clearly not in the sense of fulfilling the old sacrificial temple structures.[24]

---

[24] See Isaiah 66:1–4. Paul D. Hanson offers these helpful comments on the passage: "What, then, is the proper objective of worship? The second half of verse 2 answers this question. What God seeks is a *relationship* with human beings, an honest and open relationship free of deception and manipulation. Thus the person receptive to God's initiative is one characterized by a pure heart and a deep longing for guidance and communion: But this is the one to whom I will look, to the humble and contrite in spirit, who trembles at my word." Hanson, *Isaiah*, 249–50.

Instead, they are to be empowered with metaphorical priestly garments, signaling covenantal relationship rather than sacral efficacy, as with the attire of a bridegroom and bride (v. 10).

The text itself remains open about what a priestly covenant might entail. It is not clearly defined, other than the post-traumatic surviving community is blessed with it and equipped for it. Given the relational and restorative imagery in the text, this poetry opens connective applications similar to Isaiah 55:1–5. According to Paul Hanson, "While false prophets can claim divine authority, their deceit is unmasked by their commitment to self-gain. The prophet is validated as Servant of the Lord by being free from preoccupation with self. Power is not hoarded but is passed on to the community, enabling all members to join in the rebuilding of what had been destroyed."[25]

In working with this passage a temptation might be to settle on an overly spiritual interpretation. Such an interpretation would minimize the language of structural change envisioned,[26] that is, the transfer of priestly power from hierarchical elites to relational responsiveness within the larger community. Even more, it would betray a reluctance to take seriously the tangible concrete expectation that this new self-identity, call, and communalized organizing will, in fact, serve to "build up the ancient ruins, they shall raise up the former devastations; they shall repair the ruined cities, the devastations of many generations," (v. 4). Indeed, it is through the communalization of the office of king and priest that Jerusalem will be physically rebuilt

---

[25] Hanson, *Isaiah 40—66*, 224.

[26] "One of the most characteristic themes of chs. 56–66 is the assurance that the present unsatisfactory situation will be reversed by a divine intervention in the affairs of the Jewish community that will bring history as we know it to an end. At this point the reversal is from mourning to comfort, and assurance of its ultimate fulfillment is continued from the prophetic witness in chs. 40–55 (40:1; 49:13; 51:3, 12, 19; 52:9) and will reappear in the Matthean Beatitudes (Matt 5:4)." Joseph Blenkinsopp, *Isaiah 56—66: A New Translation with Introduction and Commentary*, Anchor Yale Bible, vol. 19B (New Haven, CT; Yale University Press, 2008), 225.

as well as the soul of the surviving post-traumatic community, individual and collective, be healed.[27]

A HEALING AND RESTORATIVE PATH

For post-traumatic survivors of clergy sexual abuse, these two passages from the Book of Isaiah might be able to foster healing, empowerment, and recovery that happens outside of structures and clericalism that were active or complicit in abuse. By way of practical summary, the following is a list of key connective and transformative insights emerging from these texts from Isaiah.

1. Since both passages arise from historical contexts of severe trauma and suffering, the most critical issues addressed in each passage are restorative justice, personal agency, and religious healing. Because of this, each passage meets a post-traumatic survivor within his or her lived reality, personally.

2. In both passages God takes the initiative toward restorative justice by rejecting the old structures of hierarchical kingship and priesthood and empowers the post-traumatic community directly to take up its own healing, restoration, and right relationships unmediated.

3. Both passages envision that as individual and communal healing takes place, a new and better community will emerge that more closely reflects the will of God for God's people. In fact, the community of healing that emerges will draw others even outside of the survivors' unique experience to its honesty, vitality, and efficacy so that it will be a light of hope and healing.

---

[27] George Knight notes the counterintuitiveness of this claim: "the thinking in a verse like this is quite other than that of the gentile world. The rebuilding of Jerusalem (cf. 49:8) out of the present ruins represents both the literal building up again of the ancient buildings and the spiritual renewal of the people who live in the city." George Angus Fulton Knight, *The New Israel: A Commentary on the Book of Isaiah 56—66*, International Theological Commentary (Grand Rapids, MI: Eerdmans, 1985), 56.

4. Crucially, God is fully and completely available to the post-traumatic survivors and in the very process of all their hurt, confusion, shame, and even guilt, God empowers and equips them with eternal covenantal relationship, healthy sustenance, and symbolic divine clothing for their violated bodies. While they may bear the marks of trauma and violation, they have full and holy access to God for themselves and for others.

Practically, and significantly, this means that survivors are not asked to trust the complicit system or even its hierarchical offices for religious healing. Access to God is theologically available immediately among the traumatized, unmediated. Pastoral practitioners accompanying those who embrace the terrifically difficult path of religious healing might serve as a prophetic embodiment of these passages, a signpost for the counterintuitive work of God. Like the prophetic voice of Isaiah 61:1–3, the task is one of unambiguous assurance and dogged commitment to name oppression; expose God's condemnation (vengeance); and offer divine healing, hope, and empowerment. This is a non-anxious loving embodiment of the passage from Isaiah that Jesus claimed as his own (see Luke 4:18).

> The spirit of the Lord GOD is upon me,
>   because the Lord has anointed me;
> he has sent me to bring good news to the oppressed,
>   to bind up the brokenhearted,
> to proclaim liberty to the captives
>   and release to the prisoners,
> to proclaim the year of the LORD's favor
>   and the day of vengeance of our God,
>   to comfort all who mourn,
> to provide for those who mourn in Zion—
>   to give them a garland instead of ashes,
> the oil of gladness instead of mourning,
>   the mantle of praise instead of a faint spirit.

They will be called oaks of righteousness,
   the planting of the LORD, to display his glory.
                                    (Isa 61:1–3)

The last line, which signifies the recognition of a new reality—
"oaks of righteousness"—probably connotes the idea of "oaks as
oaks ought to be."[28] That is, the prophetic task of accompaniment
reaches its completion when post-traumatic survivors are not only
healed but recognized as healed by others—theologically redeemed
and mirrored by a new connective community. This is nothing
less than the gospel enfleshed. Importantly, in the original context
of Isaiah 40—66, this does not happen within the old structures
mediated through traditional hierarchical theology.[29]

In sum, Isaiah 55:1–3 and Isaiah 61:1–11 might also serve as
a divine voice of accompaniment through the long and arduous
process of healing stemming from clergy abuse and institutional
minimizing. In these texts survivors are placed front and center,
but not primarily as victims. Instead, they compose the very community of hope through which the great purposes of God will
be lived out. Even more, both passages suggest that it is in the
manifold work of *healing and recovery* that God is most clearly
manifested, not in temple worship, liturgy, or representative ordained leadership. These passages strongly condemn attempts to
save the institution at the expense of the victim. They cannot be
read, as some biblical trauma literature might be, as blaming the
victim.[30] Rather, these passages suggest, in the most poetically

---

[28] Blenkinsopp, *Isaiah 56—66*, 226.

[29] Isaiah 42:9: "See, the former things have come to pass, and new
things I now declare"; Isaiah 43:19: "I am about to do a new thing; now
it springs forth, do you not perceive it?"; Isaiah 62:2: "The nations shall
see your vindication, and all the kings your glory; and you shall be called
by a new name, that the mouth of the Lord will give."

[30] "To survive, victims need interpretations, even bad ones, even false
ones, even partial ones, even self-blaming ones. . . . Explanations provide
stability and trustworthiness to the world again and create a sense of
safety, even when they are false." O'Connor, "How Trauma Studies Can
Contribute to Old Testament Studies," 216.

beautiful and theologically acute form, that the hope for future religious life of any depth and integrity falls along the healing path of the survivors, that it is they who will lead out God's good will and hope and right relationship for all people. At the right time, in the right way, these biblical texts may serve as tangible anchors of divine will by aiding in the reconstitution of faith for survivors, and they may offer a way of repentance and salvation for the church itself.

6.

Psycho-theological Functions of Laments

Giving Voice to Anger and Grief

Linda S. Schearing

Ancient Israel did not shy away from giving a voice to those who were angry at the pain and treatment they experienced. By far, the genre of lament is the most attested form of psalm in the Book of Psalms. Historically, however, theologians and ecclesial practices sometimes neutralize the anger of the lament genre. Those who analyze church hymnals note that, while laments make up many psalms in the Book of Psalms, songs with lament themes make up only a small fraction of many contemporary hymnals. Instead, praise and thanksgiving are the predominating themes of many hymns. Richard Hughes, for example, traces the decline of lament throughout church history and stresses the need for its revival.[1] The historical suppression of the anger expressed in biblical lament is not unlike that given to the suppression of contemporary sexual abuse victims' voices. This chapter argues that the psychological and theological value of the lament genre is especially significant

---

[1] Richard Hughes, *Lament, Death, and Destiny*, Studies in Biblical Literature, vol. 68 (New York: Peter Lang, 2004).

to its contemporary revival by clerical sexual abuse victims and in liturgies lamenting this crisis in the contemporary church.

LAMENTS AND TRAUMA

What is lament? Paraphrasing Michael Guinan, OFM, Sister Marion Moeser writes:

> When we feel blessed in life, . . . we turn to God in praise and thanksgiving. But what happens when we are overcome by the presence of chaos, brokenness, abuse and suffering? When we hurt physically, we cry out in pain; when we hurt religiously, we cry out in lament. Lamentation can be described as a loud, religious "Ouch!"[2]

Biblical laments deal with some type of traumatic oppression or adversity, although it is not always clear who is being troubled or the nature of the problem. What *is* clear is that the speaker does not shy away from crying out or complaining to God for what has happened. That Israel felt comfortable crying out *to* or *about* God is attested to by the presence of laments in the Psalter. Many of the 150 psalms contained in the Book of Psalms are laments.[3]

Individual Laments	3, 4, 5, 6, 7, 9-10, 13, 14, 17, 22, 25, 26, 27, 28, 31, 35, 38, 39, 40, 41, 42–43, 51, 52, 53, 54, 55, 56, 57, 59, 61, 64, 69, 70, 71, 77, 86, 88, 89, 102, 109, 120, 130, 139, 141, 142, 143.
Community Laments	12, 44, 58, 60, 74, 79, 80, 83, 85, 90, 94, 123, 126, 129, 137.

---

[2] Sister Marion Moeser, "Ouch! Why? Please! Praying with the Lament Psalms," *Western New York Catholic*, November 15, 2018.

[3] Lawrence Boadt, "Israelite Worship and Prayer," in *Reading the Old Testament: An Introduction* (New York: Paulist Press, 1984), 282.

Clearly, although ancient Israel did praise their God, they also complained to and about God quite a bit. As Gerald Arbuckle asks, "Beyond listening to and supporting victims of abuse, what can we do—as individuals, institutions and ministries—to heal our grief?" He answers, "The Scriptures have a simple, but profound, even paradoxical, answer to give words to sorrow. We actually are invited to mourn through complaining!"[4] The structure of lament psalms often follows this general pattern:

> An address to God
> A complaint
> Confession of trust and turning to God
> A plea or petition
> A vow of praise[5]

Lament psalms are important in the twenty-first century as people find them helpful in processing trauma and healing their traumatic wounds. It has been suggested that their relevance stems from the fact that "so many people have suffered trauma of various kinds."[6] Vocalizing the pain allows the speaker to process the trauma and start healing. Contemporary theories of the function of laments argue that, far from simply voicing complaints, the genre of lament psalms helps the speaker move from suffering to healing. According to D. Soelle and J. L. Herman, the movement from suffering to healing is comprised of basically three stages:

1. Muteness, isolation, and a need to establish safety
2. Becoming capable to speak of the pain with a mix of emotion and rationality, becoming capable of lament, with change becoming possible through reconstruction of a trauma story

---

[4] Gerald A. Arbuckle, "The People of God," *Health Progress: Journal of the Catholic Health Association of the United States* 101, no. 2 (2020): 47.

[5] Hughes, *Lament, Death, and Destiny*, 30.

[6] J. F. Dickie, "Lament as a Contributor to the Healing of Trauma: An Application of Poetry in the Form of Biblical Lament," *Pastoral Psychology* 68 (2019): 145.

3. Rational language and solidarity with others resulting from having been heard, reconnecting with life going forward[7]

It is the second stage of lament that allows the speaker to give voice to the "previously unspeakable agony" experienced. As Hughes so aptly explains, "Lament erupts spontaneously, sometimes convulsively, as a cry, which may be an inarticulate moaning or an accusatory question such as: 'Why is God doing this to me?'"[8]

As Moeser notes, "The radical evil of clerical sexual abuse within Christian communities, committed against its vulnerable members, elicits responses among the faithful ranging from horror, rage, shame, bewilderment and a cry for justice."[9] While initially the abused may question why God allowed the abuse to happen, the healing process (of which lament is an important element) helps the abused to lay blame on the abuser rather than on God. Indeed, a diocese of the Anglican Church in Australia declared that 2019 be set aside as a "Year of Lament" and produced a resource pack entitled "Survivors of Abuse." In the packet the writers explain their rationale:

> The idea sprung from reflecting upon how the church has failed our society in the area of child abuse. Whilst our diocese has fewer claims against it than other dioceses, some even dating back to the second world war, having just one claim would be one too many. Our "Year of Lament" has not been instigated to placate our collective guilty consciences, rather Bishop-in-Council (BiC) wants to help our parishes realise that there is a rich tradition of lament within the Scriptures that calls us to weep with those who weep and to mourn with those who mourn. BiC further recognised that there are

---

[7] Dorothee Sölle, *Suffering*, trans. E. R. Kalin (Philadelphia: Fortress Press, 1975), 142–43; Judith L. Herman, *Trauma and Recovery: The Aftermath of Violence—From Domestic Abuse to Political Terror* (New York: Basic Books, 1992), 155.

[8] Hughes, *Lament, Death, and Destiny*, 7.

[9] Moeser, "Ouch! Why? Please!"

also many other areas that should give us reason to lament. We need to weep with victims of child abuse; weep with our first peoples and refugees over their mistreatment; weep with those caught in war zones; weep with the homeless; and weep over the degradation of our environment and much more.[10]

Several biblical psalms are especially relevant to the contemporary issue of clerical sexual abuse. This chapter examines two such psalm: Psalm 55 and Psalm 88.

PSALM 55 AND SEXUAL ABUSE

Several biblical psalms are particularly useful in giving voice to the pain of the speaker. Among these, Psalm 55 stands out in relation to sexual abuse victims. In the opening verses of Psalm 55 the speaker pleads four times to God for protection from the enemy:

> [1]   Give ear to my prayer, O God;
>   do not hide yourself from my supplication.
> [2]   Attend to me, and answer me;
>   I am troubled in my complaint.
>   I am distraught [3] by the noise of the enemy,
>   because of the clamor of the wicked.
>   For they bring trouble upon me,
>   and in anger they cherish enmity against me.

The appeal implies that the speaker does not feel that God is hearing the speaker's distress. The speaker is "troubled" and "distraught." Where is God? Note that the precise nature of the trouble is unspecified, which allows readers to fill in the gaps with their own situation and identify with the speaker. One example of such personalization of these verses in situations of sexual abuse is found in the creative

---

[10] Tom Henderson-Brooks, "Year of Lament—A Pathway to God: Resource Pack–'Survivors of Abuse,'" Rockhampton Diocese, January 2019.

writing of Brad Hambrick, who takes Psalm 55 and personalizes it in the voice of a sexual abuse survivor:

1. Oh God please hear me. Don't pretend that this is not happening. I need you!
2. Be silent no longer. Say something. Let me know you are there. I am overwhelmed as I cry and convulse over what happened to me. I can't eat, sleep, or think.
3. My abuser made such awful noises. He took pleasure in my pain and degradation. He overpowered me. There was nothing I could do. He must hate me to keep doing this. What have I done?! What could cause such hatred and disregard?[11]

Hambrick explains that this creative exercise is "an attempt to rewrite Psalm 55 to put the experience of sexual abuse at the hands of a family member or trusted friend into words."[12] Such personalization allows access to the ideas and structure of the psalms tailored to specific contemporary situations. His "verse 3," for example, gives a graphic view into the act of sexual trespass and the feeling of helplessness it evokes in its victims.

Psalm 55:4–5 continues the complaint of verse 2 with five graphic, descriptive words that reflect the Psalmist's emotions (*anguish, terrors, fear, trembling, horror*).

> 4 My heart is in anguish within me,
>   the terrors of death have fallen upon me.
> 5 Fear and trembling come upon me,
>   and horror overwhelms me.
> 6 And I say, "O that I had wings like a dove!
>   I would fly away and be at rest;
> truly, I would flee far away;
>   I would lodge in the wilderness; *Selah*

---

[11] Brad Hambrick, "Rewriting Psalm 55 Reflecting on Sexual Abuse," BradHambrick.com, September 18, 2014.

[12] Hambrick.

> [8] I would hurry to find a shelter for myself
> from the raging wind and tempest."

Such descriptive words allow the speaker to give voice to the stark emotions and physical effects created by the harm, which threatens to overwhelm. Verses 6–8 lament that physically escaping the situation is not an option with a series of conditional statements—*would, would, would*. Hambrick's personalization of Psalm 55:4–8 describes graphically the despair sex abuse victims can feel:

4. My soul quakes. Heartbreak feels romantic compared to this. This is worse than death.
5. Panic attacks and the fear of panic attacks assail me. My body tremors in rebellion against me. I can't control my movements. Fear divides my heart, soul, mind, body, and will to attack them separately.
6. Like Jenny in Forrest Gump, I want to be a bird and fly away. I want to escape to a place of rest.
7. That place of rest would have to be far away, but there is one, right? I would travel however far, by whatever means, if only You promise there is somewhere I can go.
8. If you would just tell me the direction I would leave now. I would drive all night. I want peace more than sleep. Without peace sleep is useless. Sleep is just part of the storm with its nightmares and waking up realizing I've got to fake it through another day.[13]

Such personalization gives voice to the speaker's various forms of despair resulting from harm, and queries the hope that there might be deliverance. As Hambrick's "verse 7" states: "That place of rest would have to be far away, but there is one, right?"

A frequent feature of the lament genre is an appeal that God intervene and deal with the enemies. In verses 9–11, the Psalmist petitions God to "confound" the enemies' words because their

---

[13] Hambrick.

anticipated results are disastrous for the city (*violence, strife, iniquity, trouble, ruin, oppression, fraud*):

> [9]   Confuse, O LORD, confound their speech;
>   for I see violence and strife in the city.
> [10] Day and night they go around it
>   on its walls,
>   and iniquity and trouble are within it;
> [11]   ruin is in its midst;
>   oppression and fraud
>   do not depart from its marketplace.

The appeal to intervene becomes more personal and contemporary in the words of Hambrick as he gives voice to the anger felt by sexual abuse victims:

> 9. Take justice! Do to them what they have done to my soul. Don't let them multiply my shame by talking of this deed. Don't let them mock me or worse talk like nothing happened.
> 10. I can't believe I live in a world/country where this is "common." It's always being reported on the news or another documentary. Every time I hear it I am reminded. The pain echoes; worse, it flashes back.
> 11.   There is a whole industry of sexual degradation in our culture—porn. It's bigger than the NFL. They write and glorify stories like mine. There is an audience who pays for it, even with children.[14]

A poignant issue in Psalm 55 is the identity of the speaker's "enemies." They are not strangers, but people well known to the Psalmist, as is the case with the majority of survivors of sexual abuse. Verses 12–15 give voice to the betrayal trauma felt by the Psalmist due to the intimate relation with the friend who betrayed the Psalmist:

---

[14] Hambrick.

¹² It is not enemies who taunt me—
> I could bear that;
> it is not adversaries who deal insolently with
>> me—
> I could hide from them.
¹³ But it is you, my equal,
> my companion, my familiar friend,
¹⁴ with whom I kept pleasant company;
> we walked in the house of God with the
>> throng.
¹⁵ Let death come upon them;
> let them go down alive to Sheol;
> for evil is in their homes and in their hearts.

In a surprising turn, it is a trusted friend and not some stranger who is the oppressor. Although the descriptive words attached to the oppressor imply a formerly compatible relationship (*companion, friend, pleasant company*) the tone quickly changes. In verse 15 the cause of the problem shifts to the plural, and the speaker curses them with death. While the precise reason is not specified, the speaker points to the evil in their homes and hearts. Once again, by personalizing these verses, Hambrick brings the emotions of sexual abuse victims to life as they confront the sense of betrayal when abused by a trusted figure:

12. But I can't blame culture or an "industry" for my pain. It is no stranger who dined on my soul. It was not an enemy who was getting even. If it were, then I could be more protected. I could appeal to family and friends for help . . . and they might believe me.
13. But I knew him! I trusted him! My trust was used against me. My trust was the Trojan horse that let him in. How was I supposed to know?
14. We had so many good talks before that. We went to church together. We prayed together. He taught me Bible

lessons. How much of that was a lie? What does it mean to have your soul betrayed by a friend and a "friend of God"?

15.   May the death they have sparked in me explode in their own life and them live to experience it. Oh, that they would know the full degree of pain it was possible for them to create. Let their heart vomit its content into their own soul.[15]

The sense of betrayal in these words is as graphic as the anger and the wish for justice.

In verses 16–19 there is a stark turn of tone. The Psalmist shifts from a sense of betrayal at the hands of a friend to a note of trust, hope, and faith in God:

> [16] But I call upon God,
>   and the LORD will save me.
> [17] Evening and morning and at noon
>   I utter my complaint and moan,
>   and he will hear my voice.
> [18] He will redeem me unharmed
>   from the battle that I wage,
>   for many are arrayed against me.
> [19] God, who is enthroned from of old, *Selah*
>   will hear, and will humble them—
>   because they do not change,
>   and do not fear God.

Not only does the speaker trust that God will hear this complaint, but that God will also respond by saving the speaker from the enemies. In Hambrick's personalized version of Psalm 55, these emotions are expressed:

---

[15] Hambrick.

16. But I call to you God. No one is capable of handling what is before me except You. It takes omnipotence to overpower my pain, omnipresence to get your arms around it, and omniscience to fathom it. Only You can help me.
17. My pain is before me all day and at night when I am not sleeping. I don't know what else to do but cry to You. So You hear from me a lot. Everything in my life reminds me of my pain and my pain reminds me of my need for you constantly.
18. You are the one who keeps soldiers safe in the midst of battles. I am in the fight of my life and won't make it without You. My abusers, pain, memories, and fears outnumber me greatly.
19. God I trust the lies and deception do not outlive You. You hear, see, and know the truth. This sin was as arrogant against You as it was ravaging to me. He will not stand or smirk in Your presence.[16]

Verses 20–21 make explicit the nature of the Psalmist's complaint—a friend was violated and a relationship broken. The vehicle of such action was deception that violated a relationship based on trust. The deception is couched in military language (*heart set on war, drawn swords*).

> [20] My companion laid hands on a friend
>   and violated a covenant with me
> [21] with speech smoother than butter,
>   but with a heart set on war;
>   with words that were softer than oil,
>   but in fact were drawn swords.

In Hambrick's rewritten version the relationship takes on a more family/friend element:

---

[16] Hambrick.

20.   My father/uncle/friend attacked me and violated the trust of our friendship and, with it, my willingness to allow anyone to get close again.

21.   I replay his words over and over again, but cannot figure out what I should have heard. The terror of his intentions was hidden from so many. Were all of his compliments intentional instruments of death or were some of them sincere?[17]

What should be done in the face of such grooming and betrayal? The biblical speaker calls for trust, for it is God who will pull the speaker out of the situation:

> [22] Cast your burden on the LORD,
>   and he will sustain you;
>   he will never permit
>   the righteous to be moved.

Hambrick's version echoes these ideas but once again brings the specific voice of a sexual abuse victim to these feelings:

22.   This was not my fault. God calls me righteous as His child. He asks me to cry to Him. He is not ashamed of me. God is angered by anyone who would shun or condemn me for what happened to me.[18]

Psalm 55 concludes with the Psalmist voicing trust that God will punish those that have inflicted harm.

> [23] But you, O God, will cast them down
>   into the lowest pit;
>   the bloodthirsty and treacherous
>   shall not live out half their days.
>   But I will trust in you.

---

[17] Hambrick.
[18] Hambrick.

In the personalized version of Psalm 55, the nature of the enemy is clearly identified as sexual abuse, while God is safe, present, and restores trust:

> 23.   But God is more angered by my rapist. Sexual preda-
> tors will answer for their sin. Yet in His fury against them
> God is still safe for me. I will come near, leave my shame,
> look in Your eyes, and have my trust restored.[19]

Lament psalms are an invaluable tool that allows the speaker to connect with the suffering felt while not succumbing to hopelessness. A key value in applying Psalm 55 to clerical textual abuse situations is its ability to give a voice to the one being abused. This is especially significant given the fact that we are often told not to complain when we have suffered abuse. Psalm 55 contests such advice and openly advocates that the abused be given a chance to speak and their voice be heard.

PSALM 88 AND SEXUAL ABUSE

The above discussion of Psalm 55 examined how the psalm can be "personalized" to give voice to sexual abuse by a trusted person. Psalm 88 is another psalm particularly significant to sexual abuse survivors; it has been referred to as "one of the most tragic psalms in the Psalter,"[20] "the black sheep of the Psalter,"[21] and an "almost scandalous confrontation with God."[22] Moreover, it allows a "voice" to those abused without being rewritten for

---

[19] Hambrick.

[20] A. A. Anderson, *The Book of Psalms (Psalms 1–72)*, vol. 1, *The New Century Bible Commentary* (Grand Rapids, MI: Eerdmans, 1995), 612.

[21] Gina Christian, "A Psalm for Sexual Abuse," *Catholic Philly*, September 4, 2018.

[22] Sophia Stein, "I Am a Sexual Assault Survivor: The Psalms Gave Me New Words to Define Myself," *America: The Jesuit Review*, October 20, 2017.

contemporary readers. As Sophia Stein, a sexual abuse survivor, says of her own experience of Psalm 88:

> Now, my anger, my confusion, my worthlessness, my anxiety, my irrational thoughts—they were all absorbed by the terrible words written and spoken centuries before I came into being. In these ancient words I found new freedom to confront my Creator in anger, asking God a question, using the most important word I knew: "Why?"[23]

A close examination of Psalm 88 illustrates the various ways in which these ancient words speak to twenty-first-century abuse victims.

> 1 O LORD, God of my salvation,
>   when, at night, I cry out in your presence,
> 2 let my prayer come before you;
>   incline your ear to my cry.

In these opening verses the Psalmist petitions God to be heard. All too often sexual abuse survivors' voices are silenced. It is an interesting reminder of how important it is that we listen to those who have been abused rather than silencing them with quick words of simplistic consolation.

> 3 For my soul is full of troubles,
>   and my life draws near to Sheol.
> 4 I am counted among those who go down to the Pit;
>   I am like those who have no help,
> 5 like those forsaken among the dead,
>   like the slain that lie in the grave,
>   like those whom you remember no more,
>   for they are cut off from your hand.
> 6 You have put me in the depths of the Pit,
>   in the regions dark and deep.

---

[23] Stein.

7   Your wrath lies heavy upon me,
        and you overwhelm me with all your waves.
    Selah

In these verses the Psalmist utilizes a series of descriptive phrases—
"those who have no help," "those forsaken among the dead,"
"the slain that lie in the grave," "those whom you remember no
more"—to describe the pathos of the situation confronting the
Psalmist. These graphic words can be read productively as giving voice to the emotional turmoil of abandonment experienced
by those who are sexually abused. Stein explains how Psalm 88
functions in this manner for her:

> This psalm named so many aspects of being a survivor of
> sexual assault. It gave a name to the statistic I had become,
> to the gateway that would cause me to be highly susceptible
> to depression and anxiety and eventually consider suicide:
> "For my soul is filled with troubles; my life draws near to
> Sheol. I am reckoned with those who go down to the pit"
> (Ps 88:5).[24]

In verses 8–12 the Psalmist continues with a series of questions directed to God amid the pain and turmoil experienced by
the speaker:

8   You have caused my companions to shun me;
        you have made me a thing of horror to them.
    I am shut in so that I cannot escape;
9   my eye grows dim through sorrow.
    Every day I call on you, O LORD;
        I spread out my hands to you.
10 Do you work wonders for the dead?
        Do the shades rise up to praise you? *Selah*
11 Is your steadfast love declared in the grave,
        or your faithfulness in Abaddon?

---

[24] Stein.

¹² Are your wonders known in the darkness,
or your saving help in the land of
forgetfulness?

A sense of desperation resounds throughout these verses. Abandoned by friends, the Psalmist fires a series of questions to God as to whether God will even help with the issues confronting the speaker. Such a situation echoes the experience of the sexually abused.

In verses 13–18 the psalmist expresses the belief that God is the source of the Psalmist's trouble and the frustration with a God that allows such torment:

¹³ But I, O LORD, cry out to you;
in the morning my prayer comes before you.
¹⁴ O LORD, why do you cast me off?
Why do you hide your face from me?
¹⁵ Wretched and close to death from my youth up,
I suffer your terrors; I am desperate.
¹⁶ Your wrath has swept over me;
your dread assaults destroy me.
¹⁷ They surround me like a flood all day long;
from all sides they close in on me.
¹⁸ You have caused friend and neighbor to shun me;
my companions are in darkness.

It is significant that, unlike the lament in Psalm 55, this lament concludes on a series of questions and accusations hurled at God without a note of anticipated salvation. As such, it allows the person grieving a voice without silencing it with well-meant words of consolation. Stein notes of these concluding words:

Finally, the words that I had been searching for found me. Psalm 88 is a lament, an almost scandalous confrontation with God. The end of the psalm provides no expression of relief, no glimpse of hope or redemption. It complains, sighs and wails at the Creator, questioning the purpose of being created in a state of extreme suffering and separation. Through the words of a psalm, my pain had finally become incarnate. "I am a sexual assault survivor. The psalms gave me new words to define myself."[25]

CONCLUSION

Israel's biblical laments, found in the Book of Psalms, speak to contemporary clerical sexual abuse victims in a variety of ways. Most significant of these is to show that victims have voices that need to be heard. Their voices, when heard through the lament, make healing possible—theologically and psychologically—for the abused. Moreover, those who either hear or read these laments often become aware, or more aware, of such abuse. Thus, biblical laments function in an important way for today's society and should not be repressed. Not only are they a powerful and important implement to the healing of the abused, but they are also a powerful voice that needs to be heard for the healing of the theological and pastoral community.

---

[25] Stein.

7.

Malignant Narcissism and Clericalism

Psychological Perspectives on a Culture of Abuse

Fernando A. Ortiz

The Causes and Context of Sexual Abuse of Minors by Catholic Priests in the United States Study has significant implications for understanding the sexual abuse crisis in the church.[1] The study is particularly important because it has provided useful information for understanding clerical culture, specifically the maladies of malignant narcissism and character. The study describes in detail the demographic and psychological makeup of clergy perpetrators. This chapter examines this *Causes and Context* study and the risk factors associated with such clerical culture and proposes protective institutional and community-based measures to reform such culture.

Narcissism is defined as "egotism or self-absorption." According to Millon, individuals with narcissistic personalities struggle with self-regard and experience feelings of incompetence, ineffectiveness, unworthiness and inferiority.[2] Typically, others

---

[1] K. J. Terry et al., *The Causes and Context of Sexual Abuse of Minors by Catholic Priests in the United States, 1950–2010* (Washington, DC: US Conference of Catholic Bishops, 2011).

[2] T. Millon, *Personality Disorders in Modern Times* (New York: John Wiley and Sons, 2004).

describe them with feelings of superiority, arrogance, grandiosity, and lack of empathy for others. Their most distinctive characterological feature is a pervasive pattern of grandiosity, a need for admiration, and a lack of empathy, which begins in early adulthood and is clearly present in a variety of contexts. Sperry describes them as prone to over-modulated anger to the point of being enraged.[3] Behaviorally, they tend to be manipulative, and relationally, they are likely to have difficulty forming intimate interpersonal relationships. They usually relate to others only in a superficial manner and have significant empathic deficiencies. It would therefore be nearly impossible for malignantly narcissistic clergy to form and maintain healthy relationships with those whom they serve.

Narcissism, as described among clergy, is said to be less characterized by self-centeredness and more about hollowness and the need to build up a shaky self-image than about grandiosity and the belief in one's own special status.[4] Horst further postulates that narcissism is a failure to be truthful about oneself to oneself, a failure to accept the limitations of one's humanity and to accept the extent of one's capacity to influence and harm others. Moreover, narcissistic individuals develop the belief in their unquestionable righteousness, viewing those who disagree or challenge them as hostile, cruel, crazy, ignorant, or morally repulsive. Because people with narcissistic personalities believe they are always right, those who have any conflict or grievance with them are often seen as enemies, opponents, and rivals who are crazy, inferior, or morally reprehensible.

These narcissistic behaviors and predispositions are prevalent among members of the clergy.[5] Leadership positions tend to be

---

[3] L. Sperry, *Cognitive Behavior Therapy of DSM-IV-TR Personality Disorders: Highly Effective Interventions for the Most Common Personality Disorders* (New York: Routledge, 2006).

[4] P. Horst, "Abuse of Power, Part 1: Boundaries and Narcissism," *The Interfaith Sexual Trauma Institute Sun* 7, no. 2 (2001): 7–10.

[5] J. Meloy, "Narcissistic Psychopathology in the Clergy," *Pastoral Psychology* 35, no. 1 (1986): 50–55.

sought after by individuals with these strong narcissistic tendencies.[6] Multiple studies of clergy perpetrators have found that offending priests showed a marked desire for acceptance, admiration, and a need to be idealized.[7] These clergy try to use the admiration and devotion of others to bolster their false and therefore shaky self-image. When the cleric fails to receive ample admiration, submission, and devotion from the faithful, his mental hygiene begins to wane and clergy burnout or immoral acts emerge. When his needs are not met in this context, the priest abuser finds ways in which to act out feelings of childhood inadequacy. In these studies such clerics behaved like manipulative con men and were usually admired by their parishioners. They were sought out by their parishioners and by other priests as well.[8] Vitz and Vitz attributed five predominant behaviors to these priests: (1) require excessive admiration and display extreme sensitivity to criticism, (2) a sense of entitlement, unreasonable expectations of favorable treatment, (3) a belief they are superior, special, or unique, (4) arrogant and haughty behaviors, and (5) a lack of empathy.[9]

The *Causes and Context* study noted that these malignant characteristics in offending priests are a danger to our faith communities. The study instructs gatekeepers in seminaries, religious communities, and parishes to identify risk factors that contribute

---

[6] W. Cahoy, "God, Power, and Control," *The Interfaith Sexual Trauma Institute Sun* 5, no. 4 (2000).

[7] T. W. Haywood et al., "Psychological Aspects of Sexual Functioning among Cleric and Noncleric Alleged Sex Offenders," *Child Abuse and Neglect* 20, no. 6 (1996): 527–36; J. A. Loftus and R. J. Carmargo, "Treating the Clergy," *Annals of Sex Research* 6, no. 4 (1993): 287–303; G. J. McGlone, "Prevalence and Incidence of Roman Catholic Clerical Sex Offenders," in *Broken Trust: Stories of Pain, Hope, and Healing from Clerical Abuse Survivors and Abusers*, ed. P. Fleming, S. Lauder-Fleming, and M. T. Matousek (New York: Crossroad, 2003), 111–22.

[8] L. M. Lothstein, "Men of the Flesh: The Evaluation and Treatment of Sexually Abusing Priests," *Studies in Gender and Sexuality* 5, no. 2 (2004): 167–95.

[9] P. C. Vitz and D. C. Vitz, "Messing with the Mass: The Problem of Priestly Narcissism Today," *The Homiletic and Pastoral Review* 108, no. 2 (2007): 16–22.

to the creation of a narcissistically oriented clergy that may offend children and minors. The study identified the following specific risk factors, for example, as measured by the Minnesota Multiphasic Personality Inventory (MMPI), a widely used multidimensional personality assessment instrument.[10] It specifically concluded that

> collectively, results from analyses using clergy classifications based on referral information, as well as analyses based on information obtained during treatment, suggested that the strongest (though not statistically significant) personality-based risk markers for clergy sexual abuse of minors included elevations on the following MMPI subscales: Denial of Social Anxiety, Authority Problems, Persecutory Ideas, Amorality, and Over-controlled Hostility. Other possible risk markers for sexual abuse of minors included elevations on the following MMPI subscales: Need for Affection, Social Imperturbability, Imperturbability, and Inhibition of Aggression.[11]

As the study rightly points out, these risk factors should be used with caution in the formation of future priests. Figure 7.1 presents a detailed classification of these scales and their psychological interpretative meaning.[12]

From the perspective of seminary and religious formation, the profile that emerges from these clinical indicators is emotionally needy and engages in possibly ingratiating or attention-seeking behaviors to meet deeply rooted emotional vulnerabilities for intimacy, affection, and affirmation (*need for affection*). Socially,

---

[10] James N. Butcher et al., *MMPI-2. Manual for Administration, Scoring, and Interpretation,* rev. ed. (Minneapolis: Pearson, 2001).

[11] Terry et al., *The Causes and Context of Sexual Abuse of Minors by Catholic Priests in the United States, 1950–2010,* 59.

[12] Butcher et al., *MMPI-2.*; Jane C. Duckworth, *MMPI and MMPI-2. Interpretation Manual for Counselors and Clinicians* (Pennsylvania, Bristol: Taylor and Francis, 1995); Roger L. Greene, *The MMPI-2/MMPI: An Interpretative Manual* (Needham Heights, MA: Allyn and Bacon, 2000).

Figure 7.1 Personality Risk Factors
MMPI Findings

Name of Scale	Scale Label	# Items	Interpretative Meaning
Denial of Social Anxiety	Hysteria (Hy1)	6	Items on this subscale have to do with social extroversion, feeling comfortable interacting with other people, and not being easily influenced by social standards and customs. In general, these individuals deny problems with shyness or difficulty in social situations. They also value freedom of independence from the influence of others.
Need for Affection	Hysteria (Hy2)	12	Individuals with high scores on this scale describe strong needs for attention and affection from others, as well as fears that these needs will not be met if they are honest about their feelings and beliefs. They describe others as honest, sensitive, and reasonable, and they deny having negative feelings about other people. It may well be that by not having any critical attitudes towards others they seek to meet strong needs for attention and affection.
Inhibition of Aggression	Hysteria (Hy5)	7	This individual denies hostile or aggressive feelings. They report feeling sensitive about how others respond to them.
	Mania (Ma3)	8	This individual is confident in social situations. He will profess little concern about the opinions, values, and attitudes of others. In general, he does not care what others think.

Name of Scale	Scale Label	# Items	Interpretative Meaning
Amorality	Mania (Ma 1)	6	High scorers on this subscale describe other people as selfish, dishonest, and opportunistic. Because of these perceptions they may feel justified in behaving in similar ways. They may derive vicarious satisfaction from the manipulative exploits of others. In general, this person is callous towards others and feels justified in this.
Authority Problems	Psycho-pathic Deviate (Pd2)	8	High scorers on this subscale express resentment of societal and parental standards and customs, have definite opinions about what is right and wrong, and stand up for their own beliefs. They may admit to having been in trouble in school or with the law. In general, these individuals are resentful of authority and may report problems with the law.
Social Imper-turbabil-ity	Psycho-pathic Deviate (Pd3)	6	Individuals who elevate this scale express feeling comfortable, compe-tent and confident in social situations, having strong opinions about many things, and defending one's opinions vigorously.
Persecu-tory Ideas	Paranoia (Pa1)	17	This individual tends to see the world and/or other people as threatening and they often feel misunderstood and unfairly treated. He/she blames others for problems.
Overcon-trolled Hostility	O-H	28	This scale helps to identify individuals who are prone to over-controlling their hostility until they are suddenly provoked, and they consequently have sudden aggressive episodes. This scale has been particularly helpful with prison populations.

this individual will appear confident, cocky, charming, and engage in sophisticated impression management strategies to gain favors from others (*denial of social anxiety*). Remarkably, this individual will impress others as outgoing, talkative, and socially competent (*social imperturbability*). At a deeper level, however, this person is unperturbed by what others think because he is primarily motivated by satisfying his own egoist needs (*imperturbability*). On the surface he may deny having hostile or aggressive feelings. He may have learned to wear a social mask of benevolence and camouflage himself to appear in a good light before others (*inhibition of aggression*) and rigidly defend himself against any extreme aggressive impulse and eventually succumb to aggressive outbursts (*overcontrolled hostility*). What makes individuals with these profile markers particularly high risk is that they appear to be callous and unconscionable in their behavior and worldview (*amorality*). They may have had significant traumatic experiences in their lives, and consequently they view the world and other people as malevolent and threatening (*persecutory ideas*). They are particularly suspicious of those in positions of authority (*authority problems*).

EVALUATION OF PERSONALITY RISK FACTORS

Most would agree that, if these risk factors were to be significantly elevated in a candidate to religious or seminary formation, it would be very important for evaluating psychologists and formators to consider seriously the overall application of the candidate. Moreover, serious consideration would be given to a candidate for ordination whose profile presents elevations on several of these risk factors. The following are additional serious considerations based on the main themes emerging from such risky and high liability profiles.

Callousness. Callousness is often thought of in association with antisocial, sadistic, and narcissistic personalities. Callousness suggests lack of empathy, compassion, and this results in personality profiles that are highly irascible or hardhearted. In extreme cases individuals with noticeable callousness will be perceived by others as belligerent, vicious, malignant, brutal, vengeful, and vindictive.

If an evaluating psychologist were to detect a significant level of callousness, this should be probed further to determine if it is associated with a pervasive maladaptive personality structure. If this person is admitted into a formation program, he will most likely engage in behaviors charged with defiance of conventional formation rules and will interpret the tender emotions of others as signs of weakness. In a religious community he will be prone to interpret the goodwill and kindness of others as hiding a deceptive ploy to which he will react with coldblooded ruthlessness. Minors and vulnerable adults are particularly at risk with this type of callousness.

Imperturbability. Some candidates to the priesthood may be characterized by a marked air of nonchalance and feigned tranquility. They may appear coolly unimpressionable or buoyantly optimistic, except when their narcissistic confidence is shaken, at which time rage, shame, or emptiness will be displayed. This imperturbability will be self-deceptive and facile. They could also be perceived as naively self-assured and happy-go-lucky, and serious matters will not affect these individuals in formation.

Amorality. Any evidence during the screening process of unprincipled behavior should be closely evaluated. These individuals will be experienced by others as unscrupulous, exploitative, and deceptive. The psychologist should include in the report any evidence suggesting that these candidates to seminary formation have previously demonstrated a flagrant indifference to the welfare of others, willingness to harm, and fearlessness by humiliating and dominating others. A rigorous clinical interview should attempt to uncover any evidence of extreme self-interest, and, if this is coupled with any veneer of politeness and civility, this should be interpreted with caution. An evaluating psychologist could ask detailed questions to find out if the candidate has any history of behavior suggesting that he has been fraudulent or a con man and a charlatan in the past.

Neediness. Emotional neediness is another psychological vulnerability and concern in this profile. Extreme examples of dependency with a marked need for affection and approval would be highly suspect in an applicant. If the person is already in formation and appears to have an insatiable need for attention and nurturance while showing childlike behavior, he likely would be detrimental to peers in the community. This would be the case if underneath he is seething with helplessness and thoughts of revenge at those who fail to recognize his need for approval. This ineffectual dependency should be seriously considered when determining suitability for the priesthood.

Hostility. The *Causes and Context* study stated that "the experience of having been sexually abused by another youth or by an adult during childhood or adolescence was reported by more than a third of the priests in treatment for sexual abuse of children at the third treatment center."[13] This traumatic experience of abuse cannot be generalized to every priest who has been abused, but it can be considered as a risk factor for some, and it may be experientially linked to hostility. Children exposed to neglect, indifference, hostility, and physical abuse, for example, are likely to learn that the world is a cold and unforgiving place. Such children lack normal models of empathic tenderness. Rather than learning how to be sensitive to the emotional states of others, they instead develop enduring resentment and an unwillingness to reflect on the consequences of their actions. The elevated scales suggest that these individuals prone to abusing minors display an elevated level of over-controlled hostility. It is very likely that under slight pressures the pacific surface of these individuals quickly will give way to impulsive hostility. In a seminary or religious community, relating to them would be an arduous process, and in a parish or ministerial assignment it would require more patience than most people are likely to offer. They may attempt to sabotage the formation of others and may displace their hostility onto the community superior or rector of the seminary. It is very telling that the *Causes and Context* study examined the difference between priests who seek out help and those who do not, concluding that

---

[13] Terry et al., *The Causes and Context of Sexual Abuse of Minors by Catholic Priests in the United States, 1950–2010,* 60.

when differences between accused and non-accused priests were observed, it was in their willingness to reach out to peers for advice. Although a majority of priests were willing to seek advice from peers, accused priests reached out less often than non-accused priests; approximately three-quarters of accused priests reached out for work role advice and two-thirds reached out for personal advice, while about 90 percent of non-accused priests were willing to consult peers for either work or personal advice.[14]

It is very likely that priests that have over-controlled hostility toward others, who experience persecutory fears, and who endorse callousness will find it unhelpful to reach out to others for solace and emotional support.

In addition to these personality risk factors the study also identified several risk factors in the area of sexuality. It found that priests who have engaged in sexual behavior prior to, and while in the seminary, were significantly more likely to participate in post-ordination sexual behavior. This risk factor applies to both homosexual and heterosexual individuals. Masturbation and access to pornography after ordination was also correlated with other sexual behavior post-ordination. Of those using pornography, priests who access pornography post-ordination in various modalities (paper, video, internet) were more likely to have child victims than adult victims. Family formation was also found to have an influence on post-ordination sexual behavior. Priests who in their family of origin approached the topic of sex as a taboo or who were not allowed to discuss sex were more likely to engage in sexual behavior after being ordained.

EVALUATING PROTECTIVE FACTORS

The study report stated that

---

[14] Terry et al., 66.

many accused priests began abusing years after they were ordained, at times of increased job stress, social isolation, and decreased contact with peers. Generally, few structures such as psychological and professional counseling were readily available to assist them with the difficulties they experienced. Many priests let go of the practice of spiritual direction after only a few years of ordained ministry.[15]

This clearly implies that self-care for clergy should be a priority in formation. Seminarians or those in formation need to be active, especially when suffering from psychological distress, in seeking out those resources that would provide them with emotional support and guidance. Human formation programs have evolved to pay attention to the vulnerability and brokenness of those in formation. Spiritual direction and prayer can provide strength. Continuing education and learning experiences can help an individual navigate the complexities of a crisis and contribute to a sense of competence and understanding when dealing with challenging situations. Formators can encourage students to be healthy and to utilize counseling services when needed.

Stress. Clergy stress is a debilitating experience that can be harmful to both the ordained and the community. Stressful demands will always be present in the life of ministry. Formation can address this problem by encouraging individuals to develop stress-relieving practices in the form of healthy recreation and rest. This in turn can lead to resilience, which is the capacity to return to well-being after a stressful situation. The *Causes and Context* study found the following specific stressors among priests: transition to parish life, negative early parish life, uprooting (reassigned to new parishes without being asked), distance ministry (rural or roving ministries), and family stress.[16] A strong human formation program can raise awareness of these potential stressors and prepare candidates accordingly.

---

[15] Terry et al., 3.
[16] Terry et al., 70–71.

Support Systems. Formation should also encourage individuals to learn how to create and access social and emotional support systems. In the life of the ordained, this would be the network of relationships experienced as nurturing and emotionally supportive. This type of support is a basic human need, and lack of it can be a contributing factor to burnout. Those in formations should learn to prioritize the development of an adequate support system and, most important, learn how to identify relational isolation. Learning how to access family, friends, a priests' support group, professional peers, a counselor, and a spiritual director should be part of the formative development of someone prior to being in full ministry. It is worth mentioning that the *Causes and Context* study indicated that

> priests who lacked close social bonds, and those whose family spoke negatively or not at all about sex, were more likely to sexually abuse minors than those who had a history of close social bonds and positive discussions about sexual behavior. In general, priests from the ordination cohorts of the 1940s and 1950s showed evidence of difficulty with intimacy.[17]

Through the healthy formation of relationships, those in formation can learn to address needs for intimacy. Additionally, through mentoring these individuals can gain needed knowledge and understanding of stress and useful coping strategies.

Balance. Individuals doing pastoral work are deeply committed and dedicated, and this often places extraordinary demands on their lives. This can lead to exhaustion, fatigue, decreased effectiveness, negative attitudes, and other problems, as noted by the *Causes and Context* study. For example, many priests reported that they never took days off due to parish understaffing and over-commitment to too many events and responsibilities. They found it very hard to have a clear boundary between home

---

[17] Terry et al., 4.

and work. This eventually led to a poor diet and lack of exercise resulting in obesity. Therefore, a human formation program may include the development of wellness skills to teach future priests a holistic sense of balance in their lives.

Formative Growth. The study distinguished between priests who underwent human formation and those who did not. Human formation encourages individuals to look at their own areas of growth and to address these directly. For example, some candidates attracted to the priesthood may be interested in this commitment because they have a personality structure that craves admiration, and they see this pathway in their lives as a way of meeting emotional needs. Once in ministry people may notice this and demand personal sacrifices from this person while putting them on a pedestal. Entering formation with the narcissistic perspective of obtaining a position whereby one would meet personal needs at the expense of others is incompatible with an authentic religious calling. This same reasoning can be applied to those with marked low self-esteem and who are emotionally needy. These individuals may be unable to set emotional and problem-solving limits, as well as limits on time commitments when pastorally helping others. Regarding self-esteem, the *Causes and Context* study found that "when there was low esteem, accused priests were slightly more likely to have a lack of positive attitude about themselves and their priestly roles."[18] Formation is a critical experience where students can address these issues and achieve the needed formative growth prior to ordination.

Like the assessment of risk factors, especially predispositions to malignant narcissism and clericalism, individuals entering human formation should be evaluated in their capacities, competencies, and strengths. The individual arrives with some deeply seated tendencies, including an entire psychological makeup, cognitive abilities, and personality traits. Some of these predispositions have genetic and biological bases. Of specific importance to formation are personality traits, generally defined as pervasive patterns of

---

[18] Terry et al., 65.

thinking, relating, and feeling. Personality psychology has developed a comprehensive classification system for personality traits, which provides structure to the most important functional and adaptive traits mentioned by the *Program of Priestly Formation*.[19] These can be used by evaluators and formators to gauge the normal aspects of someone's personality, and more specifically the strengths that an individual brings into the formation program. One example is the Big Five Personality Trait Theory, which posits that human personality comprises five domains: *neuroticism, extraversion, openness to experience, agreeableness,* and *consciousness*. A similar system includes six similar dimensions: *honesty-humility, emotionality, extraversion, agreeableness, conscientiousness,* and *openness to experience*. Figure 7.2 is an integrated template from these two personality systems to outline the most salient traits in human formation.

Honesty-Humility. To counter the risk factor presented by hostility and rebelliousness, the preference in formation would be for individuals who score high on honesty and humility. Lee and Ashton define this psychological construct as measuring sincerity, fairness, greed avoidance, and modesty.[20] These individuals would be appropriately equipped for formation, given their authenticity and truthfulness. Formation programs are interested in individuals who are genuine in their interpersonal relations and who do not engage in manipulative behaviors. Similarly, these individuals avoid fraud, corruption, and the abuse of others. They do not take advantage of minors and vulnerable people. Evaluating psychologists can closely assess whether applicants to the seminary are interested in possessing lavish wealth, luxury goods, and signs of high social status. These can be narcissistically oriented interests. A sense of modesty would be more amenable to a healthy human formation.

---

[19] United States Conference of Catholic Bishops, *Program of Priestly Formation,* 5th ed. (Washington, DC: USCCB, 2006).

[20] K. Lee and M. Ashton, "Psychometric Properties of the HEXACO Personality Inventory," *Multivariate Behavioral Research* 39, no. 2 (2004): 329–58.

Figure 7.2 Salient Traits in Human Formation

Personality Dimension	Program for Priestly Formation Traits
Honesty-Humility Emotionality	Truthfulness, integrity, humility (#280) A person of affective maturity: someone whose feelings are in balance and integrated into thought and values...a man of feelings who is not driven by them but freely lives his life enriched by them; this might be especially evidenced in his ability to live well with authority and in his ability to take direction from another, and to exercise authority well among his peers, as well as an ability to deal productively with conflict and stress (#76)
Extraversion-Introversion	A good communicator: someone who listens well, is articulate, and has the skills of effective communication, someone capable of public speaking (#76) A man who can take on the role of a public person: someone both secure in himself and convinced of his responsibility who is able to live not just as a private citizen but as a public person in service of the Gospel and representing the Church (#76)
Agreeableness	A man who relates well with others, free of overt prejudice, and willing to work with people of diverse cultural backgrounds: a man capable of wholesome relations with women and men as relatives, friends, colleagues, staff members, teachers, and as encountered in areas of apostolic work (#76)
Conscientiousness	A person of solid moral character with a finely developed moral conscience, a man open to and capable of conversion: a man who demonstrates the human virtues of prudence, fortitude, temperance, justice, humility, constancy, sincerity, prudence, good manners, truthfulness, and keeping his word, and who also manifests growth in the practice of these virtues (#76)
Openness to Experience	A free person: a person who is free to be who he is in God's design; candidates have the potential to move from self-preoccupation to an openness to transcendent values

Emotionality. Individuals with low levels of fearfulness, emotional neediness, anxiety, and dependence will most likely do better in formation. They will be self-assured and able to deal with problems without necessarily needing the help of someone. They will maintain healthy emotional bonds with others and demonstrate empathic sensitivity to the feelings of others.

Extroversion. An appropriate level of expressiveness and social competence would also be optimal for human formation. Given the social nature of ministry, which demands being able to navigate complex social relationships, an individual in human formation will work on improving ability to enjoy conversation and social interactions. Being communicative is highly valued as well.

Agreeableness. The *Program of Priestly Formation* points out that human formation speaks to the need to have individuals who can relate well with others and are willing to work with diverse cultural backgrounds. They are characterized by forgiveness, gentleness, flexibility, and patience. They have an ability to establish friendly relations with others; are reluctant to judge others harshly; and when interpersonal conflict arises, they remain calm and open to resolving such conflicts.

Conscientiousness. The *Program of Priestly Formation* also mentions that individuals participating in human formation are individuals of solid moral character, and they demonstrate the virtues of diligence and prudence. They tend to be self-disciplined and possess an ability to deliberate carefully and to inhibit impulses.

Openness to Experience. Human formation is also about being a free person. This person has intellectual curiosity and seeks additional knowledge (philosophical and theological) with a profound interest and desire to know others.

CONCLUSION

Malignant narcissism and clericalism can be predicted and risk factors predisposing candidates to such abusive clerical culture fully evaluated. The *Causes and Context* study examined the institutional, psychological, behavioral, and contextual factors implicated in perpetuating this clericalism in the past. When there is risk for an unhealthy and destructive behavior, there is greater chance that associated problems will occur. We have all witnessed the unspeakable damage that perpetrators of sexual abuse, who were educated, trained, and formed in Catholic seminaries and religious formation programs, have inflicted on minors and vulnerable people. From a psychological perspective, then, examining potential etiologies and associated risk factors at play may help us take preventive steps. We must be realistic that some of these abusing behaviors are extremely difficult to detect, measure, and accurately evaluate. Some individuals are also very adept at deception. Therefore, it is very useful to know what experiences evaluating psychologists and formators can focus on in order to design prescriptive and preventive interventions both at the screening level prior to ordination and during formation.

Similarly, a protective factor is defined as an element or process that buffers an individual predisposed to an undesirable outcome when risk is present. It is not simply the opposite of a risk factor; instead, it interacts with a risk factor to determine the outcome. Through interaction, a protective factor moderates the effect of a risk factor and increases the likelihood of a positive result. A comprehensive human formation program attempts to reduce risk factors; aggressively promotes and enhances resilience, emotional intelligence, the improvement of problem-solving skills, and the acquisition of healthy support systems; and is committed to engendering well-integrated individuals. A rigorous psychological evaluation should focus on accurately evaluating protective factors and providing formators with usable suggestions on how to maximize the potential of these factors during human formation. We are all responsible to prevent the entry of the narcissistically oriented candidate into the priesthood and to root out the egotistical abusers from our midst. For psychologists, evaluators, and members of review boards, this chapter includes identifiable and measurable traits and behaviors. Narcissistically disordered candidates feel attracted to the seminary system where the prevalence of clericalism in the institutional church is often embraced.[21]

---

[21] D. B. Cozzens, *Sacred Silence: Denial and the Crisis in the Church* (Collegeville, MN: Liturgical Press, 2004).

8.

Understanding and Resisting Clericalism and Social Sin

B. Kevin Brown

For nearly two decades clericalism has been identified as a cause of the clergy abuse crisis in the Catholic Church. However, little attention has been paid to clericalism as a form of social sin. In this chapter I argue that understanding clericalism as a form of social sin not only illuminates how it created the conditions that allowed for the systemic cover-up of clergy sexual abuse, but also how it might be resisted and dismantled through theological renewal. In order to develop this argument this chapter proceeds in three parts. It first examines how the clergy sexual abuse crisis uncovers the phenomenon of clericalism, which is grounded in bias, in a unique way. Second, it considers how understanding clericalism as a form of social sin sheds light on its insidious nature and the ways that it might be resisted. Finally, it traces the roots of the theological bias that grounds clericalism—a theology of ministry suggesting that those who are ordained to the ministerial priesthood are uniquely ontologically conformed to Christ—and gestures toward the foundation of a renewed theology of ministry.

CLERICALISM AND THE
CLERGY SEXUAL ABUSE CRISIS

Clericalism is not the inevitable result of the presence of clergy. George Wilson notes that, sociologically, the word *clergy* refers to any group within a community that performs a particular function at the service of the rest of the community—the laity. Clergies form as societies develop into complex and structured communities, and individuals with particular skills and gifts are often called to use those skills and gifts to serve the rest of the community, the laity. Ideally, a clergy remains firmly rooted within the community, marked by differentiated service in which many clergies put their gifts and labor at the service of the common good.[1] Clericalism, however, develops when mission of service and exercise of service are distorted as the clergy becomes a class set apart from the rest of the community through a process of clericalization.

Clericalism and Bias

Clericalization is, principally, seen when members of a particular clergy are granted deference by the rest of the community simply by virtue of status or membership, prior to any authentic exercise of the service they are called to render. Wilson and Richard Gaillardetz argue that, as a result of this deference, clergy members identify primarily with the clergy rather than with the community as a whole, and a divide quickly emerges within the community. As its status becomes increasingly rarified, the clergy becomes especially sensitive to critique and hesitant to make publicly known anything that can damage the privilege of the clergy. News that might damage the image of the clergy or its members is often

---

[1] George B. Wilson, *Clericalism: The Death of Priesthood* (Collegeville, MN: The Liturgical Press, 2008), 3–36. See also Richard Gaillardetz's development of Wilson's work in Richard R. Gaillardetz, "A Church in Crisis: How Did We Get Here? How Do We Move Forward?" *Worship* 93 (2019): 209.

swept under the rug.[2] The effects of clericalization, however, are not limited to the clergy.

Clericalization facilitates the development of a clerical culture that affects the life of the whole community. Bernard Lonergan defines culture as "simply the set of meanings and values that inform the way of life of a community."[3] Clericalization results in the meaning and values that inform the life a particular community being marked by a clericalist *bias*. M. Shawn Copeland, developing the work of Lonergan, writes that bias refers to "the more or less conscious and deliberate choice, in light of what we perceive as a potential threat to our well-being, to exclude further information or data from consideration in our understanding, judgment, discernment, decision, and action."[4] The meanings and values that animate a clerical culture, which is maintained both by the clergy and by members of the laity, are distorted by a three-part bias. First, a clericalist bias presumes that members of clergy are essentially different from the rest of the community. Second, it assumes that the clergy is superior to or holds a dominant place in relation to the rest of the community because of its role in the community—a role once rooted in service. Third, it assumes that, due to the role the clergy plays in the community, it and its members are essential to the life of the community in a way that others are not. This allows other members of the community to abdicate certain rights to exercise their own responsibility for the life of the community to the clergy, who happily assumes an even greater share of power.

---

[2] Wilson, *Clericalism*, 15–35; Gaillardetz, "A Church in Crisis," 209–10.

[3] Bernard Lonergan, "A Revolution in Catholic Theology," in *A Second Collection: Papers by Bernard J. F. Lonergan, SJ*, ed. William F. J. Ryan and Bernard J. Tyrrell (Philadelphia: Westminster Press, 1974), 232.

[4] M. Shawn Copeland, *Enfleshing Freedom: Body, Race, and Being* (Minneapolis: Fortress Press, 2010), 13. See also Bernard Lonergan, *Insight: A Study of Human Understanding*, 5th ed., Collected Works of Bernard Lonergan 3 (Toronto: University of Toronto Press, Scholarly Publishing Division, 1992), 196–269; Bernard Lonergan, *Method in Theology* (New York: Herder and Herder, 1972), 214–69.

These three elements of a clericalist bias combine to generate the more or less conscious decision to protect the status, privilege, and rights of the clergy within a community to the exclusion of the well-being and rights of the community as a whole and of those community members who are not members of the clergy. Those who act accordingly refuse the corrective insight that any clergy's mission and purpose is to serve the common good of the community. Instead, they adopt the stance that the clergy is essential to the existence of the community while members of laity are nonconsequential and dependent members of the community. Thus, clericalist biases give life to cultures built on secrecy and deference. They nurture an environment in which the good of the clergy is to be protected and valued over the common good of the community at virtually any cost. The result is the emergence of a privileged elite and a superiority-inferiority division within the community. Power and authority are exercised not collaboratively but authoritatively in order to maintain power and privilege over those who are not members of the clergy. In a clerical culture marked by these realities, clericalism abounds.

As a structural reality, rooted in a clericalist bias, clericalism describes any situation in which a person or group uses its particular expertise or gifts that are meant to be put at the service of the common good of the community to protect, maintain, or establish its own privilege or superiority in relation to the rest of the community while refusing to acknowledge how that behavior might affect the rest of the community. In this sense clericalism represents a manifestation of what Sandra Schneiders identifies as a structure of domination, a two-tiered system of power and privilege in which "a few people (the rich, the political elites, the religious authorities) oppress the majority of the people for the benefit of the oppressors" through either direct exploitation or by acting in ways concerned primarily with the maintenance of their own privilege.[5]

---

[5] Sandra M. Schneiders, *Buying the Field: Catholic Religious Life in Mission to the World, Religious Life in a New Millennium*, Vol. 3 (Mahwah, NJ: Paulist Press, 2013), 467.

Clericalism and the Clergy Sexual Abuse Crisis

Before examining how clericalism is seen in the Catholic Church through the lens of the clergy sexual abuse crisis, it is helpful to recall how the church is called to live as a community. In its *Dogmatic Constitution on the Church* (*Lumen Gentium*), the Second Vatican Council speaks of the church as a community of the pilgrim people of God seeking to embody the love of the Triune God in history. Within this people particular members are called to serve the community through their participation in and ordination to the ministerial priesthood as priests (or presbyters) and bishops. But baptism, through which all members of the church participate in the one priesthood of Christ, remains the primary sacrament through which all persons in the church relate to one another (*LG*, nos. 9–11). As a result, all the baptized share a "common dignity" and "a true equality with regard to the dignity and the activity which they share in the building up of the body of Christ" (*LG*, nos. 31–32). The offices of the ministerial priesthood, then, are not to be exercised as if their holders are set apart from the community. While the ministerial priesthood is called to serve the non-ordained, with whom they continue to participate in the baptismal priesthood (*LG*, nos. 14–17), non-ordained persons in the church are likewise called to "eagerly collaborate with their pastors and teachers" (*LG*, nos. 49–50). Rather than being two classes of membership in the church, the ordained and non-ordained are called to participate together in the one priesthood of Christ. They are called to respond communally to the love of God in the world by using the distinct charismatic gifts the Spirit bestows on each person to make that love known. While some elements of Vatican II's documents reflect a more clericalist outlook (see *LG*, nos. 18–22, 28–29), one also finds this decidedly anti-clericalist vision. Yet, the clergy sexual abuse crisis has revealed that clericalism and a clerical culture protecting the ministerial priesthood—which functions, decidedly, as a clergy—can be found throughout the life of the Catholic Church.

For decades, cases in which members of the clergy sexually assaulted children were systematically covered up by bishops, provincials, diocesan staffs, and several Vatican congregations. Repeatedly, four patterns of behavior are seen in cases around the globe. First, with few exceptions, bishops and other church leaders did not report offending priests to law enforcement authorities, even after admissions of guilt. Second, bishops frequently allowed perpetrators to continue serving in positions of ministry in close contact with children after only brief periods of counseling that were repeatedly shown to be ineffective. Third, when a perpetrator was sent back into ministry or transferred to a new assignment, bishops did not inform parishioners that a priest assigned to their community had been accused of sexual abuse or that their children—or other vulnerable persons—might be in danger of being assaulted.[6] Fourth, there was a nearly complete lack of collaboration between the ordained and non-ordained in responding to sexual abuse cases. Canon law, which could have been used to consult the non-ordained in matters of governance and allow them to exercise their co-responsibility for the life of the church, was employed as a means to keep information from non-ordained members of the church and the public writ large.[7]

---

[6] Gerald A. Arbuckle, *Abuse and Cover-Up: Refounding the Catholic Church in Trauma* (Maryknoll, NY: Orbis Books, 2019), 52–60; Marie Keenan, *Child Sexual Abuse and the Catholic Church: Gender, Power, and Organizational Culture* (New York: Oxford University Press, 2012), 722–23; Nicholas P. Cafardi, *Before Dallas: The US Bishops' Response to Clergy Sexual Abuse of Children* (Mahwah, NJ: Paulist Press, 2008), 10–114; Wilson, *Clericalism*, 70–72; Thomas P. Doyle, A. W. Richard Sipe, and Patrick J. Wall, *Sex, Priests, and Secret Codes: The Catholic Church's 2,000 Year Paper Trail of Sexual Abuse* (Los Angeles: Volt Press, 2006), 3–66, 203–28; Kieran Tapsell, *Potiphar's Wife: The Vatican's Secret and Child Sexual Abuse* (Hindmarsh, Australia: ATF Press, 2014), 9–48, 95–140, 185–306; Christine Hanley and William Lobdell, "Rising above a Scandal," *Los Angeles Times*, October 3, 2002.

[7] The notable exception to this is the involvement of lay lawyers and, occasionally, psychologists. Joseph P. Chinnici, *When Values Collide: The Catholic Church, Sexual Abuse, and the Challenges of Leadership* (Maryknoll, NY: Orbis Books, 2010), 87–89, 164; Thomas P. Doyle, "Ro-

These patterns of behavior point to classic features of a clerical culture. Rather than identifying primarily with the community of God's people, those who covered up clergy sexual abuse seem to have identified primarily with their fellow clergy members and their office, including its privilege, power, and influence.[8] Moreover, the sustained effort to maintain secrecy around cases of clergy sexual abuse and to protect the reputation of bishops and priests seemingly at all costs—including the well-being of the most vulnerable members of the church community—reflects the desire to maintain the power and privilege of one's office typical of a clerical culture. Even as stories of abuse and cover-up continued to come to light and bishops publicly professed sympathy for victim-survivors, they fought to keep records of the cover-up of clergy sexual abuse from being released to the public. Internal memos reveal that bishops acted out of a fear that revealing the abuse committed by priests would result in a loss of reputation, the loss of their own pastoral office, or damage to the image of church leadership generally.[9] As Lakeland notes, such actions point

---

man Catholic Clericalism, Religious Duress, and Clergy Sexual Abuse," *Pastoral Psychology* 51 (2003): 221; Paul Lakeland, *The Liberation of the Laity: In Search of an Accountable Church* (New York: Continuum, 2003), 230; William C. Spohn, "Episcopal Responsibility for the Sexual Abuse Crisis," in *Sin against the Innocents: Sexual Abuse by Priests and the Role of the Catholic Church*, ed. Thomas G. Plante (Westport, CT: Praeger, 2004), 160; Wilson, *Clericalism*, 71–72; The Secretariat of State of the Holy See, "Report on the Holy See's Institutional Knowledge and Decision-Making Related to Former Cardinal Theodore Edgar McCarrick (1930–2017)," Vatican City State, November 10, 2020 (hereafter "McCarrick Report").

[8] James F. Keenan, "Vulnerability and Hierarchicalism," *Melita Theologica* 68 (2018): 129–42; Gaillardetz, "A Church in Crisis," 211–12.

[9] Office of the Attorney General, Commonwealth of Pennsylvania, "Pennsylvania Diocese Victims Report" (Pennsylvania, USA: Report of the 40th Statewide Investigating Grand Jury, July 27, 2018), 200, 498, 509, 536, 632, 722, 760, 767; Secretariat of State of the Holy See, "McCarrick Report," 97, 117, 123, 139, 149, 170, 173–174n580, 240, 243, 397. Reporting has revealed that, in the Archdiocese of Los Angeles, Cardinal Roger Mahony feared that the public scandal that would be caused by revealing instances of clergy sexual abuse would compromise

to a "belief, however inchoate," that "undervalues the lay lifestyle, lay talent, lay leadership, lay experience and lay spirituality."[10]

Critically, however, the clericalism revealed by the clergy sexual abuse crisis is not only seen in the actions of priests and bishops. In some instances parents, unaware of the abuse their children were enduring, thought the attention their child was receiving from a priest was a sign of blessing. Some victim-survivors and their families report feeling, at the time, as if God were choosing to spend time with them. In other cases victims did not report the crimes committed against them or they were not believed by their families because the priest or bishop who abused them was held in high esteem and there was a concern that his reputation might be damaged.[11] This dynamic should in no way be used to blame the victims, survivors, or their family for the violence perpetrated by clergy. But it is illustrative of the ways a clericalist bias affects a whole community's way of being, thinking, and acting. In this case, the priest or bishop and his reputation was to be protected and was valued more than the well-being of the individual victims or the community because the priest was seen as essential to the community.

The sexual abuse crisis is a case study illustrating the claim that a clericalist bias does not simply boost the clergy members' individual egos. It affects the life of the whole community. The actions of bishops, priests, and many non-ordained persons suggest that the clericalism and clerical culture affecting the Catholic Church involve the bias that the clergy of the ministerial priesthood holds a superior role in relation to the laity in the life of

---

his ability to advocate for social justice issues including immigration reform and the rights of migrant laborers. Victoria Kim, Ashley Powers, and Harriet Ryan, "For Roger Mahony, Clergy Abuse Cases Were a Threat to Agenda," *Los Angeles Times*, December 1, 2013, online edition.

[10] Lakeland, *The Liberation of the Laity*, 195.

[11] The Investigative Staff of the *Boston Globe, Betrayal: The Crisis in the Catholic Church:* (New York: Back Bay Books, 2015), 4, 82–88, 138–40; Office of the Attorney General, Commonwealth of Pennsylvania, "Pennsylvania Diocese Victims Report," 469; Secretariat of State of the Holy See, "McCarrick Report," 37–47.

church. Consistently, bishops and others refused the corrective insight, found in the testimony of scripture and tradition (including Vatican II), that all the baptized share an equal dignity before God and in the church. The ministerial priesthood is not set apart and deserving of special protection. Its ministry of service is meant to be exercised in collaboration with the charismatic gifts of the whole community in order to build up a communion reflective of God's nondominative love. Yet, the clergy sexual abuse crisis reveals that the ministerial priesthood has been distorted by clericalism to such a degree that the Catholic Church has come to resemble a two-tiered structure of domination.

UNDERSTANDING CLERICALISM WITHIN THE CHURCH AS SOCIAL SIN

Recognizing clericalism as a structure of domination rooted in bias illustrates that it is a social reality that affects the entire community in a deep and abiding way. It is not merely that priests get a free haircut or a tee time on an otherwise booked golf course. Clericalism affects how the entire church lives into its identity as a sacrament of both God's pilgrim people and the risen body of Jesus of Nazareth. In the last half-century theologians have typically explored the moral and theological implications of structures of domination through the categories of social sin and sinful social structures. "In its broadest sense," Kristin Heyer writes, "social sin encompasses the unjust structures, distorted consciousness, and collective actions and inaction that facilitate injustice and dehumanization."[12] Sinful social structures are the human-built structures and institutions that, animated by social sin, perpetuate systemic and structural injustice. Given this definition and the patterns of behavior just outlined, it does not take a stretch of one's theological imagination to recognize clericalism as a social sin. The importance of identifying clericalism as social sin, however,

---

[12] Kristin E. Heyer, "Social Sin and Immigration: Good Fences Make Bad Neighbors," *Theological Studies* 71 (2010): 413.

is found in the way that particular understandings of social sin suggest that it might be resisted.

Social Sin and Bias

Since the distinctions introduced by the categories of social sin and sinful social structures are nuanced and complex, they often elicit theological debate over who and what can be considered sinful in situations of social sin.[13] One view, associated with political, liberation, and praxis-based theologies, maintains that Christians cannot limit the indictment of sinfulness to human beings. Rather, oppressive social structures and ideologies must be considered sinful in themselves and in need of transformation. Certainly, individual persons sin by participating in these institutions or adhering to these beliefs, and they are responsible for building the oppressive systems in the first place. But the social ideologies and structures—even the cultures behind them—are also considered sinful. In situations of social sin it is impossible to participate without sharing in the corporate sin of the community unless one actively resists their dominative script.[14] A second view, typical of John Paul II's treatment of social sin, maintains that social ideologies or social structures cannot be considered sinful because they are not individual persons making concrete moral decisions. They are only seen as sinful analogically. In this view, sinful social structures or ideologies are the cumulative result of

---

[13] For a helpful overview of this debate, see Heyer, 415–25.

[14] Broadly speaking, this first position has developed out of Latin American liberation theology, Black liberation theology in the United States, feminist theology, the thought of Bernard Lonergan and his students, and post-war European political theology. Foundational figures in these theological movements include Gustavo Gutiérrez, Jon Sobrino, José Ignacio González Faus, Ignacio Ellacuría, James H. Cone, M. Shawn Copeland, Bernard Lonergan, Patrick Kerans, Piet Schoonenberg, Johann Baptist Metz, and Eugen Drewermann. Building on the work of these thinkers, theological ethicists Bryan Massingale and Megan McCabe have recently argued that cultures can be considered sinful as well.

the personal sins of individuals, are sustained by personal sin, and cause individuals to commit further personal sins. But the indictment of sinfulness is limited to individual acts of persons with moral agency, not institutions or ideologies.[15]

A third view, articulated by Daniel Finn, seeks something of a middle ground between these two positions. Like the liberationist approach, Finn challenges John Paul II's view that sinful social structures are primarily the consequences of personal sin. Drawing on the critical realist school of sociology and Karl Rahner's theology of original sin, he illustrates that social structures are indeed causal, inclining people to sin and limiting, to a certain extent, their moral agency. In this way, he argues, "the sin that can exist in social structures," like original sin, "is sin only analogically."[16] Finn helpfully draws out how institutions shape the moral agency of persons, leading to the perpetuation of sin, without obliterating free will. But by his own admission, he does not address how culture or ideology shape these institutions or are propagated by these structures.[17]

In contrast, the liberationist approach emphasizes that situations of social sin and sinful social structures are sustained by sinful ideologies.[18] Schneiders suggests that these ideologies stem from the fear that sits at the heart of what she identifies as the sin

---

[15] See Pope John Paul II, *Reconciliation and Penance*, no. 16; and *Sollicitudo Rei Socialis*, nos. 35–37.

[16] Daniel K. Finn, "What Is a Sinful Social Structure?" *Theological Studies* 77 (2016): 155.

[17] Interestingly, Finn notes that his conclusion has much in common with the approach found in Pope Benedict XVI's encyclical *Caritas in Veritate*. This marks a significant development in Benedict's thought, given his earlier critiques of liberation theology; as Cardinal Joseph Ratzinger, he argued with John Paul II that sinful social structures are not causal of sin but consequences of personal sin (Finn, 136–53). See also, Pope Benedict XVI, *Caritas in Veritate* (2009); "Instruction on Certain Aspects of the 'Theology of Liberation'" (August 6, 1984), chap. IV; and Congregation for the Doctrine of the Faith, "Instruction on Christian Freedom and Liberation" (May 22, 1986), nos. 15, 74.

[18] See, for example, Gregory Baum, *Religion and Alienation: A Theological Reading of Sociology*, 2nd ed. (Maryknoll, NY: Orbis Books,

of the world. Drawing on the work of Eugen Drewermann, she writes that the sin (singular) of the world is humanity's refusal to accept God's unceasing invitation to share in God's communion of love that sustains life even through death due to our existential fear of our mortality as contingent beings. Accepting this love would entail sharing in God's gratuitous love by building up a community of mutual flourishing with and for all creatures through the realization of the common good. However, as we fail to recognize that God sustains our existence as an eternal act of self-giving love, we become preoccupied with securing our existence and refuse to accept fully the love offered by God. This refusal to accept God's self-sustaining love affects the way we live in relationship with others. By breaking right relationship with the God who sustains all that exists and calls all creatures back to God through God's creative act of love, we turn our concern away from those with whom we do not identify. In turn, we build up structures of domination, or the *sins* (plural) of the world, to provide for the apparent social, political, economic, and spiritual security of our in-group while ignoring the ways these systems trample upon other persons and communities, especially the most vulnerable.[19]

In essence, the sin of the world that Schneiders identifies as sitting at the heart of all structures of domination is a bias. Recall that Copeland defines bias as "the more or less conscious decision to refuse corrective insights or understandings, to persist in error. Bias, then, is the arrogant choice to be incorrect."[20] This bias reflects the

2006), 174–75, 200–203; Jamie T. Phelps, "Communion Ecclesiology and Black Liberation Theology," *Theological Studies* 61 (2000): 699.

[19] Schneiders, *Buying the Field*, 129–31; Sandra M. Schneiders, *Jesus Risen in Our Midst: Essays on the Resurrection of Jesus in the Fourth Gospel* (Collegeville, MN: The Liturgical Press, 2013), 154–56; Sandra M. Schneiders, "The Lamb of God and the Forgiveness of Sin(s) in the Fourth Gospel," *Catholic Biblical Quarterly* 73 (2011): 6–9.

[20] M. Shawn Copeland, "Toward a Critical Christian Feminist Theology of Solidarity," in *Women and Theology*, ed. Mary Ann Hinsdale and Phyllis Kaminski, The Annual Publication of the College Theology Society, vol. 40 (1994) (Maryknoll, NY: Orbis Books, 1995), 24.

refusal of the corrective insight of God's own love—God's salvific invitation to share in the divine life by building up a community of agapeic love. This foundational bias spins off into countless derivative biases providing seeming ideological foundations for the social, political, economic, and spiritual structures we build up to provide for our privilege and apparent existential security at the cost of others. As in the case of the clericalist bias outlined above, they shape entire cultures and condition a community's set of meanings and values in ways that allow the dominant group to maintain power and privilege at the expense of others. As a result, these biases account for three of the most pernicious and insidious dynamics of social sin. First, they incline human beings to believe that effects of social sin appear to be the natural order of things. They become "baked" into our ways of thinking and living to such a degree that we refuse to acknowledge how our privilege or power is maintained at the expense of the well-being of others, especially the most vulnerable among us. Second, since biases shape the values of a community, they can lead even those who do not benefit from the dominative system they underlie to think and act according to their superiority-inferiority and privileged-nonprivileged scripts. Third, these biases harm all persons within the community. Obviously, they harm most those persons against whom the violent structural and personal manifestations of a particular bias are directed. But these biases also injure the humanity of the dominant group—including those who are passively privileged—by preventing them from living into the fullness of the creaturely communion that God invites all of creation to share. Therefore, as José Ignacio González Faus notes, in instances of social sin "any personally sinful human being is both responsible and a victim."[21] Such a person is in need of both transformation and liberation from the biases and ideologies that incline the world toward sin.

---

[21] José Ignacio González Faus, "Sin," in *Mysterium Liberationis: Fundamental Concepts of Liberation Theology*, ed. Ignacio Ellacuría and Jon Sobrino, 532–42 (Maryknoll, NY: Orbis Books, 1993), 536.

Each of these three elements of social sin, rooted in bias, is seen in the clericalism that the clergy sexual abuse crisis has revealed within the Catholic Church. Clericalism has led to a way of living as church in which the ministerial priesthood has come to be seen as so essential to the life of the community that the reputation, power, and privilege of it and its members have been protected at the cost of the well-being of the rest of the community. While this bias has been upheld most directly by members of the ministerial priesthood, as I noted above, non-ordained members of the community certainly have acted to maintain systems, structures, and ways of acting in accord with this bias. As a result, some of the most vulnerable members of the community have been made to suffer due to the cover-up of clergy sexual abuse and the reassignment of known predators. In the process the entire community was prevented from living into its baptismal dignity through which each person shares a common dignity and is called to participate in the building up of the church through his or her particular charismatic gifts.

Addressing the Social Sin of Clericalism

While much of the debate over social sin is often framed in terms of personal and social culpability, it raises the question of how a community might turn away from social sin and toward a life reflective of the communion into which God invites all of creation. I am convinced that Christian theology must adopt the view that emerges out of liberation theologies if it is going to address adequately the social evils that mar creation and society, like the form of the clericalism affecting the Catholic Church. This approach suggests that transformation is necessary at three levels if clericalism is going to be addressed and resisted within the church.

As with any sin, conversion away from social sins requires personal repentance. The entire church is called to conversion and repentance because each member is complicit in clericalism in some way. But not all people are equally complicit. Those who are denied access to power in dominative structures are often denied the opportunity by those in power to bring about any meaningful change. Thus, as Jesus illustrates in his ministry, the oppressors and the oppressed are both called to different types of conversion by Jesus's invitation to communion. Both active oppressors and those passively privileged by situations of social sin are called to leave all they have behind—to divest themselves of the privilege they gained through their participation in an unjust system (see Mk 10:17–31; Lk 19:1–10). The oppressed are called to no longer live in a way that is defined by the systems that denied their humanity and identity as children of God (see Lk 7:36—8:3). Resisting clericalism demands that members of the ministerial priesthood refuse to exercise their ministry according to the clericalist bias and the non-ordained refuse to be denied the right to exercise their baptismal responsibility to participate in the life of the church. At this level there is some agreement between the liberationist approach to social sin and that of John Paul II. However, as Heyer notes, by suggesting that social transformation is possible through personal conversion alone, John Paul II overlooks the extent to which structures and ideologies limit personal agency.[22]

Therefore, social structures and institutions must be transformed if personal conversion is going to have any affect. Unless the clerical structures of leadership and ministry that allowed for the cover-up and perpetuation of abuse are uprooted, clericalism will continue to mar the church and these structures will continue to incline individuals and communities toward sin. Here, Finn finds common ground with the liberationist approach to social sin. But he does not account for the ways culture, ideology, or bias inhibit the ability of individuals and communities to work for structural change.

Accordingly, if structural transformation *and* personal conversion are going to be effective, the sinful biases underlying social sins must be challenged and deconstructed.[23] In the case

---

[22] Heyer, "Social Sin and Immigration," 419. See also *Reconciliatio et Paenitentia*, no. 16.

[23] Heyer, 422.

of clericalism, so long as members of the ministerial priesthood are seen as distinct from and/or superior to the rest of the church, a vision of the church wherein all the faithful might claim their baptismal co-responsibility has no chance of taking root. A renewed theology of ministry is necessary.

The need to attend to the underlying biases of clericalism are particularly acute given who and what the church is called to be. In her theological interpretation of the Johannine resurrection narrative, Schneiders argues that the church is called to continue the salvific mission of Jesus of Nazareth, who takes away the sin of the world. Jesus does this not only by inviting all of creation to share in the nondominative love of God through his inauguration of the reign of God but also by refusing to resist his unjust death violently, instead trusting that the love of God would sustain him even through death. As the risen Jesus returns to his disciples through the Spirit, he commissions them to live as his risen body in the world and continue his mission by taking away the sins of the world. Schneiders suggests that this mission entails working to deconstruct structures of domination that mar creation and striving to embody, in its own communion, the nondominative love of God's life that it is called to invite all of creation to share.[24] A clericalist bias that conditions the church to live as a community marked by clericalism, then, inhibits the church's ability to live into its truest identity as a sacrament of the risen body of Jesus. Until the church is able to transform the bias that sits at the heart of clericalism, no amount of personal or structural conversion—whether in the form of seminary reform, collaborative and

---

[24] Schneiders makes this argument through a critical engagement with each scene of the Johannine resurrection narrative, drawing out the author of the Fourth Gospel's employment of Hebrew imagery found in both Genesis and Ezekiel. Sandra M. Schneiders, "Touching the Risen Jesus: Mary Magdalene and Thomas the Twin in John 20," *Proceedings of the Catholic Theological Society of America* 60 (2005): 13–35; Sandra M. Schneiders, "The Raising of the New Temple: John 20:19–35 and Johannine Ecclesiology," *New Testament Studies* 52 (2006): 337–55; Schneiders, "Lamb of God and the Forgiveness of Sin(s) in the Fourth Gospel"; and Schneiders, *Jesus Risen in Our Midst.*

consultative leadership, or zero tolerance policies—will allow it to live into this call and dismantle the clerical culture that allowed the clergy sexual abuse crisis to unfold.

RESISTING CLERICALISM THROUGH THEOLOGICAL RENEWAL

Identifying the bias at the root of clericalism is critical to resisting it and ultimately dismantling it. In the remainder of this chapter, I briefly trace how the clericalist bias affecting the Catholic Church is rooted in a theology of ministry that distorts the Christian tradition. Once this has been identified, I suggest how an alternative theology of ministry, rooted in the ancient Christian tradition and the ways that the Spirit's invitation to share in God's nondominative love has and continues to unfold in the history of the tradition, might lay the foundation for an anti-clericalist understanding of the church.

The Theological Roots of Clericalism

In order to understand how a clericalist bias took root in the Catholic tradition despite the ways it distorts the church's identity, it is helpful to note how the church understands itself to be priestly people and to review briefly how the categories of clergy and laity developed in the Christian tradition in relation to the theological notion of priesthood. Jon Sobrino argues that priesthood is, at its heart, a matter of mediating the presence and saving activity of the Holy Other to creation.[25] While he was never a Temple priest, Jesus is understood in the Christian tradition to be the great High Priest, fully mediating God's saving activity in

---

[25] Jon Sobrino, "Toward a Determination of the Nature of Priesthood: Service to God's Salvific Approach to Human Beings," in *The Principle of Mercy: Taking the Crucified People from the Cross*, trans. Robert R. Barr (Maryknoll, NY: Orbis Books, 1994), 112–13.

creation. Thus, the church understands itself, as the risen body of Christ, to be a priestly people (see 1 Pt 2:9–10) called to mediate God's presence on earth.[26]

Within this people there was not an immediate distinction made between a clergy and a laity. Alexandre Faivre notes that while the New Testament refers to community leaders and ministers, the only references to a *kleros* (roughly translated as "clergy"), or people set apart, are references to the entire church who are made a part of God's people through Christ. Even among its varied organizational and theological contexts, the primitive communities were too Christocentric to admit strong distinction between those who exercised ministry and the rest of the community. By virtue of baptism, each person was understood to offer a co-equal, though distinctive, *diakonia* ("service or ministry") to the community through his or her charismatic gifts, some of which were ordered into offices.[27]

By the third century, however, an identifiable clergy and laity had emerged. In most local churches the clergy consisted of those who exercised ministries of oversight, leadership, and service

---

[26] While this is typically how the church's priestly identity is portrayed in church teachings, it is important that the church's priestly identity not be described in a way that contributes to supercessionist biases in the church. Therefore, it is important to note that the church's priestly identity is rooted in the priestly identity of biblical Israel, whom the church does *not* replace as God's people. Rather, as Willie James Jennings notes, through the person of Jesus, the church, in its Gentile identity, is grafted onto and woven into the people of God—not as a replacement but as second readers of God's salvific promise to all creation. See Willie James Jennings, *The Christian Imagination: Theology and the Origins of Race* (New Haven, CT: Yale University Press, 2011), 250–59.

[27] Alexandre Faivre, *The Emergence of the Laity in the Early Church*, trans. David Smith (New York: Paulist Press, 1990), 3–42, 210–11. See also Edward Schillebeeckx, *Ministry: Leadership in the Community of Jesus Christ*, trans. John Bowden (New York: Crossroad, 1981), 38–46, 70–71; and Edward Schillebeeckx, *The Church with a Human Face: A New and Expanded Theology of Ministry*, trans. John Bowden (New York: Crossroad, 1985), 125–33.

through the offices of bishop, presbyter, and deacon.[28] Yet, Edward Schillebeeckx notes, as references to the clergy and laity emerged, "this terminology in no way indicated a difference of status."[29] These officeholders were seen neither as set apart from the community nor as receiving a special power handed down by Christ. Rather, they were empowered by the Spirit-filled community to serve and lead the church from within its communion through their charismatic gifts.[30] As they led the community and coordinated its life as God's priestly people, bishops and presbyters in particular were understood to exercise a type of ministerial priesthood. In a community in which each disciple was understood to mediate Christ's presence through charismatic cooperation with the Spirit, these ministers were understood to mediate the presence of Christ, head of the church, through their charismatic ministry of pastoral leadership and oversight. Through this presidential ministry of leadership, they in turn presided over the community's sacramental life.[31]

This development, however, was by no means universal. Some bishops in the third century exercised their episcopal ministry

---

[28] As the offices of bishop, presbyter, and deacon developed, they were recognized as *apostolic* offices that facilitate the church's efforts to remain faithful to the apostolic tradition by ordering the charismatic ministries of oversight, leadership, and service. At times, in some local churches, instituted readers (lectors), instituted widows, subdeacons, and deaconesses *may* have also been considered clergy or held in liminal spaces between the clergy and laity. Schillebeeckx, *Ministry*, 38–48; Schillebeeckx, *The Church with a Human Face*, 125–39; Faivre, *The Emergence of the Laity*, 69–120; David Noel Power, *Mission, Ministry, Order: Reading the Tradition in the Present Context* (New York: Continuum, 2008), 117–208.

[29] Schillebeeckx, *Ministry*, 70.

[30] Faivre, *The Emergence of the Laity*, 43–51, 70–71; Schillebeeckx, *Ministry*, 5–52; Schillebeeckx, *The Church with a Human Face*, 40–156; José Ignacio González Faus, *Builders of Community: Rethinking Ecclesiastical Ministry*, trans. María Isabel Reyna and Liam Kelly, Series Traditio (Miami, FL: Convivium Press, 2012), 34–39. Faivre notes that at least in some communities laity did not refer to all of the non-ordained but to a clearly defined subset of the non-ordained (Faivre, 43–71).

[31] Schillebeeckx, *Ministry*, 49.

through dialogue and consultation with the rest of the faithful. But, in other churches, like the Syrian church that produced the *Didascalia*, the bishop exercised his office as a benevolent monarch who was called to mediate God's presence while the people, who were not depicted as exercising any priestly function, were called to be totally submissive to their bishop.[32] As Faivre notes, "The logical consequence of this attitude is that the laity came to be treated as inferior."[33] A clericalist bias had begun to take root.

Over the next several centuries these roots deepened and spread. As church ministers adopted Roman honorific titles and bishops began to be seen as princes and the laity as subjects, ministries of ecclesial authority were no longer understood in terms of service of the community. Instead, the community was compelled to serve those in authority.[34] Concurrently, in Western Christianity the office of deacon as a stable ministry slowly began to fall out of practice. Increasingly only presbyters and bishops were understood to be the clergy of the community. Additionally, several ecclesial practices were distorted in ways that deemphasized the priestly identity of the whole church and emphasized the priestly ministry of presbyters (now called priests) and bishops.[35] More often, they alone were seen as *the* priests of the community: Christ was mediated in the community through their liturgical

---

[32] Schillebeeckx, *The Church with a Human Face*, 133–39; Faivre, *The Emergence of the Laity*, 72–133.

[33] Faivre, 90.

[34] Schillebeeckx, *The Church with a Human Face*, 141–63; Faivre, 145–57.

[35] While such practices are found throughout the church's history, several major developments began to take shape in the late fourth century. Practices such as regular presbyteral presidency at the Eucharist, the gradual formalization of liturgical ritual, and ascetic monasticism were paired with the clerical adoption of Roman titles of honor and dress to create two distinct classes within the church. Thomas P. Rausch, *Towards a Truly Catholic Church: An Ecclesiology for the Third Millennium* (Collegeville, MN: The Liturgical Press, 2005), 103–4; Michael L. Papesh, *Clerical Culture: Contradiction and Transformation* (Collegeville, MN: The Liturgical Press, 2004), 20–32; Schillebeeckx, *The Church with a Human Face*, 140–62.

presidency at the Eucharist and as they acted *in persona Christi* to lead the community as its head. While the clergy were to care for the laity, the clergy were also to be revered above the laity as uniquely holy.[36] The growing association of priest-presbyters and bishops with the priestly work of Jesus as the affirmation of the whole church's participation in his priestly work fell out of the church's lexicon. It provided an apparent—albeit deficient— theological justification for the deepening clerical bias. This bias suggested that members of the ministerial priesthood were set apart because they were more like Christ than other members of the church and therefore had a greater inherent dignity and worth.

A theology of ordained ministry that developed early in Christianity's second millennium reinforced the apparent theological justification of the clerical divide within the church. This theology emerged out of a theological landscape that had seen shifts in both eucharistic theology and the understanding of the relationship of the priest (and bishop) to the Eucharist. Beginning in the sixth century there was a growing tendency to understand the ministerial priesthood primarily in relation to the celebration of the sacraments. The focus on this relationship was only deepened as theologies of the Eucharist, beginning in the ninth century, tended to focus primarily, and sometimes exclusively, on the transformation of the eucharistic elements of bread and wine into the body and blood of Christ. Falling out of view was an understanding that the Eucharist is celebrated by the entire community, as the church is reconstituted as Christ's risen body through its encounter with the risen Christ in the eucharistic banquet.[37] The theology of ordained ministry that developed early in the second millennium emphasized the individual priest's or bishop's sacramental power, handed down in the sacrament of ordination by Christ, rather than the minister's service within

---

[36] Schillebeeckx, *Ministry*, 48–52; Schillebeeckx, *The Church with a Human Face*, 140–41, 163–94; Faivre, *The Emergence of the Laity*, 189–208.

[37] Schillebeeckx, *Ministry*, 48–58; Schillebeeckx, *The Church with a Human Face*, 161–67, 189–94.

the community.[38] Gaillardetz notes that such an understanding of ordained ministry is "metaphysically underwritten with what we might refer to as a 'substance ontology.'"[39] It suggests that the ontological substance of the individual is transformed, enabling the person ordained to act *in persona Christi* and "confect" the Eucharist. This theology provides an even deeper—albeit again flawed—theological grounding for the clericalist bias shaping of how the relationship between the ordained ministers of the church and the rest of the community was understood.[40] It suggests that the non-ordained members of the community participate in the Eucharist only through the power and activity of the ordained. Moreover, it reifies the idea that priests are more like Christ than other members of the church. And, since it intimates that the clergy are somehow more able to act *in persona Christi*, it suggests that power and responsibility for the life of the community should be concentrated in them so they can rule over the laity.

This bias would be hardened in the Catholic tradition with the development of the French School of clerical piety in the

---

[38] For an example of this theology, see Thomas Aquinas, *Summa Theologiae*, trans. Fathers of the English Dominican Province, Latin-English ed., vol. 9: Tertia Pars, Q. 60–90; Supplement Q. 1–33 (Scotts Valley, CA: NovAntiqua, 2018), ST III, q 63, a 3.

[39] Richard R. Gaillardetz, "The Ecclesiological Foundations of Ministry within an Ordered Communion," in *Ordering the Baptismal Priesthood: Theologies of Lay and Ordained Ministry*, ed. Susan K. Wood (Collegeville, MN: The Liturgical Press, 2003), 40.

[40] This bias is classically expressed by Pius X: "The Church is the mystical body of Christ, ruled by the Pastors and Doctors—a society of men containing within its own fold chiefs who have full and perfect powers for ruling, teaching and judging. It follows that the Church is essentially an unequal society that is a society comprising two categories of persons, the Pastors and the flock, those who occupy a rank in the different degrees of the hierarchy and the multitude of the faithful. So distinct are these categories that with the pastoral body only rests the necessary right and authority for promoting the end of the society and directing all its members towards that end; the one duty of the multitude is to allow themselves to be led, and, like a docile flock, to follow the Pastors." *Vehementer Nos* (May 22, 1906), no. 8.

seventeenth century. Edward Hahnenberg notes that this spirituality was well intentioned as a means to nourish the spiritual lives of priests so they might be empowered to nourish the spiritual lives of the communities they led. However, it is centered on the idea the priest is uniquely an *alter Christus*, conformed by ordination to Christ so that the priest might act "directly for Christ."[41] Therefore, it reinforces the notion that the priest or bishop is set apart from the rest of the community and uniquely able to act *in persona Christi*.

This clericalist bias, with roots now in the theological and spiritual traditions of the Catholic Church, has proven to be especially insidious. Despite the anti-clericalist understanding of the church found in the documents of Vatican II noted above, the council's teaching is marred by clericalist bias in other places. This bias is seen not only in the council's discussion of the power and nature of ordained ministry (*LG*, nos. 18–22, 28–29) but also in its treatment of the common priesthood and the ministerial priesthood. *Lumen Gentium* states:

> Though they differ essentially and not only in degree, the common priesthood of the faithful and the ministerial or hierarchical priesthood are none the less interrelated; each in its own way shares in the one priesthood of Christ. The ministerial priest, by the sacred power that he has, forms and governs the priestly people; in the person of Christ he brings about the eucharistic sacrifice and offers it to God in the name of all the people. (no. 10)

For Schillebeeckx, the first sentence of this passage affirms the work of the ministerial priesthood as a unique ministry within the priestly community of the baptized, ordered according to particular charismatic gifts, while not implying that it elevates a person to a distinctive state. However, in the next sentence the council draws on a theology of substantial ontological change, suggesting

---

[41] Edward P. Hahnenberg, *Ministries: A Relational Approach* (New York: Crossroad, 2003), 47.

that the ministerial priesthood has received a sacred power to form and govern the baptismal priesthood.[42] More recently, a clericalist bias could be found in the teaching of John Paul II on the nature of the ministerial priesthood when he spoke in *Pastores Dabo Vobis* of "the specific ontological bond" a priest or bishop shares with Christ (no. 11). Admittedly, such teachings may well be, at least in part, well-intentioned efforts to encourage bishops and priests to emulate Christ in their ministry. But the pernicious effects of such a bias on the life of the church are made evident in clergy sexual abuse. Government reports and victim-survivor testimonies have indicated that the unique association of the priest with Christ, as "Christ's representative on earth," as a result of a perceived ontological change affected through ordination, is a major factor leading to the systemic cover-up of abuse on the part of church officials and a hesitancy to report abuse on the part of survivors.[43] Beyond its inability to represent an authentic development of the tradition that calls the church to live as a community that reflects and embodies the nondominative love of God, this bias inclines the church to live in ways marked by structural and social sin—to refuse the corrective insight of God's invitation to love. As Lakeland writes, "When we have a Church built on an ontological divide . . . we are almost guaranteed to be out of step with God."[44] So long as a theology of substantial ontological change presents the ordained as uniquely close to or representative of Christ—and therefore set apart from the community and uniquely indispensable to the life of the community—there is little chance that the church can live in a way that is not marked by clericalism. What is needed is a theology of ministry rooted in the tradition and scripture that can ground a new way of recognizing

---

[42] Schillebeeckx, *Ministry*, 70.

[43] Investigative Staff of *The Boston Globe*, *Betrayal*, 44. See also *Royal Commission into Institutional Responses to Child Sexual Abuse: Preface and Executive Summary* (Barton, ACT: Commonwealth of Australia, 2017), 68.

[44] Paul Lakeland, *A Council That Will Never End:* Lumen Gentium *and the Church Today* (Collegeville, MN: The Liturgical Press, 2013), 140.

the charismatic contributions of both the ordained and the non-ordained to the life of the church.

Toward Theological Renewal

The full elaboration of a theology of ministry that resists the clericalist bias outlined above is beyond the scope of this chapter.[45] However, in the space that remains, I would like to point to the foundation of a theology of ministry that allows the church to live into Vatican II's affirmation of the ancient Christian tradition's conviction that all the baptized share an equal dignity and co-responsibility for the life of the church. This foundation is found in Schneiders's interpretation of the Johannine foot washing (Jn 13:1–20). Schneiders argues that, when Jesus washes the feet of his disciples (not the Twelve but the whole community), he performs this act of service in the context of friendship. She notes that, by demanding the gift of oneself to the other and the reception of the other's reciprocal gift of self, friendship is "the one human relationship based on equality. . . . Service rendered

---

[45] Gaillardetz, Hahnenberg, and Susan Wood have made important contributions to the development of a theology that moves beyond the idea of substantial ontological change by proposing that all persons exercising a formal ministry in the church undergo a type of relational ontological change that reaffirms the fundamental equality of all the baptized. I find Hahnenberg's development, which draws on the relational ontology of classical Greek trinitarian theology, to be especially compelling. However, given what I have outlined above, I worry that maintaining the idea that persons ordained to the ministerial priesthood undergo any sort of ontological change, even while framing it in terms of their charismatic cooperation with the Spirit and ecclesial relationality, remains at risk of being coopted to suggest a superior status of the ordained. See Gaillardetz, "The Ecclesiological Foundations of Ministry within an Ordered Communion," 35–48, quote at 39; Richard R. Gaillardetz, "The Shifting Meanings in the Lay-Clergy Distinction," *Irish Theological Quarterly* 64 (1999): 133–39; Hahnenberg, *Ministries*, 87–97, 122–50, 176–210; Susan K. Wood, "Priestly Identity: Sacrament of the Ecclesial Community," *Worship* 69 (March 1995): 123n31.

between friends is never exacted and creates no debts, demands no return but evokes reciprocity, and never degenerates into covert exploitation."[46] Thus, the act of service in this pericope is based on neither subordinate admiration nor one person's ability to serve another, who cannot reciprocate the service. In both situations the service rendered is rooted in a relationship of inequality perpetuating a "structure of domination, however benevolently exercised."[47] Rather, by washing his disciples' feet and telling them, "I do not call you servants any longer, . . . I have called you friends" (Jn 15:15), Jesus abolishes any pretense of inequality between them. Schneiders argues that Jesus, Sophia Incarnate, "has transcended and transformed the only ontologically based inequality among human beings, that between himself and us."[48]

Peter's resistance to Jesus washing his feet, then, is not out of embarrassment for Jesus. It is a refusal or an inability to see beyond a world marked by domination and subordination. Schneiders maintains that in this act of service, wherein he divests himself of his own claim to superiority and domination, Jesus "is subverting in principle all structures of domination."[49] Thus, Schneiders argues, "What definitively distinguishes the community that Jesus calls into existence from the power structures so universal in human society is the love of friendship expressing itself in joyful mutual service for which rank is irrelevant."[50] This does not

---

[46] Sandra M. Schneiders, *Written That You May Believe: Encountering Jesus in the Fourth Gospel*, rev. exp. ed. (New York: Herder and Herder, 2003), 193–94; Sandra M. Schneiders, "The Foot Washing (John 13:1–20): An Experiment in Hermeneutics," *Catholic Biblical Quarterly* 43 (1981): 86.

[47] Schneiders, *Written That You May Believe*, 192–93; Schneiders, "The Foot Washing," 84–86.

[48] Schneiders, *Written That You May Believe*, 195; Schneiders, "The Foot Washing," 87.

[49] Schneiders, *Written That You May Believe*, 195; Schneiders, "The Foot Washing," 87.

[50] Schneiders, *Written That You May Believe*, 195; Schneiders, "The Foot Washing," 87.

mean that the Johannine Jesus divests himself of his divinity or his unique, personal identity shaped by his relationships with others. Similarly, this does not deny the need for offices and ministries of leadership within the church. But it does suggest that friendship, "with its delight in mutual service that knows no order of order importance,"[51] not only should characterize the relationships shared by Jesus's disciples but also is the means by which they will be recognized as his risen body, commissioned to take away the sins of the world. All disciples are called to relate to one another as friends—as co-equal participants in the life and work of the risen Jesus—albeit through each person's particular charismatic gifts, several of which are properly ordered through formal offices such as the ministerial priesthood.

These offices ought not be exercised dominatively or non-collaboratively but through a ministry of accompaniment. Roberto Goizueta argues, "By definition, the act of accompaniment suggests going with another on an equal basis and thus implies the transgression of barriers. . . . To accompany another person is to *walk with* him or her. . . . It is, above all, by walking with others that we relate to them and love them."[52] Jesus's way of being in relationship—of being in friendship—was one of accompaniment, of journeying together, of living into a shared life with his companions. All members of the church must respond to the Spirit's call to use their charismatic gifts to build a church that transgressed the borders erected within the communion of Christ's body by claims of supposed ontological superiority or distinction. Each ministry—whether exercised through the ministerial priesthood or another ecclesial ministry—must be exercised with the deliberate aim of making the accompaniment typical of Jesus's friendship with his disciples a visible reality within the life of the church. For

---

[51] Schneiders, *Written That You May Believe*, 196; Schneiders, "The Foot Washing," 88.

[52] Roberto S. Goizueta, *Caminemos Con Jesús: Toward a Hispanic/ Latino Theology of Accompaniment* (Maryknoll, NY: Orbis Books, 1995), 206.

only when the friendship symbolized in the act of washing one another's feet becomes visible through our cooperation with the Spirit are we, as church, able to be recognized as the risen body of the crucified Jewish prophet from Nazareth.

9

Worship among the Ruins

Foundations for a Theology of Liturgy and Sacraments
"after Abuse"

Joseph C. Mudd

Our church lies in ruins, and ghosts lurk amid the rubble. How will we rebuild the church? For the last thirty years the Roman Catholic Church has sat with these questions as revelations of abuse, violence, and cover-up continue to pile up. This chapter asks whether we can worship in truth amid a ruined and haunted church. The specters of recent history—histories of clergy sexual abuse and cover-up, of gossip and scandal, of dissembling and evasion, of disclosure and deflection—hover over us. Indeed, these are *our* histories. The victim-survivors of clergy sexual abuse testify not only to the unholy lives of perpetrators and their protectors, but to the responsibility of all of us in the church who have been complicit in a culture of secrecy and silence. To put things right, the culture must change. But what of our liturgical life? Reflecting on our experience of the liturgy today, we might wonder how our liturgies reinforce a culture that encourages secrecy and silence. Do we worship in truth, or do our liturgies sacrifice the truth for a lie? How might our rituals bring healing to the traumatized body of Christ? To begin answering these questions, I analyze the foundations of clericalism in the church in terms of dramatic bias. Following this analysis, I propose a re-appropriation of the language of sacrifice in Catholic liturgy. Finally, I ask how the sacraments of reconciliation and anointing might mediate a renegotiation of our ecclesial life.

CLERICAL CULTURE
AND THE DIALECTIC OF AUTHORITY

Clearly, not all Catholics are responsible for clergy sexual abuse. But cultures have a way of invading our psyches and shaping our imaginations. Before we arrive at the moment of critical engagement with them, we are carried along on a current of meanings and values we inherit from our traditions. Only at a later interval do we disavow or embrace them as our own. A critical appropriation of one's tradition is itself only a probable occurrence depending on the relative cultural and social power of the authorities that mediate that tradition.

Clericalism refers to a culture, a pattern of actions, a set of meanings and values and the intellectual and affective responses to these meanings and values that inform a common way of life. Clericalism is not exclusive to Catholicism, Christianity, or religion; it is a human phenomenon observable across cultures. Clericalism emerges in any context in which authority is attached to office.[1] There are clerics in the academy, technology, finance, and government. Once a clerical caste emerges, it begins to control discourse, to define who speaks with authority based on criteria derived from the routinization of knowledge

---

[1] Bernard Lonergan, "Dialectic of Authority," in *A Third Collection*, Collected Works of Bernard Lonergan, vol. 16, ed. Robert M. Doran, SJ, and John Dadosky (Toronto: University of Toronto Press, 2017), 5. For an analysis of the dynamics of clerical culture, see Donald Cozzens, *Sacred Silence: Denial and the Crisis in the Church* (Collegeville, MN: Liturgical Press, 2002), 112–23. Cozzens distinguishes between clerical culture and clericalism as a distortion of that culture. For a thorough analysis of clericalism see Chapters 7 and 8 in this volume.

in bureaucratic structures that constitute human institutions. Of course, establishing credentials in specialized fields of knowledge is not inherently bad; it is basic to any society complex enough to divide labor according to specialized skills. But with the routinization of authority in the form of offices and the establishment of credentials distributed by officials, the potential for clericalism emerges. Clericalism, therefore, is not only a pattern of action, or an attitude, but it is also a culture, a set of meanings and values informing a way of life. Moreover, clericalism thrives in historical settings dominated by a classicist notion of culture.[2]

According to classicist interpretations of history, culture is an achievement to be repeated in every place and at every time; it is the opposite of barbarism. A classicist conception of culture assumes "that one and only one set of meanings and values was valid for all mankind."[3] Religious traditions often rely on a classicist notion of culture to establish and maintain their authority. In this view, it is only by doing things the way they have "always been done" that we can avoid the calamity of barbaric anarchism; it is only by continually replicating the mechanisms of some perceived high point of culture that we can avoid societal collapse. Of course, there are good reasons to conserve traditions from ages past. Indeed, the very basis of human culture is memory. But classicism reduces living memory to memorization, and tradition to a storehouse of prefabricated answers that reinforce existing authority structures and patterns of acting, even when those structures and patterns are oppressive or corrupt. There results a crisis of authority.

As we seek to live according to conscience, we begin to ask questions about ourselves and our traditions. In addition to our individual quests for authenticity in relation to the traditions in which we have been formed, there is also the matter of "the authenticity that justifies or condemns the tradition itself."[4] We

---

[2] On the distinction between classical and empirical notions of culture, see Bernard Lonergan, *Method in Theology* (Toronto: University of Toronto Press, 1990), 120.

[3] Lonergan, 120.

[4] Lonergan, 77.

wonder whether we are truly Christian. We might answer in the affirmative and be correct. But we can also miss those areas in which our way of living diverges from the ideals of Christian tradition. Furthermore, the Christian tradition as we receive it is a mixture of authenticity and unauthenticity, for it too is the net result of individuals in community struggling toward authenticity. As a result, we find ourselves authentically realizing unauthenticity without adverting to that fact. Simply doing what has always been done is no guarantee that one is upholding the ideals, the meanings, the values of a tradition. I hasten to add that the same is true for merely keeping up with the times, for the times may be evil. But the question of authenticity cannot be evaded. The history of clericalism in the church should raise questions about the authenticity of Christian meanings and values as we have received them in the present. Clericalism, among laity and clergy alike, is often an authentic realization of unauthenticity.[5] Many in the church are simply trying to live out their faith as they have received it, but part of what they have received includes showing deference and respect to clergy simply as clergy or imagining that clerics are uniquely qualified to speak for God because they are closer to God. These are examples of authentic realizations of unauthenticity in the tradition.

Of course, not all authority is infected with the kind of un-authenticity we are identifying with clericalism. Just as there are authentic clergy in the Roman Catholic Church there are authentic professors in universities, authentic government ministers, and authentic business leaders. Authority alone does not lead to clericalism. In addition to the merely clerical power that comes from office, there is the authority that comes from authenticity. This clarification by no means suggests that one is unauthentic

---

[5] It is worth noting that clericalism may also be an unauthentic realization of unauthenticity. One can act in bad faith. One can understand that one's authority is based on a lie and yet still exercise that authority as mere power over others. Indeed, one's insecurity over one's standing in the community may lead one to hold on to power even more aggressively.

simply because, for example, one pursues ordination or religious life. Far from it. The many good and holy priests and bishops who minister in the Catholic Church give ample evidence against such simplistic assessments. Nevertheless, goodness and holiness are not properly predicated of clergy because they are clerics but because they are authentic. Lonergan explains: "Authenticity makes power legitimate. It confers on power the aura and prestige of authority. Unauthenticity leaves power naked. It reveals power as mere power. Similarly, authenticity legitimates authorities, and unauthenticity destroys their authority and reveals them as merely powerful."[6] The resort to mere power leads to a crisis of authority.

According to Lonergan, authenticity means living in fidelity to the unrestricted dynamism of the human spirit toward self-transcendence as it unfolds in the activities of experiencing, understanding, judging, and deciding.[7] This unrestricted dynamism, manifest in our asking and answering questions, can suffer aberrations, but when it unfolds attentively, intelligently, reasonably, and responsibly it unfolds authentically, that is, without being distorted or overridden by biases.[8] Moreover, authenticity is not some permanent achievement but the flight from unauthenticity.[9] Four biases regularly inhibit our quest for authenticity: dramatic bias, individual bias, group bias, and general bias.[10] Individual and group biases refer to our tendency to put ourselves or our group at the center of our intellectual and moral concern. General bias

---

[6] Lonergan, "Dialectic of Authority," 6.

[7] See Bernard Lonergan, *Insight: A Study of Human Understanding*, Collected Works of Bernard Lonergan, vol. 3, ed. Frederick E. Crowe, SJ, and Robert M. Doran, SJ (Toronto: University of Toronto Press, 1992). See also "Cognitional Structure," in *Collection*, Collected Works of Bernard Lonergan, vol. 4, ed. Frederick E. Crowe, SJ, and Robert M. Doran, SJ (Toronto: University of Toronto Press, 1993).

[8] Lonergan correlates the four levels of his cognitional structure (experiencing, understanding, judging, deciding) with four transcendental precepts by which each of those levels is fulfilled authentically (be attentive, be intelligent, be reasonable, be responsible). See Lonergan, *Method in Theology*, 52.

[9] Lonergan, 237.

[10] See Lonergan, *Insight*, 214–31, 244–69.

identifies the way in which the common sense of a given culture claims competence over all fields of knowledge and mocks the highbrow "theories" of the elites. The notion of dramatic bias reveals how clericalism functions in the church.

Clericalism and Dramatic Bias

Dramatic bias impedes the process of asking and answering questions from the start, for "just as insight can be desired, so too it can be unwanted. Besides the love of light, there can be a love of darkness."[11] The refusal to ask certain questions that make one uncomfortable or that challenge the imagination to confront data that elicit revulsion can undercut progress, because "to exclude an insight is also to exclude the further questions that would arise from it, and the complementary insights that would carry it towards a rounded and balanced viewpoint. To lack that fuller view results in behavior that generates misunderstanding both in ourselves and in others."[12] Dramatic bias refers to an "aberration of understanding" that establishes a blind spot in one's horizon; it is the seedbed of misunderstanding and, in the long run, of paranoid fantasies and conspiracy theories.[13] Of course, we all suffer blind spots because of the limited range of data available to our experience, but the scotoma of dramatic bias arises in "the censorship that governs the emergences of psychic contents."[14] We react to unwanted insights with "distaste, pride, dread, horror, revulsion."[15] Normally, censorship functions in the psyche constructively by selecting and arranging "materials that emerge in consciousness in a perspective that gives rise to an insight."[16] This constructive function also entails a "negative aspect" as it eliminates data that are not relevant to the emergence of an insight.

---

[11] Lonergan, 214.
[12] Lonergan, 214.
[13] Lonergan, 215.
[14] Lonergan, 215.
[15] Lonergan, 215.
[16] Lonergan, 216.

The psychic censor can suffer an aberration of the negative aspect by repressing relevant questions. For example, if one's identity is heavily invested in an authority structure through which one's being in the world is made meaningful, data—and the images derived from those data—that indicate corruption within that authority structure will be unwanted because they call into question one's heretofore established identity. One experiences dread, horror, distaste, pride, and revulsion at the thought of the corruption of these authorities and one's complicity in their corruption. Pride, the refusal to admit a mistake in one's reasoning or acting, takes over, and one becomes defensive. One is quick to point out the corruption to be found in other, perhaps rival, authority structures. The refusal of insight hardens into a blind spot. Furthermore, pride will often not only repress questions regarding the authority structure, it may even amplify its authority. The dramatic bias of those in the authority structure may manifest in rhetoric that feeds the pride and defensiveness of those under their authority. This doubling down on authority through pride reduces authority to a function of mere power. Only those with the requisite credentials or position in the authority structure know the real story; only *they* can tell *us* the truth. Only those in authority can keep us safe, sustain our cultural achievements, and prevent us from sliding back into chaos. When dramatic bias takes hold in this way, authorities, indeed the authority structure itself, are seen as ultimately unquestionable. The cycle leads unavoidably to authoritarianism and suppression of dissent, the preconditions for oppression. The history of clergy sexual abuse and cover-up in the Catholic Church clearly shows how these dynamics work. As a form of dramatic bias, clericalism refuses to be honest with reality because that would require attending to the testimony of victims, which clergy and laity alike may experience with dread, horror, revulsion, distaste, and pride.

Lonergan's analysis of dramatic bias takes us to the deep roots of clericalism in the repressive function of the psyche.[17] Certainly, we can find individual bias among the clerical caste

---

[17] See Lonergan, 214–31.

and, of course, we have ample evidence of group bias shaping the actions of clerics, whether political, medical, or religious leaders. But clericalism is a symptom of a deeper psychic dysfunction plaguing human societies and it infects the church in a uniquely damaging way, for clericalism is not an attitude of clergy alone. Clericalism depends on a particular image of authority; it is the fruit of an image of the church that operates in tandem with a classicist understanding of culture found among laity and clergy alike—a classicist view of the church as a timeless, unchanging body of teachings and practices works hand in glove with clericalism. If Catholics are angry about clericalism among the clergy, we might also consider how deeply clericalism runs among the laity. Clericalism is a distinctively ecclesial illness, and many justifiably wonder whether there is any cure to this disease without razing the structure to the ground.

Ecclesial Illness and Psychic Conversion

There are two ways of being conscious. Dramatic bias has to do with the first way of being conscious in which "we undergo rather passively what we sense and imagine, our desires and fears, our delights and sorrows, our joys and sadness."[18] As noted above, the primary drivers of consciousness at this level are images and feelings. A second way of being conscious emerges when "we consciously inquire in order to understand, understand in order to utter a word, weigh evidence in order to judge, deliberate in order to choose, and exercise our will in order to act."[19] Symbols or affect-laden images set the conditions in the first way of being conscious for what emerges in the second way of being conscious. In a healthy psyche the first way of being conscious supports the

---

[18] Bernard Lonergan, *The Triune God: Systematics*, Collected Works of Bernard Lonergan, vol. 12, trans. Michael G. Shields, ed. Robert M. Doran and H. Daniel Monsour (Toronto: University of Toronto, 2007), 139.

[19] Lonergan, 139.

second way, as the psychic censor selects and assembles the images and affective dispositions that prepare the way for insights. But because of human historicity, healthy psyches are rare, and therefore "we can speak of a statistical near-inevitability of distortion precisely in the spiritual dimensions of human operation."[20] Robert Doran calls this distortion of the psyche a "radical ontological sickness."[21]

The entire sacramental economy of the church, with its emphasis on healing, is ordered toward curing such ontological sickness. The dynamic of repentance and forgiveness that suffuses every sacrament both reveals our disease and offers a cure, the mediation of healing grace. Under the influence of a clericalist imagination, however, forgiveness can be construed exclusively in terms of power, which can turn the priest into a forbidding psychiatrist, the confessional into a "torture chamber,"[22] and the altar an abattoir. By the same token, revulsion at one's own being can lead to rivalry and hostility toward all clergy among the laity. These distortions create a situation of mimetic rivalry that afflicts the mystical body of Christ.

This ecclesial illness shows us up in a variety of dynamics that obtain between clergy and laity. Some lay people are exceedingly deferential to clergy as clergy, and some clergy are only too happy to arrogate power to themselves and wield it arbitrarily. On the other hand, some lay people routinely dismiss all clergy as corrupt,

---

[20] Robert M. Doran, *The Trinity in History: A Theology of the Divine Missions*, vol. 2. Missions, Relations, and Persons (Toronto: University of Toronto Press, 2019), 21.

[21] Doran, 22. Following Girard's analysis of mimetic desire, Doran argues that because we are keenly aware of our finitude and emptiness, we frequently identify in others what we perceive to be a fullness of existence we lack in ourselves. This dynamic heads toward rivalry and violence, because we not only imitate others' desires, we claim them as our own. As a result, we desire not only *what* another has, but *who* the other is. Doran identifies in this dynamic a kind of masochism that transmutes very easily into sadism and abuse of power.

[22] Elise Harris, "Pope: Sacrament of Confession Is Not a Torture Chamber," Catholic News Agency, October 25, 2013.

while some clergy profess not to have the powers they do in fact have. This rivalry shows up on one side as idolatrous fawning over clergy and on the other as derisive mockery of clergy and of the priesthood as an institution.[23] These warped dynamics inform the concrete practice of the church, especially at the level of image and affect. The fact that many Catholics imagine that priests are closer to God because in certain situations they act "in persona Christi"[24] creates twisted relationships between clergy and laity. Such elevated language, if not carefully examined and understood theologically, reinforces power dynamics that have the potential to turn into a sadomasochistic nightmare. Those who casually dismiss such elevated language, on the other hand, often injure their fellow Christians who have trusting, loving, and familial relationships with clergy. The effects of the ecclesial illness uncovered by histories of clergy sexual abuse are exceedingly grave.

Doran argues that the cure to our ontological sickness begins with psychic conversion. What he means by psychic conversion is the transformation of the repressive role of the psychic censor to a constructive one. Like any conversion this is ultimately the work of grace, but we cooperate with God's healing of our psyches through an ongoing psychic self-appropriation born of regular practices of discernment and examination of consciousness, individually and as an ecclesial body. Discernment facilitates "access to one's own symbolic system and through that system to one's affective habits and one's spontaneous apprehensions of possible values."[25] Because the psyche operates on symbols, "on

---

[23] For an example of the latter, see Garry Wills, *Why Priests? A Failed Tradition* (New York: Viking, 2013).

[24] See Chapter 8 in this volume, which takes up the question of the theological significance of this phrase.

[25] Robert M. Doran, *Theology and the Dialectics of History* (Toronto: University of Toronto Press, 1990), 61. A complete treatment of Doran's notion of psychic conversion is beyond the scope of this chapter. Doran's development of Lonergan's thought in this area spans three major studies: *Subject and Psyche* (Milwaukee, WI: Marquette University Press, 1994), *Theological Foundations* (Milwaukee, WI: Marquette University Press, 1995), and *Theology and Dialectics of History*.

images and their concomitant affects,"[26] our failure to attend to the symbolic and affective dimensions of consciousness increases the probability that dramatic bias will continue to afflict the church. This is especially the case when we begin to investigate the symbols of Christian liturgy, for in the liturgy and sacraments of the church we discover symbols that can evoke either liberation or oppression depending on the images and affects that inhabit one's consciousness. Without discerning that difference, our rituals can exacerbate the illnesses of repression and oppression.

Redeeming Sacrifice after Abuse

What do we imagine we are doing when we are worshiping? Do our liturgies alleviate our "radical ontological sickness" or aggravate it? These are difficult questions to face, but we must face them if we are to be faithful to the experiences of victim-survivors of clergy sexual abuse whose physical, psychological, and spiritual wounds constitute a trauma in the body of Christ.[27] As Johann Baptist Metz framed his political theology as taking its bearings from the dangerous memories of victims of the Shoah—a theology "after Auschwitz"—so too our theologies of the liturgy and sacraments today should take their bearings from the memories of victim-survivors of clergy sexual abuse—a liturgical theology "after abuse."[28] How does such a perspective in solidarity with

---

[26] Doran, *Theology and the Dialectics of History*, 60.

[27] In Chapter 2 in this volume, Jennifer Beste rightly questions the tendency to suggest that the whole body of the church is suffering traumatic consequences of clergy-perpetrated child sexual abuse. The trauma suffered by victim-survivors is unique and should not be ascribed to the whole body.

[28] This theological posture is not meant to indicate that an era of clergy sexual abuse is over. It is not. It continues. Theology, explicitly framed as "after clergy sexual abuse" reflects the concrete situation of the church in history and the concrete biographies of persons who have suffered clergy sexual abuse. See Johannes Baptist Metz, *A Passion for God: The Mystical-Political Dimension of Christianity*, trans. J. Matthew Ashley

the suffering of victims-survivors transform our theology of the liturgy? First, the experiences of victim-survivors urge us to consider the ways in which the church has historically deployed the language of sacrifice in order to ennoble or even compel silent suffering at the expense of truth-telling. Second, the memories of suffering urge that we do not abandon the language of sacrifice but reinterpret it in terms of the event in which evil is transformed into good by the concrete self-offering of the whole ecclesial body in solidarity with victims.

The language of sacrifice evokes violence—the immolation of a victim. As a result, many contemporary Christian theologians have attempted to approach the cross by emphasizing Jesus's nonviolent confrontation with religious violence.[29] Because of the association with violence, many liturgical theologians struggle with how to understand Christian worship in a nonviolent way while retaining the existing sacrificial language in the rites.[30] Taking into account our discussion of the role image and affect play at the level of the psyche, we might ask whether the symbolism of sacrifice promotes a repressive or constructive role in the psyche of Christian worshipers.

(New York: Paulist Press, 1998), 122–24. See also M. Shawn Copeland, "Turning Theology: A Proposal," *Theological Studies* 80 (2019): 753–73.

[29] See Raymund Schwager, *Jesus in the Drama of Salvation: Toward a Biblical Doctrine of Redemption*, trans. James G. Williams (New York: Herder and Herder, 1999); S. Mark Heim, *Saved from Sacrifice: A Theology of the Cross* (Grand Rapids, MI: Eerdmans, 2006); J. Denny Weaver, *The Nonviolent Atonement* (Grand Rapids, MI: Eerdmans, 2011). See also William Loewe, *Lex Crucis: Soteriology and the Stages of Meaning* (Minneapolis, MN: Fortress Press, 2016). For accessible and concise articulation of this theological problem, see Charles C. Hefling Jr., "Why the Cross? God's at-one-ment with humanity," *Christian Century* (March 2013): 24–27.

[30] See Robert J. Daly, *Sacrifice Unveiled: The True Meaning of Christian Sacrifice* (New York: T & T Clark, 2009). See also, David N. Power, "Words That Crack: The Uses of 'Sacrifice' in Eucharistic Discourse," *Worship* 53 (1979); and David N. Power, *The Sacrifice We Offer: The Tridentine Dogma and Its Reinterpretation* (New York: Crossroad, 1987).

Idolatry and Deviated Transcendence

René Girard's psychology of mimesis provides theologians a unique lens through which to reread Christian revelation and to confront the dramatic bias at the root of our ecclesial illness.[31] The mimetic instinct that allows for the survival and flourishing of human beings also contains within it the basis of the kind of rivalry described above. Bringing resolution to rivalries has historically entailed acts of scapegoating violence.[32] Only when the victim is sacrificed is peace restored.[33] Girard proposes that at the heart of all religion we find acts of flagrant or sublimated scapegoating violence that bring temporary relief to human communities in the throes of mimetic rivalry. Because the relief is only temporary, religions routinize violence into a *cultus* sanctioned by deities who require victims to restore peace in the community.[34]

The projection of the cultic mechanism into the divine realm means that the distorted desires that give rise to scapegoating violence remain hidden. In addition, the "religious act of sacrifice reveals a double transference: a shift of blame to the victim and yet a paradoxical divinization of the victim, who gets credit for peace and prosperity."[35] The dialectical orientation toward the

---

[31] For a compact comparison of Girard's and Lonergan's approach to the theology of redemption, see Robert M. Doran, "The Nonviolent Cross: Lonergan and Girard on Redemption," *Theological Studies* 71 (2010): 46–61.

[32] See René Girard, *The Scapegoat*, trans. Yvonne Freccero (Baltimore: Johns Hopkins University Press, 1986).

[33] For a compact introduction to Girard's theory in relation to Christian theology, see James Alison, *Raising Abel: The Recovery of the Eschatological Imagination* (New York: Crossroad, 2000). For an analysis of Girardian theory in relation to Christian sacrifice, see Daly, *Sacrifice Unveiled*.

[34] See Nikolaus Wandinger, "Religion and Violence: A Girardian Overview," *Journal of Religion and Violence* 1, no. 2 (2013): 127–46.

[35] Randall S. Rosenberg, *The Givenness of Desire: Concrete Subjectivity and the Natural Desire to See God* (Toronto: University of Toronto Press, 2017), 188.

victim, as rival and god, reveals a profound distortion of desire. The rival becomes the object of envy. The desire to be like the victim leads to what Girard calls, according to Doran, "deviated transcendence."

Deviated transcendence refers to a distortion of desire in the direction of the perceived power of the rival/victim.[36] These dynamics are on full display in the history of religions, in which religious sages, kings, holy women, and holy men whose being was believed to be superior to one's own and whose proximity to the gods gave them the power over life and death. Yet in Christianity, Girard claims, this whole hidden mechanism is laid bare. Following a trajectory set by Israelite tradition's sublimation of violence in animal sacrifice, the Gospels continue exposing the scapegoating tendency latent in human communities and manifest in religious violence. In the New Testament the victim is no longer silent but speaks. Jesus's teaching and ministry prove his innocence. He speaks the truth. He exposes the distorted religious impulses of those invested in the exploitation of religion as a means of acquiring and maintaining civil or cultic power. By comparison, Jesus does not lord his power over others but bids them keep it secret. In offering himself in friendship to others, he invites them to share his desire for the kingdom of his Father, the reign of God, and not the power of human authorities. Ultimately, Jesus's self-offering is the fulfillment of his own radical fidelity to a kingdom that triumphs by non-violence.[37]

To reappropriate the language of sacrifice for liturgical theology "after abuse," we have to attend to the dynamic of *self-offering* that is the substance of eucharistic sacrifice.[38] Christ's exercise

---

[36] This is the source of the radical ontological sickness identified by Doran above.

[37] See Doran, "The Nonviolent Cross," 56–57.

[38] A full elaboration of the theology of eucharistic sacrifice lies beyond the scope of this chapter. Elsewhere I have written about the Eucharist as the fullness of the incarnate meaning of Christ and of the cross and altar as symbols of his sacrificial attitude. See Joseph C. Mudd, *Eucharist as Meaning: Critical Metaphysics and Contemporary Sacramental Theology* (Collegeville, MN: Liturgical Press, 2014). See also, Eugene R. Schlesinger,

of his priesthood in self-offering is the paradigmatic case of all Christian priesthood, both baptismal and ministerial.[39] Christian sacrifice, if it is not to slide into a form of sublimated religious violence, needs to attend carefully to the unique self-offering of Christ that continues to expose the scapegoating mechanism in history. A clericalist mindset among clergy and laity alike distorts this uniquely Christian understanding of sacrifice and reinscribes the desire for deviated transcendence into Christian ritual.

Sacrifice as Self-Offering in Christ

Sacrifice is a participation in a historical dynamic by which God in Christ Jesus reconciles the world to God's self by the transformation of evil into good. Lonergan calls this dynamic intelligibility through which we can make sense of myriad cases of evil transformed into good the "Law of the Cross."[40] It is a law in the sense that it explains an intelligible pattern in history. But it is also a supernatural solution to the problem of evil for the revelation of this law inserts into human life "truths beyond human comprehension [and] values beyond human estimation."[41] Gilles Mongeau brings together Lonergan's Law of the Cross and Girard's analysis of foundational violence:

> This total offering of self out of love . . . functions to reorient the interpersonal knowing that has refused to acknowledge the reality of foundational violence; to express and release divine Love to constitute a community that has the form of

---

"Eucharist Sacrifice as Anti-Violent Pedagogy," *Theological Studies* 80 (2019): 653–72.

[39] See *Lumen Gentium*, nos. 10, 62; and *Sacrosanctum Conclilium* nos. 14, 48.

[40] See Bernard Lonergan, *The Redemption*, Collected Works of Bernard Lonergan, vol. 9, trans. Michael G. Shields, ed. H. Daniel Monsour, Jeremy D. Wilkins, and Robert M. Doran, SJ (Toronto: University of Toronto Press, 2018).

[41] Lonergan, *Insight*, 747.

the Suffering Servant, which is the form divine Love takes in a world of sin and violence; and to mediate to the disciples in a once-for-all and total way the non-acquisitive desire that overcomes acquisitive mimesis. The state of grace is thus understood to include in an ongoing way the Law of the Cross. This means that the new divine-human interpersonal situation that is brought into being can only be properly understood, as Girard points out, from the point of view of the victims.[42]

The liturgical self-offering of the church in and with Christ the head again and again reveals the Law of the Cross as the substance of the redemptive vector in history through which the mischief of decline is undone by establishing a new divine-human interpersonal situation.[43] The language of sacrifice as self-offering is essential to the church's mission in history, but it is self-offering in and with Christ, whose sacrificial attitude provides the unique intelligibility of Christian sacrifice because it is understood from the perspective of the victim. Moreover, Christian sacrifice is the work of the baptismal priesthood.

Rather than reinscribe rivalry between clergy and laity, our shared baptismal priesthood places clergy and laity in a shared mission of overcoming evil with good through self-offering. Reflecting on liturgy "after abuse," Eugene Schlesinger observes, "The notion of [baptismal] priesthood strongly reasserts the agency of survivors of abuse. Although abusers, through coercion and violence, would steal away the agency of those whom they abuse, reducing them to victims, the priestly and agential dignity of the baptized remains ineffaceable because baptismal character is indelible."[44] Indeed, the

---

[42] Gilles Mongeau, "The State of Grace and the Law of the Cross: Further Insights into Lonergan from René Girard," *Theoforum* 45, no. 1 (2014): 132.

[43] The "redemptive vector" is Lonergan's way of identifying the historical causality of Christ and the church. This vector is to be distinguished from those of progress and decline. See Bernard Lonergan, "Healing and Creating in History," in *A Third Collection*, 94–104.

[44] Eugene Schlesinger, "Eucharist as Nonviolent Pedagogy," *Theological Studies* 80, no. 3 (2019): 671.

indelible character conferred in baptism marks the faithful with a priestly identity that enables the whole body of believers to offer itself in union with Christ. Sacrifice, in Christian understanding, is, therefore, a participation in the sacrificial "attitude" of Christ the head who mediates his interior experience of fidelity both to his Father and to his friends through the symbols of cross and altar.

As Mongeau indicates above, the sacrificial attitude of Christ is central to the interpersonal situation or "state" of grace. Understood in terms of a dynamic historical intelligibility rather than a static concept of the soul, the state of grace is a divine-human interpersonal situation of mutual self-offering in solidarity with the victims of suffering. Such an understanding of sacrifice as self-offering resists any sense that victim-survivors of abuse should suffer silently. As an interpersonal situation the state of grace emerges when we bring our whole selves into relationship with one another. Indeed, the church's self-offering if it does not include an open acknowledgment in solidarity with the suffering of victim-survivors, the church's self-offering is in danger of failing to embody properly the sacrificial attitude of Christ. If this is the case, should not every mass explicitly remember victims of clergy sexual abuse? If explicit references to victims are not regularly included in our liturgies, why not? Does refusal to admit the experiences of victim-survivors a place in our liturgical prayer undermine the very meaning of the liturgy? Answering these questions will require honesty with reality, beginning by attending to the voices of victims in liturgical planning.

SACRAMENTS AND HEALING AFTER ABUSE

In addition to the church's eucharistic self-offering in imitation of the self-offering of Christ, the sacramental economy includes specific rites of healing that hold untapped resources for addressing the crisis of meaning that deepens with each revelation of abuse and cover-up. Bruce Morrill suggests that we reorient our thinking about the sacraments of healing as proper acts of worship that are integral to the eucharistic center of the sacramental economy.[45] These sacraments take us to the heart of suffering and begin to enact ritually a changed historico-ecclesial situation in which reconciliation begins. The sacraments of anointing and reconciliation embody the Law of the Cross as they transform the evils of sin and suffering into the goods of healing and creating in history. In this section I raise questions regarding how the sacraments of reconciliation and anointing might be reimagined in a historical context after abuse.

Reconciliation: Transformation of Histories of Suffering

The sacrament of reconciliation can easily be reduced to a matter of private concern. Sin elicits a concrete historical situation of absurdity. Therefore, when we imagine the sacrament of reconciliation as addressing the state of grace of an individual soul, we run into confusion. And while only individuals incur culpability for sin, degrees of culpability depend on a range of psychological, sociological, and cultural factors. A deep examination of conscience, therefore, entails not only quasi-private venial or mortal sins, but it also adverts to one's various entanglements with the whole of reality, "the personal, natural, social, political, cultural, and economic reality that one encounters in history."[46] We are enmeshed in patterns of behavior and languages that are not our own, and our expressed values are often at odds with our affective responses to our own deepest desires. Furthermore, the influence of dramatic bias in our biographies may make it nearly impossible adequately to recognize this enmeshment. Our entanglements with culture can bring it about that our appropriation of a scale of values remains distorted despite our best efforts.

---

[45] Bruce T. Morrill, *Divine Worship and Human Healing: Liturgical Theology at the Margins of Life and Death* (Collegeville, MN: Liturgical Press, 2009), 3.

[46] Todd Walatka, "Uniting Spirituality and Theology: Jon Sobrino's Seeking Honesty with the Real," *Spiritus: A Journal of Christian Spirituality* 13, no. 1 (2013): 78.

Lonergan proposes that feelings respond to values in accord with some scale of preference.[47] He distinguishes "vital, social, cultural, personal, and religious values in ascending order."[48] Our affective responses to values develop with other aspects of our human being through the dialectics of subject, culture, and community.[49] But affective responses not only mature, they also suffer aberration, especially as ressentiment distorts the scale.[50] Combined with the mimetic rivalry identified by Girard, Lonergan's account of ressentiment points to the re-feeling of a clash with someone else's value qualities.[51] This re-feeling intensifies the pride and defensiveness described above in relation to dramatic bias. Ressentiment is directed at another who one subconsciously acknowledges is "one's superior physically or intellectually or morally or spiritually."[52] This attitude of ressentiment is like an undertow that is "neither repudiated nor expressed."[53] Ressentiment

> attacks the value-quality that the superior person possessed and the inferior not only lacked but feels unequal to acquiring. The attack amounts to a continuous belittling of the value in question, and it can extend hatred and even violence against those that possess that value-quality. But perhaps its worst feature is that its rejection of one value involves a distortion of the whole scale of values and that this distortion can spread through a whole social class, a whole people a whole epoch.[54]

These are the roots of sin: a roiling resentment of goodness and holiness that takes cover in rationalization, in pride, in defensiveness.

---

[47] Lonergan, *Method in Theology*, 31.

[48] Lonergan, 31.

[49] Doran, *The Dialectics of History*, 93.

[50] Lonergan, *Method in Theology*, 33.

[51] Lonergan, 33.

[52] Lonergan, 33.

[53] Lonergan, 33.

[54] Lonergan, 33.

The sacrament of reconciliation can expose the mischief of this evil, but it requires an ecclesial rather than an individual effort. Envy, jealousy, pride, calumny, resentment—the church is rife with the sins that result from distortions in the scale of values. Human moral impotence means that combatting these distortions of the scale of values is profoundly difficult.[55] The sacrament of reconciliation is meant to mediate both the grace of healing and to reorient human desire in such a way that it begins to engage in the creative work of redemption in history. Morrill explains, "Healing is needed when communal relations, whether vertical or horizontal or both, are somehow broken off, eliciting the need for reconciliation and forgiveness not only among people but with God."[56] The abuse crisis in the Catholic Church has fueled ressentiment between and among bishops and priests, clergy and laity, clergy and victim-survivors. While it is one thing to lament the abuses of power laid bare by the journalistic and legal investigations of the last decades, it is another to plumb the depths of the deeper disorders of dramatic bias and ressentiment afflicting the church. These deeper disorders plague our parishes and apostolates.

While the sacrament of reconciliation normally takes place privately, at the present time there are sins afflicting the entire ecclesial body that cry out for public penance and collective absolution. Certainly there are differing degrees of entanglement in the sexual abuse perpetrated by clergy and covered up by bishops. Individuals will have to discern for themselves what sins to bring to confession. But cannot the whole body in a collective act express its deep regret and sorrow over the sins of sexual abuse, and cannot this happen with some frequency?[57] Liturgies of lament and masses offered for reconciliation provide resources for

---

[55] See Lonergan, *Insight*, 651.

[56] Morrill, *Divine Worship and Human Healing*, 31.

[57] This is already happening in the form of various liturgies of lament that have occurred over the past twenty years, including at my own institution, Gonzaga University, March 6, 2019. See also, "Irish Archbishop Repents for Clergy Sex Abuse," *Catholic News Service* (2011).

ongoing ritual enactment of communal repentance and reconciliation. But further reflection on the sacrament of reconciliation will be required before many Catholics will feel comfortable in the dynamic created by private auricular confession. If we listen to victims, especially those for whom the confessional became a torture chamber, how might we reconfigure the administration and indeed the theology of this sacrament?

Healing and Worship

In addition to the sacrament of reconciliation, the body of Christ yearns for the kind of healing that sacramental anointing can offer. In one way or another the vast majority of Catholic Christians are suffering through the histories of clergy sexual abuse and the patterns of cover-up that follow. Of course, victim-survivors of abuse have been uniquely traumatized. They have suffered in their bodies what others who embrace solidarity with them have suffered in mind and heart. But the physical, emotional, and spiritual wounds run deep in the church. Can sacramental anointing begin to heal the psychic trauma and moral injury afflicting the church?[58]

While anointing was historically reserved for those near death, the post-conciliar rite is open to all who are seriously ill.[59] The sacrament of anointing is for those who find themselves at the

---

[58] Moral injury has emerged as a distinct but related category to trauma through which to assess the impact of clergy sexual abuse on both victims and the larger church. Recently, a team of scholars at Xavier University began developing a set of analytic tools to assess experiences of moral injury in the church (see "Creating a Tool for Measuring and Responding to Moral Injury Caused by Clergy Sexual Abuse," a project of Xavier University and supported by Fordham University's "Taking Responsibility: Jesuit Educational Institutions Confront the Causes and Legacy of Clergy Sexual Abuse"). Scholars exploring the moral injury of clergy sexual abuse have proposed the category of "sacred moral injury" to identify the unique harm done to victims. See Len Sperry, "Moral Injury in Christian Organizations: Sacred Moral Injury," in *Christianity and Psychiatry*, ed. J. R Peteet et al. (Cham, Switzerland: Springer, 2021).

[59] Morrill, *Divine Worship and Human Healing*, 161.

limit of what they can bear without the aid of God's healing grace. Morrill suggests that "the sacrament of anointing the sick serves [a] profound need for a *renegotiation* of one's life, the desire to know something of God's love and presence and one's own value and purpose in relation to others and the world around oneself" (emphasis added).[60] How many in the church yearn for such a renegotiation of life? How can the sacrament of anointing be implemented to assist the faithful as they renegotiate their identity as members of the body of Christ after abuse?

Healing here can be helpfully understood in terms of the reintegration of the normative scale of values after the distortion of ressentiment has ravaged the psyches of the faithful confronted with betrayal and scandal. Our discussion of psychic conversion above helps explicate the meaning of healing I intend here. The healing mediated by the sacrament of anointing inaugurates a new set of images and affects that enable honesty with reality. The sacrament of anointing, therefore, provides rich resources for addressing the experience of spiritual, emotional, and psychological illness. Nevertheless, there remains an ambiguity in the norms for administering the sacrament regarding whether it can be offered to those experiencing mental or spiritual illness.[61] Crucially, inasmuch as clergy sexual abuse inflicts violence on bodies, a wholly disembodied way of entering into solidarity with victim-survivors seems profoundly inadequate. Might we not consider ways of treating bodies with reverence, whether through the sacrament of anointing or some other practice of recognizing the embodied aspects of both abuse and healing? Making the sacrament of anointing available to all the faithful in light of the psychic trauma of the last few decades might offer the church an opportunity to reconcile the psychic suffering that may be manifesting in terms of ressentiment or a desire for deviated transcendence.

---

[60] Morrill, 161.

[61] See "Pastoral Care of the Sick: Rites of Anointing and Viaticum," in *The Rites of the Catholic Church* (New York: Pueblo, 1983), no. 53, which makes only brief reference to mental illness.

CONCLUSION

Unless the church addresses the psychic suffering and trauma caused by clergy sexual abuse with every means available to it in the sacramental economy, the sacraments cannot but be diminished in the eyes of the faithful as expressions of mere power. To avoid confronting the history of clergy sexual abuse in the face of the ongoing effects of psychic trauma risks making the church a structure of denial and repression. If the church is to be a place of truth-telling and liberation in the midst of sinful human histories, especially the church's own history, then we should continue to reflect on how rituals might provide unique possibilities to enact reconciliation and healing.

I have tried to show in this chapter that the illness afflicting the mystical body runs deep. It is not the case that clericalism and all its ramifications can simply be rooted out. The roots take nourishment from distorted desires and the love of deviated transcendence that animate the concrete history of sin. They are in all of us. What is needed is a complete reconfiguration of how authority is expressed in the church, built on a new foundation, namely, authenticity. We will have to deal squarely with the dramatic bias that undergirds the culture of clericalism in the church and the need for psychic conversion. We must confront the various ways in which our rituals reinforce a love of deviated transcendence. But we can also discover how liturgical self-offering, reconciliation, and anointing offer important resources for navigating the present crises. Of course, this whole conversation is complicated by the fact that the church's liturgies are led exclusively by clergy. But the presence or absence of clergy alone does not determine the degree of clericalism in a community. As B. Kevin Brown proposes in Chapter 8 herein, clergy and laity can work in a spirit of collaboration and indeed in friendship as together they minister to the needs of the body of Christ. A healthy friendship between clergy and laity will be the fruit of growing in authenticity through ongoing psychic conversion: listening to victim-survivors, asking uncomfortable questions about our own complicity in cultures of clericalism, reimagining sacraments and ministry in light of the Law of the Cross. Perhaps then, our worship be in truth, and even as we worship among the ruins of an idealized past, we will be closer to the kingdom and to the reconciliation and healing we all so deeply desire.

Contributors

Hans Zollner, SJ, is Full Professor and Director of the Institute of Anthropology: Interdisciplinary Studies on Human Dignity and Care (IADC) of the Pontifical Gregorian University in Rome, Italy.

John N. Sheveland, PhD, is Professor of Religious Studies and the Flannery Chair in Catholic Theology at Gonzaga University in Spokane, Washington. He currently serves on the United States Conference of Catholic Bishops National Review Board.

Heather T. Banis, PhD, is the Victims Assistance Coordinator for the Archdiocese of Los Angeles in Los Angeles, California.

Jennifer Beste, PhD, is Professor and the Koch Chair in Catholic Thought and Culture in the Theology Department of the College of Saint Benedict and Saint John's University in Collegeville, Minnesota.

Cristina Lledo Gomez, PhD, is the Presentation Sisters Lecturer at BBI–The Australian Institute of Theological Education (TAITE) and a Religion and Society Research Fellow at Charles Sturt University's Public and Contextual Theology Research Centre (PACT) in Pennant Hills, New South Wales, Australia.

Scott Starbuck, PhD, is Senior Lecturer of Religious Studies at Gonzaga University in Spokane, Washington.

Linda S. Schearing, PhD, is Professor of Religious Studies, Emerita, at Gonzaga University in Spokane, Washington.

Fernando Ortiz, PhD, MBA, ABPP, is Director of Psychological Services at Gonzaga University in Spokane, Washington. He formerly served on the United States Conference of Catholic Bishops National Review Board.

B. Kevin Brown, PhD, is Lecturer of Religious Studies at Gonzaga University in Spokane, Washington.

Joseph C. Mudd, PhD, is Associate Professor of Religious Studies and Director of Catholic Studies at Gonzaga University in Spokane, Washington.

Index

abandonment, 31, 68, 74, 152
abuse
    cover-up of, 47, 51
    enabled by clericalism, 48,
        105
    importance of acknowledg-
        ing, 18, 27–8, 31, 34–5
    and need for admiration, 22,
        156–7
    need for affection as risk
        marker, 158–9, 162
    prevention of, 64–6
    risk factors, 6, 61, 66, 155,
        157–8, 161, 163–4,
        167–8, 170–1
abuse of power, and clerical-
    ism, 2, 61–2, 87, 90,
    92, 100, 108, 110,
    112–13, 220
accompaniment, 4, 18–19, 64,
    67–8, 73, 75, 117, 126,
    136, 199
accountability, 18, 21, 31, 33,
    38, 79, 90, 98, 108,
    112
agency
    of abusers, 75
    and clericalism, 118
    and healing, 32, 76, 123,
        130, 216

    and moral patency, 58
    personal, 31, 118, 125, 134,
        187
    spiritual, 118
    and trauma, 23, 25, 42, 50,
        125
aggression, 158–9, 161
    and narcissism, 159, 161
    sexual, 107
agreeableness, 168–70
alternative moral universes,
    103–5
amorality, 158, 160–2
anchors
    and accompaniment, 117
    need for in healing, 117–18,
        137
    spiritual, 124
anger
    and biblical lament, 138
    and hyperarousal, 95
    and loss of faith, 122
    towards clergy, 21, 46, 50
    as trauma response, 20,
        43–4, 47
Annual Reports: Findings and
    Recommendations,
    6–8, 65
anointing, sacrament of, 202,
    218, 221–3

anxiety
    and emotionality, 170
    and PTSD, 25
    and trauma, 41, 68–9, 152
Arbuckle, Gerald, 43, 140
Archdiocese of Los Angeles's
        Office of Victims Assis-
        tance Ministry, 17
Asch, Solomon, 87–9, 115
asymmetric relationships, 78,
        106, 111–12
attunement, 18–20, 29, 67

Baldwin, Jennifer, 18–19, 22–4,
        30, 32–3, 35, 38
Banis, Heather, 80–1, 85
baptismal priesthood, 177, 196,
        215–16
Beste, Jennifer, 68, 121
betrayal
    healing from, 4, 146, 222
    and loss of faith, 122
    in Psalms, 147, 149
betrayal trauma, 18, 31, 37,
        145
bias
    and authenticity, 205
    and clericalism, 173–5,
        180–1, 185, 187–9,
        193–6
    group, 205
    individual, 205, 207
    and social sin, 182, 184,
        186
Bidwell, Duane, 70
Big Five Personality Trait Theo-
        ry, 168–70
blame, of victims, 127, 136
Blue Knot Foundation, 100,
        115–16
Buddhism, 70, 85–6

Calhoun, Lawrence, 56
callousness, 70–2, 160–2, 164
canon law, 89, 102–5, 107, 178
Causes and Context of Sexual
        Abuse of Minors by
        Catholic Priests Study,
        The, 155
Causes and Context Study, 6
celibacy, 105–6
censorship, 98–9, 206
Cesareo, Francesco, 6–8
charismatic gifts, 181, 186,
        190–1, 195, 199
Charter for the Protection of
        Children and Young
        People, 4, 6–7, 65–6
clergy
    anger towards, 21, 46, 50
    and authenticity, 205
    and burnout, 46, 166
    and clerical culture, 155,
        170, 175–7, 179–80,
        189, 202
    and clericalism, 70, 174–6,
        204, 208–10
    and fatigue, 46–7, 166
    human formation programs,
        162, 165, 167–8,
        170–1
    vs. laity, 190, 192–4
    and narcissism, 71, 156–7
    protected by superiors, 178
    and self-care, 165
    as shepherd, 53, 112, 119–
        20, 127
clergy-perpetrated sexual abuse
        survivors. See CPCSA
clericalism
    and abuse of power, 2–3,
        61–2, 87, 90, 92, 100,
        108, 110, 112–13, 220

and arrogance, 57, 156
and authenticity, 204
and baptism, 110, 177, 190
and clericalization, 174–5
as culture, 203, 208, 223–4
definition, 174, 202
as dramatic bias, 207
and enabling of abuse, 48, 105
and healing, 134
and infantilization of laity, 107, 113–14
and liberationist approach, 186–7
and liturgy, 64, 81, 201
and narcissism, 64, 70–1, 161, 163, 167, 170–2
and need for admiration, 22, 156–7
and obedience., 112
and prophetic texts, 118
and religious authority, 107, 120, 176, 203, 207
as social sin, 173, 181, 188
theological roots, 189, 196, 202
clericalist bias, 173–6, 180–1, 185, 187–9, 192–7
closed systems, 108–9, 115
coercion, 99, 216
compassion, 24, 86, 161
complacency, 7, 58, 62, 110
complex post-traumatic stress disorder. See CPTSD
complicity
among bystanders, 52, 56
among clergy, 56, 58, 61
and church structure, 81, 94, 119, 121, 134, 201, 207, 223
in systems, 117, 135

confession, 24, 83, 104–5, 209, 220–1
control
and authority, 112
and spiritual abuse, 99–100
and trauma, 41–2, 68
Copeland, M. Shawn, 175
corrective insight, 176, 181, 185, 196
counseling, 70, 165–6, 178
CPCSA (clergy-perpetrated sexual abuse survivors), 39, 43–4, 46–50, 56–7
CPTSD (complex post-traumatic stress disorder), 91, 94–6, 115
culpability, 47, 58, 218
culture
of abuse, 59, 87–8, 94, 98, 113, 115, 155
church, 6–9, 43, 64–6, 81, 89–90, 201
and clericalism, 3, 155, 176, 185, 187, 202–3, 208, 223
definition, 175
of safety, 7, 104
and social sin, 182–3
total institutions, 101–2, 110, 114

deep listening, 64, 70, 73, 80
denial
of social anxiety, 158–9, 161
of survivor experience, 68, 113
and trauma, 31, 44, 47, 56, 223
depression, 25, 68, 152
Deusen Hunsinger, Deborah van, 67–70, 118

deviated transcendence, 214–15, 222–3
Diagnostic and Statistical Manual. See DSM-IV
discipleship, 39, 47–8, 59, 62–3
dissociation, 41, 44–5, 47, 56, 63, 68, 95
Dogmatic Constitution on the Church. See Lumen Gentium
Dombo, Eileen, 85–6
domination, structures of, 176, 181, 184, 188, 198
Doran, Robert, 209–10, 214
dramatic bias, 202, 205–8, 211, 213, 218–20, 223
DSM-IV (Diagnostic and Statistical Maual), 53

Easter narratives, 25, 29–30, 33
ecclesial body, 210, 212, 220
ecclesial illness, 208–10, 213
emotional dysregulations, 41, 47–8
emotional intelligence, 65, 80–1, 171
emotionality, 168–70
empathy, 24, 47, 156–7, 161
    low, 70–1, 81
empowerment, 69, 116–18, 126–7, 130–1, 134–5
Eucharist, 106, 193–4
everlasting covenant, 126, 128–9, 132
evil, moral, 50–1, 54, 56, 60, 62–3

faith
    loss of, 24, 32, 121–2, 124
    and original grace, 23

reconstituting, 118, 137
    and trauma, 33, 43
Faivre, Alexandre, 190, 192
families
    disbelieving, 27, 146, 180
    maligned, 48
    support from, 166
    and trauma, 43, 52
family, violence in, 92, 95
Feldman, Valerie, 87, 92, 101–8, 113–14
Final Report: The Role of Organisational Culture in Child Sexual Abuse in Institutional Contexts, 87, 92, 101–2, 104
Finn, Daniel, 183, 187
forgiveness, 3, 34, 48, 105–6, 170, 209, 220
Francis (Pope), 1–2, 116
Francis, Mark, 71
Frawley-O'Dea, Mary Gail, 44, 56–7

Gaillardetz, Richard R., 194
Gaudium et Spes, 114
Girard, René, 213–16, 219
Goffman, Erving, 101–2
Goizueta, Roberto, 199
González Faus, José Ignacio, 185
Good Friday, 25–6. See also Easter narratives
grace
    and healing, 20–1, 32, 35, 37, 48, 62, 126–7, 210
    and reconciliation, 218
    and self-offering, 216–17
grandiosity, 156
Gray, Cathleen, 85–6

Guinan, Michael, 139
Gundry-Volf, Judith, 59–60

Hahnenberg, Edward, 195
Hambrick, Brad, 143–9
Hanson, Paul, 128, 133
Hartill, Mike, 109
healing
   and church culture, 65–7
   communal, 65, 69, 71–2,
      119, 130, 134
   conditions for, 4–6, 21, 28,
      31, 37, 62, 64
   definition, 35
   and empowerment, 118,
      127–8
   and grace, 20–1, 32, 35, 37,
      48, 62, 126–7, 210
   and imagination, 29, 32,
      34–6, 38
   and liturgy, 81–3, 85–6,
      201, 211–12, 216–17
   and need for anchors, 117–
      18, 137
   and ontological sickness,
      209–11
   and original grace, 23–4
   process, 20, 24–5, 35, 57, 141
   and Psalms, 140, 154
   and reconciliation, 18, 31,
      223–4
   religious, 134–5
   and sacrament, 209, 217–
      18, 220–4
   and sense of safety, 25, 122
healing and reconciliation, 28,
   30–1
Herman, Judith, 27
Heyer, Kristin, 181, 187
holding environments, 69–70,
   72, 77–8

Holy Saturday, 19, 25–6, 29–
   30, 36. See also Easter
   narratives
honesty-humility, 168–9
Hughes, Richard, 138, 141
human formation programs,
   162, 165, 167–8,
   170–1
hyperarousal, 40, 47, 95
hypoactivity, 95
hypoarousal, 95

imagination
   collective, 19, 36–7
   and healing, 29, 32, 34–6,
      38
   and original grace, 24
   paschal, 19, 34
imago Dei, 110, 112
inhibition, 158–9, 161
isolation
   relational, 166
   social, 68, 165
   and trauma, 24, 31, 33, 68,
      99, 140

Jesus Christ, 30, 59–61, 125,
   131, 181, 188, 198,
   214
   and children, 59–61
   and clericalism, 110, 189–
      91, 193–6, 198, 214
   and Easter narratives, 30
   and healing, 32, 34, 37, 49,
      58, 79, 130, 135
   and moral responsibility,
      62
   and original grace, 23
   sacrificial attitude of,
      216–17
   and self-offering, 215–17

and social sin, 187–8
and witnessing, 26–8
John Paul II, 111, 182, 187, 196
Jones, Serene, 18–21, 29, 32, 35–6

Kansteiner, Wulf, 53
knowing ministry, 26, 73, 75–6

laity
    vs. clergy, 190, 192–4, 204, 208
    infantilization of, 107, 113–14
Lakeland, Paul, 179, 196
liberation theologies, 182–3, 186–7
liturgy
    and clericalism, 64, 81, 201
    and healing, 81–3, 85–6, 211–12, 216–17
    of lament, 72, 81, 83
Lonergan, Bernard, 175, 205, 207, 215, 219
Lumen Gentium, 79–80, 177, 195

Martin, Jennifer, 101
Martin, Michelle, 45
Mary Magdalene, 26–8, 33
McCarrick, Theodore, 2, 7, 31, 80
McEwan, Tracy, 97
McKibbin, Gemma, 87, 92, 101–8, 113–14
McNally, Richard, 53
media, and coverage of clergy sexual abuse, 52, 62, 72
meditation, 85–6

Milgram, Stanley, 89, 112, 115
mimetic rivalry, 209, 213, 219
Minnesota Multiphasic Personality Inventory (MMPI), 158
Moeser, Marion, 139
Mongeau, Gilles, 215
moral agency, 58, 62, 183
moral evil, 50–1, 54, 56, 60, 62–3
Morrill, Bruce, 217, 220, 222

Nakashima Brock, Rita, 23
narcissism, 64, 71, 81, 155–6
    and dependency, 162–3
    malignant, 155, 161–3, 167, 170–1
    pathological, 3, 70
    personalities, 156, 161
    traits, 71

Oakley, Lisa, 91, 98–9
obedience
    and authority, 89, 99, 115
    and total institutions, 111–12
    and clericalism, 112
O'Connor, Kathleen, 124
ontological change, theology of, 195–6
ontological sickness, 209–11
organizations
    behavior, 108, 116
    and containment, 78–9
    high reliability, 64, 78
original grace, 23–4
over-controlled hostility, 158, 161, 163–4

Palmer, Donald, 87, 92, 101–8, 113–14

paralysis, as trauma reaction, 45–50, 54, 58, 63
paranoia, 95, 160, 206
Pastores Dabo Vobis, 111, 196
Paul VI, 111
Pennsylvania grand jury report, 2, 7, 80
perpetrators
    and accountability, 117
    acknowledgement of abuse, 34
    church protection of, 48, 50, 104, 178
    and clericalism, 171
    and healing, 24, 28, 32
    and self-deception, 61
    and trauma, 43–5, 52, 54, 56, 122
in persona Christi, 107, 193–5, 210
pilgrim church, 79–80
post-traumatic communities, 125–8, 132, 134
post-traumatic growth, 56–7
post-traumatic stress disorder. See PTSD
power
    abuse of, 2–3, 27, 61–2, 87, 89–90, 92, 100, 107–8, 110, 112–13, 220
    and clericalism, 106, 176, 179, 185–7, 194–5, 205, 207, 209–10
    communal, 133, 175
    dynamics, 6
    and Jesus, 214
    and perpetrators, 28
    relational, 22–3
    sacred, 195–6
prayer, 48–9, 81–3, 85, 119, 142, 151, 153, 165

Preparatory Document for the 16th Ordinary General Assembly of the Synod of Bishops, 1–3
prevention, of abuse, 64–6
priesthood
    baptismal, 216
    biblical conception, 130
    and narcissism, 162–3
    screening for, 65, 167, 171
    Sobrino on, 189
    and total institutions, 102
Program of Priestly Formation, 168–70
PTSD (post-traumatic stress disorder)
    assessment criteria, 40, 53, 58
    symptoms, 25, 34, 47–8, 56, 94

Rahner, Karl, 69, 183
Rambo, Shelly, 18–19, 22, 26–33, 36
reconciliation
    and companionship, 30
    and healing, 18, 31, 223–4
    sacrament of, 105, 122, 202, 218, 220–1, 223–4
redemption, 64–5, 67, 72–3, 85, 127, 153, 220
relational home, 69–70
repentance, 48, 83, 105–6, 137, 186, 209
Rerum Novarum, 61
ressentiment, 219–20, 222
retraumatization, 91, 95, 105, 110, 122
review boards, 4, 8, 65, 171
Ricketson, Matthew, 101
righteousness, 121, 131–2

Rolheiser, Ron, 18–19, 21, 32, 34–7

sacrament
    and healing, 209, 217–18, 220–4
    of reconciliation, 105, 122, 202, 218, 220–1, 223–4
sacramental economy, 209, 217, 223
salvation, 69, 85, 105–6, 114, 131–2, 137, 151
scapegoating, 213, 215
Schillebeeckx, Edward, 191, 195
Schlesinger, Eugene, 216
Schneiders, Sandra, 176, 183–4, 188, 197–8
Second Vatican Council. See Vatican II
secrecy, 88, 99, 103, 108–9, 176, 179, 201
self-agency, 118, 123, 127
self-blame, 23, 41, 68
self-deception, 62, 70–2
self-esteem, 68, 167
self-loathing, 31, 41, 68
self-love, 25, 75, 84
self-offering, 214–17, 223
self-protection, 40, 96
seminaries, 104, 157–8, 161–4, 168, 172
service, acts of, 197–8
shame
    and CPTSD, 94
    and narcissism, 162
    and non-offending priests, 50
    and public disclosure of abuse, 56
    and self-blame, 23, 41

and spiritual abuse, 98
and women, 97
shepherds, clergy as, 53, 112, 119–20, 127
Shooter, Susan, 26, 73–7, 79, 81
sin
    concept of, 22
    and healing, 24
    and Jesus, 60, 188, 199, 216
    Rahner on, 183
    and reconciliation, 105–6, 218–20
    Schneider on, 184
    and Second Vatican Council, 79
    and trauma, 47–8
sins, original, 23–4, 32, 183
Sobrino, Jon, 189
social anxiety, 158, 161
social sin, 173, 181–3, 185–7, 196
    and bias, 182, 184, 186
    categories, 181–2
    situations of, 182–3, 187
sociology, 108, 115–16, 183
soul murder, 34, 68
spiritual abuse, 90–1, 96–100, 109–10, 115
    and controlling behavior, 97–100
    and retraumatization, 110
Stein, Sophia, 151–3
Suffering Servant, 216
suicide, 32, 41–2, 152
survivors. See victim-survivors
synodality, 1–2, 4–5, 116

Terry, Karen, 6, 66, 81
theological renewal, 173, 189, 197

theology
    and clericalism, 189, 193–6
    and healing, 38, 70
    liturgical, 211–12, 214
    of ministry, 173, 189, 196–7
    and reconciliation, 221
    and trauma, 30, 32–3, 116
    victim-centric, 2, 9
transcendence, 128–30
transparency, 18, 33, 38, 46, 90
trauma
    and anxiety, 41, 68–9, 152
    betrayal, 18, 31, 37, 145
    and control, 41–2, 68
    coopting, 52, 55
    generational, 117
    and grace, 32
    interpersonal, 40
    and isolation, 24, 31, 33, 68,
        99, 140
    and paralysis, 45–50, 54,
        58, 63
    psychic, 221–2
    research, 39, 49, 51, 54, 57,
        68
    response, 20, 43–4, 47
traumatic wounding, 2, 32–3,
    65, 67–9, 82, 85
traumatization
    and child development, 42
    dynamics of, 63, 68
    extending claims of, 39, 43,
        49–50, 52, 55–6, 63
    and healing, 62
    and post-traumatic growth,
        57
    and PTSD, 40
    Zollner on, 58
trust
    and authority, 112, 117
    and betrayal trauma, 31

    and healing, 38, 82, 116–18,
        135
    and interpersonal trauma,
        40
    and loss of faith, 121–2, 124
    and relationships, 42
    and spiritual abuse, 99
    and traumatic wounding, 68

unauthenticity, 204–5
United States Conference of
        Catholic Bishops (US-
        CCB), 5–7, 78

Vatican II, 79, 114, 177, 181,
        195, 197
victim assistance coordinators,
        25, 65, 69, 80
victim-centric approaches, 2, 4,
        9, 18, 20, 76, 81–2
victimization, 43–4, 52, 55, 122
    secondary, 62, 180
victims, and blame, 127, 136
victims assistance ministry, 18,
        20, 30, 37–8
victims-first approach, 64, 67,
        74, 83
victim-survivors
    and clericalism, 179–80,
        223
    and companionship, 30
    and healing, 21, 25, 29, 32,
        37, 67, 222
    and knowing ministry, 26
    and liturgy, 81–2, 211–12,
        217
    and original grace, 24
    and PTSD, 25
    and reconciliation, 220–1
    and self-blame, 23
    and self-offering, 217

and sin, 22, 24
and synodality, 2
theological responses to, 9, 19, 31
and victims assistance ministry, 18, 38
and witnessing, 4, 27–8, 33

Wilson, George, 174
witnessing, 4–5, 21, 26–30, 33–4, 36, 38, 40, 62, 111, 117, 126

Woman and Man: One in Christ Jesus, 97
women, and clerical abuse, 72–3, 75–8, 93, 96–7, 169

Zelyck, Lorne, 60
zero tolerance policies, 87, 90, 189
Zimbardo, Phillip, 89, 102, 108, 115
Zollner, Hans, 3, 44–6, 58